*An Appreciation*

Dr. Barnes of Merion

BY HENRY HART

New York: Farrar, Straus and Company

DR. BARNES OF MERION

Carl Van Vechten

I

As I write this, a decade has passed since the automobile accident which killed "Dr. Barnes of Merion."

In those ten years people he snubbed or insulted, or told the truth about, have forgotten nothing and learned nothing, and many of them still attempt to publicize an image of Dr. Barnes as a poor boy who, by chicanery or a fluke, discovered an antiseptic that could be used on mucous membranes and spent the resulting fortune accumulating works of art he did not want the public to see.

Nothing could be more untrue, and it is important for contemporary intellectuals, and those who come after us, to realize this. For Dr. Barnes tried to do something which needed doing, still needs doing, and always will need doing. He tried to get people to rid themselves of the ignorances, preconceptions, sentimentalities and rationalizations which prevent them from appreciating the *fact* that beauty pervades *all* life, and that art brings efficacy and grace to *every* human activity, no matter how prosaic.

Why did Barnes want to do this?

The answers to that question are not simple, but neither are they incomprehensible. They involve the personal psychology of a knowing and dynamic personality; the rapidly shifting and changing mores of American life; and the intellectual ramifications of "the decline of the West."

The answers, I hope, will be found in what follows.

 II

I first met Albert Coombs Barnes in 1927. He was fifty-five and had invented Argyrol long before, had assembled his great collection of paintings, had built the beautiful building in Merion, Pennsylvania, which houses them, and had written *The Art in Painting*. I was twenty-three, unaware of my ignorances and something of a literary snob.

I was also a reporter on the Philadelphia "Record," the only paper, in a then overwhelmingly Republican city, which supported the Democratic Party. It was owned by Rodman Wanamaker, the esthetic son of John Wanamaker. He took no interest in it whatever, and in 1928 sold it to those who were even then promoting the Presidential ambitions of Franklin D. Roosevelt.

Though salaries on the "Record" were low, the working conditions were ideal, for there was no pressure, neither from the absentee owner nor the gentlemanly editors. And except for obscenity, libel and anti-capitalist propaganda, it was possible to write as one pleased. This helped a friendship between Dr. Barnes and myself to burgeon.

The "Record" was a morning paper and the reporters who covered "general assignments" got to the city room between one-thirty and two o'clock each afternoon. On my arrival one Spring day the city editor handed me a printed folder which said, in effect, that unless a certain unscrupulous building contractor ceased and desisted from erecting a "slum" adjacent to the Barnes Foundation in Merion its art collection would be transferred to the Metropolitan

Museum in New York and the gallery would be converted into an educational institution for Negroes.

"See what it's all about," the city editor said.

I no longer remember much about my first meeting with Dr. Barnes, which took place in the small factory in Philadelphia, at Fortieth and Filbert Streets, in which Argyrol was then manufactured, packaged and shipped. But I still remember my surprise when I saw modern paintings on most of the walls and noticed that the offices were furnished more like a home than a place of business.

Dr. Barnes could not have been more affable, and this too surprised me, for all I had heard about him had given me the impression he was irascible and even irrational. When he went out of his way to put me at ease I thought it merely the usual courtesy extended a reporter by people who want the reporter to be well disposed toward their side of the story. But, in addition to amiable informality, there was in his manner an intensity of bearing and speech that gave force to what he said, and was new to me. I was aware of a power in him I was too inexperienced to identify.

Barnes said, I remember, that he did not expect the community to rally to his side but that it should. When I asked the price of the houses the building contractor intended to erect, he mentioned $15,000 to $18,000 in a tone of voice which told me he knew his use of the word "slum" was a bit rhetorical (in 1927 the dollar was worth at least twice what it is today). And when I remarked that transforming the Foundation buildings into a school for Negroes sounded more like a threat than philanthropy, a slight hesitation, before he admitted it might seem so, told me the possibility of such an interpretation had occurred to him too.

"The University of Pennsylvania could have had that whole tract," he said bitterly. "I offered to buy it and put up a building if they would equip a laboratory for experiments in horticulture and they turned it down."

I did not want my native city to lose the Barnes collection

and the "Record" took the line that a solution should be found which avoided such a loss. One was. A neighbor whose property also abutted the prospective "slum" suggested that he and Barnes protect themselves by building a stone wall. They tossed a coin to see who would pay for the wall. Barnes built quite a beautiful one.

As this story, from the city editor's point of view, "petered out," I was assigned to another one, and was surprised when Dr. Barnes expressed an interest in it.

A young Baptist minister with no regular church had been supplementing his income by working as a part time instructor in the State Normal School at West Chester, some twenty miles southwest of Philadelphia, and had annoyed the local post of the American Legion by airing pacifist opinions. A move to have him fired had been gaining headway in the community, and the "Record" assigned me to begin a campaign on the minister's behalf. I did so. The New York "World" took it up and the American Civil Liberties Union, then under Roger Baldwin, offered its services.

Dr. Barnes offered his. He induced John Dewey to come from New York to Philadelphia and address a protest meeting, and paid for the hall and all the promotional material, including advertisements in all the newspapers.

As a result the young minister obtained a better teaching position in a better institution.

The "Record" then assigned me to do a series of articles on the State of Pennsylvania's mental hospitals, and once again Dr. Barnes went out of his way to be helpful. First, he lent me some books, including Bernard Hart's *The Psychology of Insanity*, a classic it would profit everyone to read. Second, he offered to accompany me on my inspection of the State hospital nearest Philadelphia.

This was at Norristown, some seventeen miles northwest of Philadelphia. Barnes drove me there in his Packard roadster and went with me through all the buildings, wards and rooms. He had interned more than thirty years before in the

State Hospital at Warren, in northwestern Pennsylvania, and he made sure I understood the diagnoses proffered by the Norristown doctors. As a result, I wrote a much better article than I could have had Barnes not guided my advance reading and enriched my understanding of what I saw clinically. In fact, the whole series of articles was better because he had taken the trouble to teach me what I didn't even know I needed to know.

By this time I was convinced the public's conception of "the eccentric Dr. Barnes" was as ill-informed as are most of the public's ideas about exceptional men.

I did not, of course, then understand him, and therefore was not comfortable with him. But I had enough sense to realize I had come into contact with an unusual intellect, and with a man of even more unusual will and purpose.

The association was not easy. I did not fully comprehend many of his ideas, and of course was totally ignorant of their wellspring. Whenever I ventured a half-baked opinion he did not hesitate to knock it flat. Which would make me feel aggrieved, and cause me to work up face-saving charges against him. If I expressed them, he quickly flattened me anew.

In those early days of our acquaintance I must have been a great trial to him. I once burst out in anger and exclaimed that it was self-defeating, if he *really* was interested in educating people who didn't even know they needed educating, to make them feel small.

His reply was harsh and unfeeling, but—*in the long run* —helpful.

He said that, like most young fools, I used my mind to perpetuate delusions and thereby spare myself the pain of realizing how little I knew. Sparing my feelings would not encourage me to learn, he continued, but would merely allow me to flounder about in sentimental miasmas which, in my ignorance, I mistook for rational ideas. Unfortunately, I was the kind of romantic who had to be bludgeoned before a new idea could reach his attention. Furthermore, the amount of time he, Barnes, could spare for suffering fools gladly was strictly limited. If he could knock sense into my swelled head and teach me something, fine. But he had neither the time nor the inclination to coddle an ignorant youth who resented being told he didn't know anything.

"If you want to learn," he said in a kindlier tone, "you will, and if you don't, God help you. I certainly won't."

 III

In the years since Barnes spoke those blunt words I have often wondered what enabled that twenty-three-year-old youth to surmount his egoism and realize that the strictures and exhortations of the older man were not only just but essentially well-meaning. At various stages of my friendship with Barnes I entertained different hypotheses on this important point, and I now proffer the one on which I have come to rest. It is that I came out of a similar background and sensed beneath his intolerances that he espoused the ethics and ideals I too had derived from an enfeebled Protestantism in a shrewdly oligarchic Philadelphia. Since I shall discuss this later, when dealing with some of the hereditary and environmental factors that influenced the formation of Barnes' psyche, I shall now say only that the weltenschaung of pre-World War I Protestant Philadelphia, lurking at the bottom of both of us, resulted in an unspoken mutual respect, which survived quarrels and other disillusioning experiences.

It was while I was traveling about Pennsylvania getting material for my articles on its mental hospitals that Barnes suggested, in a letter, that I leave the "Record" and become the editor of the "Journal of the Barnes Foundation," which he was then publishing irregularly.

Barnes had started it several years before and its first issue (April '25) came out almost simultaneously with the opening of the gallery of the Barnes Foundation (March 19, '25). The half dozen issues that had been published contained contributions from only six authors—Barnes, John Dewey, three members of the Barnes Foundation staff, and Paul Guillaume, the Paris art dealer Barnes then used and had made "foreign secretary" of the Foundation.

I recently re-read the "Journal of the Barnes Foundation" and was assailed by poignant memories—not only of Barnes' hopes that the "Journal" would be an effective means for the dissemination of his ideas on art and art's meaning for the least of men, but also by memories of how his ideas had influenced my own intellectual evolution. I was also impressed by the vitality of the ideas, by how little, if at all, the passage of time has diminished them.

Most of his basic ideas were stated, and reiterated, in the pages of that brave little "Journal," the circulation of which was miniscule, and, I now suspect, largely gratis.

Here, for example, is his most basic assumption, the idea upon which all his others rested:

Art is not something apart, not something for the few, but something which can give deeper meaning to any and every human activity, even the humblest, and the most routine.

This formulation of Barnes' basic credo is John Dewey's, and I quote it, from memory, from the dedicatory address Dewey delivered at the opening of the Foundation's gallery, which was later published in the "Journal."

Here is a variation on this idea from one of the "Journal's" essays ("Art and the Ivory Tower" by Laurence Buermeyer): "To make human nature intelligible to itself—that is the real purpose of art, that, and not the construction of some sanctuary for those who find the real world of practical affairs too much for them."

9

And here is a third variation on this all important idea, from another of the "Journal's" essays: "Art is a record of experience, and education in art must take into account the human attributes of both the artist and the student."

Ah, those human attributes! How rich the little "Journal" is in allusions to them, definitions of them, clarifications of them. And warnings of how easy it is for the intellectual to go astray. Listen to Buermeyer, in the essay he called "Art and the Ivory Tower":

"Art and day-dreaming are alike in that they both show us a world nearer to the heart's desire than is the actual world. Otherwise, they are antithetical. Art is conduct and feeling, enlightened by 'fundamental brain-work,' which enters, by sympathy and imagination, into the wider world of Nature and man. But day-dreaming is conduct and feeling so dull or so feeble they can only shrink into a private cell."

The chief aim of art education, says another essay, should be "the development of the individual's own esthetic powers, with emphasis on clear, spontaneous feeling, and the ability to organize experience creatively, rather than on memorizing facts about art, or acquiring technical skill along stereotyped lines."

And what is "education" as Barnes conceived it? Another essay in the "Journal" supplies the answer: Education is the "complete and harmonious development of all the capacities with which an individual is endowed at birth, a development which requires, not coercion or standardization, but guidance of the interests of every individual towards a form that shall be uniquely characteristic of him."

Accordingly, the writer continued, the Barnes Foundation hopes to further education that shall be free, that shall not be "as too often, a lifeless erudition or inculcation of meaningless uniformity, but an encouragement of initiative, of independence, of personal distinction, in all the relations and activities of life."

Education is successful, says another essay, when an individual's *interest* is elicited, and "interest" is defined as an anxiety about future consequences which impels an individual to actions leading to better consequences and the avoidance of worse ones. In short, effective education shows an individual *how* it benefits him to use *intelligence* in each and every thing he does. Intelligence was defined as "the purposive reorganization, through action, of the material of experience."

Paintings, said John Dewey in one of the "Journal's" most interesting essays, "Affective Thought in Logic and Painting," can be a very advantageous educational tool because they are examples "not only of the integration of the special factors found in paintings as such, but also an integration of deep and abiding and harmonized human experience. In other words, paintings, when taken out of their specialized niche, can be the basis of an educational process free of the compartmental divisions and rigid segregations which so confuse and nullify our present life."

Dewey then explained *why* paintings are especially efficacious in bringing about a genuinely educational result.

He began by enunciating the second most fundamental idea which Barnes had proffered in his *The Art in Painting*. This was the criterion Barnes used in evaluating a painting: a *good* painting is one in which the plastic means—line, light, color and space—are integrated into a consistent and meaningful whole.

From the psychological standpoint, Dewey pointed out, the successful integration of line, light, color and space, means that "a correlative integration is effected in our organic responses to the painting. Eye-activities arouse allied muscular activities, which, in turn, not only harmonize with, and support, eye-activities, but evoke further experiences of light and color, and so on. Moreover, as in every adequate union of sensory and motor actions, the background of visceral, circulatory and respiratory functions is also consonantly called into action. In other words, the successful integration of the plastic means in a painting permits, and ensures, a corresponding integration of organic activities. Hence the peculiar well-being, relaxation in the midst of excitation, and vitality in peace, which are the characteristics of esthetic enjoyment."

Dewey then indicated some of the social implications of Barnes' conception of painting and education.

Unless some integration occurs of our scientific and intellectual systems with those of art, he said, "the always increasing isolations and oppositions, consequent upon the growth of specialization in all fields, will in the end disrupt our civilization. That art, especially as manifested in painting, and its appreciation, is itself an integrating experience, is the constant thesis of *The Art in Painting* and the Barnes Foundation."

I did not understand all of the foregoing thirty-five years ago, when Dr. Barnes sent me copies of the "Journal" and invited me to become its editor, but there was one thing proclaimed in the "Journal" that I did understand at the immature age of twenty-three. This was the third basic idea in Barnes' personal philosophy.

"Democracy," said one of the essays in the "Journal," "means the sharing of all the interests of a group by every member of the group, and the full and free interaction of all the groups making up a society."

And further:

"Democracy and culture are not incompatible ideals, and the common man, if properly instructed, and given a flexible environment, may hope not only to enjoy, but also to contribute to, the spiritual values of civilization."

 IV

When Barnes suggested I leave the "Record" and edit the Foundation's "Journal" he was preparing to leave with Mrs. Barnes for a summer in Europe, to which, at that time, he went twice a year. He suddenly invited me to accompany him. "We can discuss the magazine on the boat," he said, "and the trip will change your environment and enlarge your mind." He said he would pay my passage over and back and give me a hundred dollars a month while I was there, and that we could discuss a permanent salary on our return. I accepted eagerly.

We sailed on the "Leviathan" on May 20, 1927, the day Lindbergh took off on his solo flight across the Atlantic. The following evening, when it was announced that Lindbergh had landed in Paris, Barnes said, in an accolade tone of voice, "He's an artist—with guts."

There was much talk by Barnes about the nature of an artist on that trans-Atlantic crossing, only some of which I understood, not only because of our age difference, with all that means in terms of experience, and of *funded* experience, to use a favorite phrase of his, but also because of the quality of Barnes' mind. It was perceptive of the least nuance, well informed and disciplined, fearlessly realistic, and completely intolerant of the weaknesses, and rationalizations, of others.

For example, I discovered by reading the passenger list that Herbert Adams Gibbons was on board and I looked him up. He had published a life of John Wanamaker the year before and I had met him when he descended upon the Philadelphia "Record" to make an analysis of its functioning for

Rodman Wanamaker. Gibbons said he was going to Paris to prepare for Admiral Byrd's trans-Atlantic flight, of which Rodman Wanamaker was one of the backers. He had been a foreign correspondent of the New York "Herald" and of "Harper's" and "Century," and a lecturer for the French foreign ministry and our own War College. I thought Barnes might find him interesting and suggested he invite Gibbons for a drink.

Bringing them together proved to be a mistake. Gibbons was an apologist for the status quo and was annoyed when Barnes ribbed him about it. Afterward they made revealing comments about each other. "There's madness there—the madness of genius," said Gibbons of Barnes. "He's the foam on a glass of beer," Barnes said of Gibbons.

Barnes, I was to learn, often dismissed many people he knew only casually, or by reputation, just as brutally. I also was to learn that he was equally uncompromising with those who were close to him. On that trans-Atlantic crossing he spent quite a bit of time analyzing things I said and explaining why I said and thought them. It's easy now to see how right he was, but it wasn't easy at the time, and his efforts to improve me all too often elicited nothing but defensive anger.

One evening at dinner we were discussing André Siegfried's *America Comes of Age*, which I had lent him. He said I had not understood the book, that I was almost totally uneducated, and was prevented from recognizing that fact by the superficial information and misinformation of the newspaperman.

"Don't be so hard on him, Albert," said Mrs. Barnes.

Dr. Barnes brushed her intercession aside. "Don't coddle him," he said impatiently. "He'll never grow unless he's forced to—like most human beings."

But Barnes also had a gentler side. One morning we caught sight, from our deck chairs, of a green shore-line.

"La belle France," he said with affection, and then, observing the absorption in my gaze, added kindly: "Votre premiere vue." The tone of his voice made me turn and look into his eyes. They were odd eyes, and the brown irises, behind rimless spectacles, always seemed contracted. At that moment there was a smile, and understanding, in them.

 V

In Paris the Barnes stayed at the Royal Monceau and I went to a Left Bank hotel which Herbert Adams Gibbons frequented, the Malherbe, on rue Vaugirard near the Luxembourg. Barnes told me to wander about and familiarize myself with Paris and meet him in a few days at Paul Guillaume's gallery on the rue le Boetie.

On the appointed day I arrived at Guillaume's ahead of Barnes and Guillaume asked if I cared to see what he had hanging on his walls. He was a dapper and dynamic little man, and, as they say in the theatre, he was "always on." I was not oblivious to this, and was on my guard. But Guillaume could turn on the charm, and he went out of his way to be pleasant.

As I wandered around looking at the examples of modern art he had for sale, a thin and elderly Frenchman of scholarly mien came in and also began scrutinizing the paintings. I cannot recall what painting I paused before—Guillaume's best pictures were displayed in his home and not in his gallery—when Guillaume clapped me on the shoulder and said, in a tone audible to the Frenchman some feet away: "No, Capitaine Lindbergh, that is not for you."

I turned around and he gave me a quick wink. In turning I saw, out of the corner of my eye, the astonishment on the Frenchman's face. At that instant Guillaume took me by my arm and propelled me out of the room and into his office. "I had to get you out of his sight before he discovered you don't really look like Lindbergh," he said with a laugh.

I asked who the Frenchman was and the way he evaded giving the name made me wonder if the incident had had other than a joking purpose. I mentioned this suspicion to Barnes that night as we sat at a cafe on the Place de Terte on Montmartre. Barnes thought the incident had been a joke, not a ruse. "Guillaume doesn't have to resort to such tricks," Barnes said, "he *has* arrived."

The conversation then turned on how I could study James, Santayana and Dewey with the greatest profit to myself, and to the Barnes Foundation. He told me again, as he had many times before, and as he continued to do throughout his life, that James taught him how to think, Santayana had taught him how to feel, and Dewey had taught him what is involved in educating people to new ways of thinking.

I asked Barnes what it was that impelled him to *want* to convert people to his way of thought—why he bothered. He said the motives were various, and he named, in the following order, a desire for a kind of immortality,* pleasure in the exercise of power, and an esthetic desire for unity.

Although it was late when he got back to his hotel, he appeared at mine the following morning at 8:30, having promised to go with me to the National City Bank in order to facilitate my opening an account there. He said he had been up since 5:30 and predicted that we would arrive at the bank before it was open. We did, and as we stood on the pavement waiting Barnes exclaimed with a laugh: "Look at me! This is Barnes in Europe—always waiting for things to open."

Afterward we went to the Louvre, and he showed me some of its treasures and explained why they were such. In front of Titian's "Man with a Glove," for example, he patiently and skillfully showed me what "losing a line" meant. He leaned

* Each life he helped to change for the better, he thought, set in train other changes for the good, which extended into other lives, and subsequent generations.

16

close to the canvas, and, wholly engrossed, pointed to the line of the shoulder which was almost indistinguishable from the background. Almost, but not quite. "Your eye sees a line that isn't there," Barnes said. "No one knows how Titian did it."

I was fascinated by his intensity and absorption and as he turned away from the canvas he caught my scrutiny of him before I could hide it. He smiled sheepishly and stalked off, exclaiming over his shoulder: "Pay attention to what I say, not to how I say it!"

That evening the Guillaumes included me in a dinner they were giving for Dr. and Mrs. Barnes. Mme. Guillaume, then in her late twenties or early thirties, was a chic Parisian sophisticate in full bloom. Both Dr. and Mrs. Barnes liked her, and she went out of her way to please them. The dinner was perfection, and after it Mme. Guillaume proposed the movies, of which she professed to be fond. Her husband demurred, but she insisted, and we went to see Leni Riefenstahl in *La Sacre Montagne*.

There was much to enjoy in that now forgotten film—especially Riefenstahl's dancing and the excellent photography of mountain precipice and snow. But the plot was melodramatic and at its most gripping moment, as two men fell off a precipice, Guillaume burst into mocking applause. Infuriated hissing came instantly from all sides.

Barnes was amused. "You see how wrong you were about him," he said later, as he and I sat at La Rotonde over coffee. "He's like a child—he can't confine his attention to one thing for any length of time."

I was not convinced that M. Guillaume was quite so simple, and we argued the point back and forth good-naturedly. As we did so Barnes kept watching what went on around us and he suddenly pointed out a young man and girl who were very obviously in love.

"That's the time of happiness," he said wistfully. "It's ten to one they're not yet married and that they make love every night and morning."

He was so patently right I said kiddingly: "You must be psychic."

The banality of my remark offended his esthetic sense and he upbraided me for using such a phrase. He said it proved how superficial, sentimental and lazy I was, and how much I needed to learn and change and grow.

Fortunately, Barnes then noticed a pedestrian he thought was Leo Stein and he yelled: "Leo!" The man turned his head and Barnes saw he had made a mistake.

This led him to reminisce about Leo and his sister Gertrude, whom Barnes regarded as intellectual sports. One day, he said, on his way to Gertrude's apartment, he had met Leo coming away from it. Leo was agitated and told Barnes he had just had a fight with Gertrude, adding: "You know, of course, she's crazy." On entering Gertrude's apartment Barnes found *her* extremely agitated. "I've just had a fight with Leo," she exclaimed, and added: "You know, of course, he's crazy."

"It's a loose word," Barnes said seriously. "Some people call me crazy."

Then, with cold and accurate objectivity, he added: "If I ever went over the line I'd be a paranoiac."

 VI

In addition to taking me with him to the Louvre and the Luxembourg, Barnes also had me accompany him to some of the dealers' galleries.

Guillaume's, at 59 rue le Boetie, was his Paris headquarters, and dealers often sent there pictures they wanted him to buy, and split the commission with Guillaume. But Barnes also liked to drop into their galleries unexpectedly and catch them off balance.

"They're crookeder than a dog's hind leg," he said on our first day out, "and I wouldn't trust one of 'em with a plugged nickel. Except Paul." Barnes declared that Guillaume always told him exactly what he had paid for a picture, or what another dealer had paid for it, and that he and Guillaume then came to an agreement on how much mark-up Barnes should pay.

"Paul will never double-cross me." Barnes said confidently. "He knows I'd advertise it all over Europe and he'd be finished."

Which was true, for at that time Barnes was directly responsible for about seventy-five per cent of Guillaume's business, and indirectly responsible for much of the remainder. Guillaume was well aware of this, and each issue of "Les Arts à Paris," which he published to advertise himself and his wares, had one or more articles about Barnes, his collection of pictures, and the educational work of the Barnes Foundation.

"What of Mme. Guillaume?" I asked.

"Don't think I haven't given that some thought," Barnes replied quickly. "I've warned Paul to keep her on a short leash." He was silent a few seconds and then somberly added: "I doubt that he will. Or could."

Whenever we arrived and a dealer was out, and a subordinate did not recognize him, Barnes amused himself by clowning. If the subordinate were a decent fellow, Barnes drew him out, asked his opinion of canvases on the walls, and gently led up to the sometimes touchy subject of the pictures the gallery had that weren't on public display. But when a subordinate was pretentious, Barnes egged him on to praise a patently dubious canvas, or otherwise to make himself ridiculous.

If the dealer was in when we arrived Barnes adjusted his manner to the man's temperament. With most of them he affected a down-to-earth, let's-level-with-each-other attitude. He did not hesitate to allude to any past derelictions of theirs he happened to know about, nor to praise Guillaume to them for "protecting me from you wolves." But with dealers whose minds he respected he took a different tack. Several, I noticed, asked his opinion about canvases they knew he had no interest in, and did it neither to arouse his interest nor to flatter, but as a favor one professional asks of another.

Of course a dealer's guile was occasionally so well dissimulated that Barnes was temporarily deceived. Sooner or later, however, he was undeceived, and thereafter he never let pass an opportunity to tell exactly what the dealer had done. Needless to say, he made enemies thereby, and some of the most scabrous stories that have circulated about him were started by conscienceless dealers he had publicly denounced.

 VII

Barnes was working that summer on pre-Durer German, French and Flemish painting, in order to add a chapter to a new edition of *The Art in Painting*, and to get material for a book he had in mind on the French primitives. In the course of these researches he was arranging to visit the museums in Amsterdam and Cologne, and the National Gallery in London, where there is so fine a representation of Flemish canvases. Also, the London dealers wanted to show him a Greco, a Ruysdael and some Italian primitives—none of which, it turned out, he bought.

He therefore had less and less time for me, but before he

left for Amsterdam we had a long talk, and our first serious quarrel. Unexpectedly finding himself free for a few hours, he came to my hotel. I was out, but he discovered from the concierge that I was probably to be found in the Luxembourg Gardens, where I usually read in the late afternoon. Barnes found me there.

I was reading Dewey's *Democracy and Education* and Barnes asked if it was "touching" me. I replied it was hard going.

The remark annoyed him. "I knew you were young and inexperienced and ignorant of psychological fundamentals," he said, "but I didn't know you were lazy."

"It isn't that I'm lazy," I said combatively, "it's that Dewey writes so badly."

"Dewey writes so badly!" He mimicked my pronunciation with withering scorn, took the book out of my hand, tapped the opened page with a rapidly wagging index finger, and, his angry eyes fixed on mine, told me that only nit-wits rationalize an unwillingness to put forth mental effort by alleging the teacher doesn't explain things clearly.

"Everybody knows Dewey writes badly," I said resentfully.

"It doesn't matter a tinker's damn!" Barnes exclaimed. "The important thing is he thinks clearly!"

He then questioned me about specific ideas in the chapters I had read. My answers convinced him I *had* understood at least something and he let his anger ebb away. He told me, with kindly intent, but also impatiently, that I preferred going on emotional jags instead of facing problems realistically, analyzing their components, utilizing intelligence to find hypothetical solutions, and having the guts to test the hypotheses in the real world.

I did not reply to this for I knew much of what he said was true. Sensing that my resistance was capitulating, he became paternal and told me not to despair, that I was young and would soon acquire the experience that would enable me to "substitute intelligence for sentimentality." He did not fail to recall Santayana's definition of a sentimentalist: one who has too much emotion and too few ideas.

Whereupon he proposed that we walk to La Rotonde and have an aperitif. He was the kind of heavy-set man who is light on his feet, and he liked to walk at a good clip. He was observant, and interested in everything he saw, no matter how trivial, and when walking his conversation was different from what it was at other times. When strolling he talked chiefly in free association, and with little of his inveterate didacticism. His comments on whatever life presented were apt, and often picturesque. But when he was sitting down he was not so free and easy.

At La Rotonde, after a quick survey of the people at the other tables, and a few remarks about the more bizarre personalities, he turned to me and said out of the blue:

"Now that you know a little something of what the Foundation is trying to do, have you any concrete ideas worth our consideration?"

I hemmed and hawed and took a long swig of vermouth cassis. "Not really," I muttered.

"How about unreally?" he said, with a hint of a smile.

"Well," I said reluctantly. "I think your public relations would be better if you let the public see your pictures."

This released, as I expected, quite a barrage. He said the problem had been thoroughly explored and that the policy of non-admittance was a considered one. He said anyone with a genuine interest in painting would be admitted to the Foundation's classes and could *study* the Foundation's paintings. Even I, he assumed, was aware that most "art-lovers" are indolent dawdlers, time-killers and poseurs. Besides, he said, he had tried it. "We lent some pictures to the Pennsylvania Academy of Fine Arts," he explained with disgust, "and all that happened was old ladies from the Main Line called us degenerates for showing such things and a psychiatrist named Dercum said he was certain the artists were insane."

22

"From what you've told me about Utrillo, Modigliani, Pascin et al he may have had a point," I said with a smile.

He shot me a quick glance, got up and stalked off toward a taxi, calling over his shoulder: "Please pay the check."

The next morning I received a penciled note from him. He said I was not ready to take on the "Journal," that he was off to Amsterdam, that we would talk it all over when both of us had returned to the United States, and that the books of James, Santayana and Dewey were tools that could transform the journalist I had been into the creative personality he hoped I might still become.

These early interchanges between Barnes and myself illustrate not only his efforts to spur *me* to "get a re-education," as he put it, but also his life-long attempts to do the same for others, and, through the Foundation, for whole groups. How diffident, resistant, and ungrateful, most of us proved to be!

The memories of what he was actually like when he was trying to teach me what life had taught him, are tainted with the sadness that comes over us when we realize that one generation is unable to give its wisdom to the next, and everything has to be learned all over again, the hard way. I could absorb intellectually the ideas of James, Santayana, Dewey and Barnes himself, but it was life, not ideas experienced only intellectually, which ultimately taught me what Barnes wanted me to learn. And, as so often happens, I did not even approach his knowledge of life, of men, and of art, until around the time he died.

He endured similar disappointments from others whom he thought had promise, and might be developed into effective personalities capable of helping him to spread the all-important truth that art exalts the least of men, as well as the artist.

The key to Barnes' personality was that he believed in human perfectibility and was messianic about it. He believed in it because he was convinced he had proved its possibility in his own life. He had come from nothing, and, without help or influence from others, had discovered Argyrol, made a fortune, created one of the world's great collections of paintings, written *The Art in Painting*, and established the Foundation. All, he never tired of saying, because he had embraced, and utilized, ideas that have validity in the real world. The determining difference between effective and ineffective people, he believed, lies in the ideas they elect to live by, and in the habits the ideas originate and solidify.

Barnes never doubted that he had molded his own destiny, and that he had done so by means of ideas derived from James, Santayana and Dewey. Had he embraced other ideas, he believed, he would not have been the man he was. Nor, he was sure, and not immodestly, so effective a human being.

The essential ingredients of Barnes' philosophy are to be found in James' *The Will to Believe*, which states the primary pragmatic principle—an idea is true if it works; in Santayana's *The Sense of Beauty*, which defines beauty as "a pleasure in the eye of the beholder" and declares that beauty is "objectified good"; and in Dewey's *Human Nature and Conduct*, which asserts that an individual's habits explain his relation to society, and account for the kinds of societies men create.

Barnes also believed ideas should lead to action, and that if we fail to act we stultify ourselves and in time become permanently paralyzed psychologically. Much of Barnes' pugnacity, which caused him to be so widely misunderstood, was the result of this belief that failing to act and react leads to mental, moral and physical degeneration.

There was more to Barnes' philosophy, as will presently appear. For the moment, keep only this in mind: he *believed* it is possible for human beings to transform themselves, to release themselves from the bondage of their ignorances and preconceptions, to lead lives more wonderful than anything poets have imagined. He believed this is possible *now*, and that *he* understood how individual men and women can bring it to pass. He wanted to help them do so. He was messianic about it, and a bit possessed. He did not succeed. But he tried.

 VIII

When I returned to the United States Barnes informed me that since I wasn't up to editing the kind of magazine he wanted the "Journal" to become, and he didn't have time to teach me how to do it, he had been thinking how my abilities could be used in ways that would help me to grow, and had concluded I should make a study, for the Foundation, of political corruption in Montgomery County, and especially in that portion of it containing Lower Merion Township, in which the Barnes Foundation is located. He said he would pay me $325 a month and that I would be on my own, except for periodical reports, which he and I would discuss and analyze in order to determine whether or not I was on the right track.

Needless to say, nothing came of this. What contacts I had with Philadelphia and Pennsylvania politicians were of the cat-and-mouse sort, with me, the young reporter, as the mouse, and the politicos as the very knowing cats. After several weeks of interviewing people whom I thought might help me make a beginning, I came to the conclusion that I not only did not know how to go about it but wouldn't get very far even if I did. Politicians really don't believe in explaining to strangers how the wheels go round.

When I told this to Barnes he accused me of being the prisoner of habitual indolence and fear of the new, and of being unwilling to forsake the genteel world of the intellectual for the hurly-burly of life as it actually is.

He was right, and I was right, and it was an impasse. So I sent back the third pay check. He returned it and said our agreement had stipulated that I would be paid monthly and that I was entitled to it. I sent it back again and he replied that my peace of mind was more meaningful to him and would be decisive. I would not take it, and he respected me for not doing so.

He then proposed that I accept one of the eight-month scholarships at $100 a month which the Foundation gives to those who want to study its paintings and the method of art appreciation that is detailed in *The Art in Painting*. I accepted gladly, and though I resigned the scholarship two months later, my study of the pictures in the Barnes Foundation is one of the major, and most profitable, experiences of my intellectual life.

At that time the collection consisted of a hundred Renoirs, including one of the most joyous pictures ever painted ("The Bathers"); fifty Cézannes, including "The Card Players"; numerous examples of Daumier, Manet, Sisley, Puvis de Chavannes, Van Gogh, Gauguin and other men of the end of the nineteenth century; examples "in the dozens" of Matisse, Picasso, Utrillo, Modigliani, Soutine, Kisling, Derain, Pascin, Laurencin, and other "moderns." There were at least a hundred examples of such American painters as Glackens, Prendergast, Lawson, Demuth, Maurer, et al, and many canvases representing all the traditions of painting, on which Barnes later concentrated in the '30s. There were no examples of the early American and "Pennsylvania Dutch" handicraft he concentrated on in the '40s.

I did not then, and do not now, agree with all of Barnes' evaluations of individual items in his collection, which is an aggregation of artistic significance unequalled by any other assembled by a single individual. But what he said about his pictures always had point, for not only was his aesthetic sense

26

sophisticated, but he spoke from a highly integrated knowledge of physiology, psychology and philosophy as well.

The procedure for scholarship students at that time—at least in my case—was this:

On Tuesdays there was a lecture, in front of pictures, but at other times students were on their own. When the lecture was given by Barnes, it was a rewarding intellectual experience, but when given by one of the three women he was then trying to transform into teachers it was a manifestation of everything, I thought, to which he was opposed. I was aghast at their ineptitude, and astonished that he did not appear to be aware of it.

He was only too aware of it. But he would not admit it, not even to himself. He did admit it years later, in one of the most revealing moments I ever had with him.

The explanation of his failure to train effective teachers is to be found in the fact that, like most of the movers and shakers who have stormed across the rim of this cooling globe, he was not the *proponent* of an idea, but the *creator* of one. There is an important difference between the two. The proponent of an idea, provided he is not a fanatic, objectively appraises what dissenters have to say, and is even willing to grant their right to say it. But the creator of an idea is personally, and paternally, involved. Dissent and disagreement, however minor, asperse his child. Barnes' child was his belief that he knew the actual steps that lead to human perfectibility. He constantly strove to make his belief come true, he constantly battled on behalf of his child. Hence, he was always striving to make reality conform to his conviction. It seldom did. Whereupon Barnes would become disillusioned with *people*. There'd be a fight, and a potentially able teacher would be lost.

Barnes liked to talk, and to be told he talked well—who doesn't? But that was about the extent of his grasp of the teaching art. Aside from an innate, and lifelong, *willingness* to share his knowledge, and his acumen, he was everything a teacher ought not to be—intolerant of stupidity, impatient with the first confused efforts to learn, suspicious of difference of opinion, niggardly with praise.

These attitudes were hard enough on students, but they were doubly so on those whom Barnes tried to train to be teachers at the Foundation. Over the years there was a procession of protegés, almost all of whom, sooner or later, would evince an independence of judgment at which Barnes would take alarm, or offense. Sometimes, of course, he was wholly right in doing so.

There was one man, however, whose own ideas agreed with Barnes' completely. This was Laurence Buermeyer, a student of John Dewey's whom Barnes met when he began going to New York each week to attend Dewey's classes at Columbia (years after Barnes had become a millionaire). Buermeyer had a brilliant philosophical mind and a gift for exposition that is the sine qua non of a good teacher. His little book, *The Aesthetic Experience*, which the Barnes Foundation published, is one of the best definitions of that subject ever written, yet it probably hasn't been read by more than a few thousand people.

Buermeyer is an example of the tragic waste of talented intellectuals. He was born in Reading, Pennsylvania, of "Pennsylvania Dutch" stock—a background Barnes appreciated and approved. While teaching at Princeton he fell in with the epicenes who are tolerated, at such disastrous cost, in and around our best schools and colleges. I do not deny there were things in Buermeyer's background that explain such association. Be that as it may, he later resorted to alcohol, which led to a breakdown. Barnes tried to help him in every way he knew, and to this day the Foundation cares for him in a sanitarium.

When Barnes noticed that my attention wandered at the Tuesday lectures of his feminine associates, he took me to task. I did not know how to explain, for, after all, the women were doing their best, and what they thought he wanted.

28

Then, one Sunday afternoon—at that time Barnes frequently had me for the weekend—John Dewey came over from New York for I forget what purpose. He and I fell into conversation in the Barnes' living room and Dewey asked how my studies were progressing. I told him they weren't, and when he asked why not, I told him the women Barnes hoped to make teachers were not up to it. I also said I had no gift for dissimulation and that when Barnes asked my opinion I gave it, and that the result was usually a fight.

Barnes caught sight of us and demanded to know what we were talking about. Dewey gave me a beseeching look, but what do the young know of the mutual discretions and understandings of the mature? I was unable to dissimulate even for Dewey.

"We were talking about you," I said apprehensively. Barnes demanded to know what had been said, and I told him.

To our surprise he said nothing, but the next morning I received a letter he must have dictated after I had left the previous evening.

The burden of it was that on a clean-cut issue between us I "had run to the childish equivalent of papa." My mind, Barnes said, was critical, not receptive, and my criticisms had nothing to do with factual thinking. My mind was also so "buttoned up" it was impossible for him to provide me with the background I so badly needed. It was clear, he declared, that I had come to the Foundation too late. Instead of allowing him to change my self-defeating habits, I wanted to change him. I was, in short, wasting my time.

I of course resigned the scholarship and in the letter in which I did so I merely remarked that since we were both egoists we had better go separate ways.

I did not think Barnes would bother to write to me again and was surprised to receive a letter in which he said I reminded him of William James' story about an old judge's advice to a young one: "Give your decision, it will probably be right, but don't give your reasons, they will probably be wrong." Barnes added that I shouldn't worry about being an egoist—"Cézanne was the star one of his age"—provided I made sure that the motor power of my egoism was "experience and not pipe dreams."

So I wrote him my reasons, and, with all the presumption of youth, analyzed his character in the same terms in which he had been analyzing mine.

This elicited the vituperation it no doubt deserved. His letter concluded with this: "Your howl of ill-digested book excerpts differs in no essentials from those of other sore-heads we kept in their place. All it proves is that our method is as efficient in eliminating the unsuitable as it was in producing a lot of pictures, some fine buildings, and a program that is being carried out. A consistent feature of twenty years' practise of our method has been the total disregard of all criticism that is divorced from intelligence or experience. We have lived, have had fine adventures, have had no bosses, and, as a Harvard professor says, have 'the most exciting place in America.' It's already a legend, and will soon be a tradition that may benefit all mankind."

To which I did not reply.

About ten days later he wrote a long letter of kindly, disinterested advice, in which he told me he had sent our whole correspondence to Dewey, who had said that maybe he, Barnes, had let me be by myself too much.

"Dewey may be right," Barnes declared, and then, in pencil, added: "My latch-string is always out for you."

 IX

In the weeks preceding this interchange of accusatory and recriminatory letters I had learned a great deal about Dr. Albert C. Barnes, and could have learned much more had I been older. I have often wondered whether my inadequacy seemed as regrettable to him at the time as it has since seemed to me. My conclusion is it simply exasperated him.

I cannot recall his ever making a conscious effort to bridge "the gap between the generations." Yet, after that first serious quarrel had been patched over, he did occasionally elude his messianic daemon and realize that my inability to give him the intellectual understanding and companionship he wanted was not entirely due to my willful refusal to change my mental habits, or to lazy disinclination to put forth the effort that would make me a more effective human being.

Our most relaxed hours, at that time, occurred on Sunday morning walks in and around Merion, then one of this country's loveliest suburbs, and adjacent parts of Overbrook and Narberth. Barnes had walked those streets, lanes and shortcuts for a quarter century and knew a surprising amount of their lower, middle and upper class gossip and lore, much of which related to the Philadelphia out of which both he and I had come.

Barnes had been born, on January 2, 1872, in a small two-story row house, No. 1466 Cook (now called Wilt) Street, in the Kensington section of Philadelphia, then, as now, a predominantly factory district. It was not a slum, as has been said, but a very self-respecting neighborhood, which it still is, almost a century later.

His father, John Jesse Barnes, had started out in life as a butcher in a slaughterhouse and had worked at the bench next to P. A. B. Widener, long before that ambitious and re-sourceful man began amassing street car franchises. On February 5, 1864, Barnes' father, then twenty years old, enlisted in the 82nd Infantry Regiment of Pennsylvania Volunteers, and, four months later, in the bloody fighting at Cold Harbor, Virginia, had his right arm so badly shot up it had to be amputated. He was awarded a pension of $8 a month, but he was not the kind of man who becomes a public charge. In fact, he was so self-reliant he later learned to take a clock apart with his left hand. He succeeded in finding a variety of jobs, and ultimately one in the circulation department of the Philadelphia "Public Ledger" which provided his family with a modest, but by no means an impoverished, existence.

He was a letter carrier when, on April 4, 1867, he married Lydia A. Schafer, two years his junior. They had four children—all boys. The first born, Charles, and the third, Albert Coombs, survived. The second, John J., born Jan. 4, 1870, lived less than a year. The fourth, George W., born Feb. 8, 1881, died on April 16, 1883.

I cannot recall Barnes ever saying much about his mother, but I did gather she had been the parent who did the disciplining. Once, however, when we were discussing the nature of mysticism, he paid a tribute to the simple Methodist faith to which she had passionately clung. "It was narrow," Barnes said almost wistfully, "but it worked—for her. And for millions of other Americans." After which he recalled, with all the nostalgia a half century can generate, the good times they had when his mother took him to Methodist camp meetings at Merchantville, New Jersey, where she had been born, and, in summertime, at Ocean Grove, on the Atlantic shore, just south of Asbury Park.

I also gathered that he had been her favorite, and that she had early determined he should be a doctor, as was one of her cousins. His brother, Charles, became a lead worker.

Early in Barnes' childhood the family moved to a three-story house at 1331 Tasker Street in South Philadelphia. It was a middle-class, and better, neighborhood, and Edwin S. Stuart, who became Mayor of Philadelphia, and later Governor of Pennsylvania, lived around the corner on Broad Street, and was a friend of Barnes' father.

When he was thirteen Barnes entered Philadelphia's Central High School, the second oldest high school in the country and the only one which gave—and gives—B.A. and B.S. degrees. When I attended it, some thirty odd years after Barnes, we were told the curriculum had considerably declined. If so, the curriculum in Barnes' time must have provided an education indeed, for in my day the curriculum of the "Latin Scientific" course consisted of four years of Latin; three of French; four of mathematics; three each of chemistry and physics; one each of biology, geology and astronomy; one of ancient history, two of American history, and one of modern world history; one of English composition and grammar, one of philology, one of American literature, and two of English and world literature. Plus extra-curricular lectures in philosophy for any who desired them.

There were three boys in Barnes' class at Central High who later won a place in the annals of American art—John Sloan, Robert Preston and William J. Glackens. The last became Barnes' life-long friend.

Barnes graduated from Central High twenty-fourth in a class of twenty-six, but mere graduation from that school in those days meant superior intelligence. Moreover, he had had much less time to study than the other boys. Throughout his four years in high school he had gotten up at four in the morning to deliver papers on the route his father had been granted by the Philadelphia "Public Ledger."

After graduation, in obedience to his mother's desire, he enrolled in the University of Pennsylvania's Medical School, where the course was then only three years. His marks were so good the first year he won a scholarship, which, plus

33

money he earned by tutoring, paid the cost of his medical education.

He got his M.D. degree in 1892 and interned at the State Hospital for the Insane at Warren, in northwestern Pennsylvania. His experiences there bred a lifelong interest in psychiatry and psychology, and also, I believe, led to the first formulation of the ideas which became the warp and woof of his personality and intellectual being. The patients at Warren, he once told me, revealed to him how wrong beliefs and habits cause sane people to "lose their minds," and convinced him that the process could be reversed, and that the non-organically and non-chemically insane would have their sanity restored if they could be led to accept valid ideas and acquire new attitudes and habits.

I once asked Barnes why he left Warren as soon as the intern requirements had been met. He replied curtly that he didn't have a slave make-up. I asked what kind of make-up he had and he replied: "I'm a chance-taker." I asked what the components of a chance-taker's make-up are.

From the way he replied—without an instant's hesitation —it was clear he had often pondered the point. "A chance-taker knows that change, not permanence, is the fundamental fact of the universe," he said, and added: "It's struggle, not acceptance, that makes life worth living."

I asked if he had known all that when he was an intern at Warren. "I've always known it," he said grandiloquently, but he had the grace to add: "Subconsciously, of course."

When he left Warren he made the first of his many trips to Europe, and spent the summer of 1893 in England and the Isle of Man. On his return to Philadelphia he hung out a shingle at 1331 Tasker Street and practised there for several years. But he didn't like it. "Most of the ills I treated were imaginary," he said, "or would have cured themselves, and I didn't like bluffing my way through the hard ones. Besides, I wanted to go to Europe again."

By 1896 he had saved enough money to do so and sent his

mother a wireless from the boat—a freighter—to tell her he was bound for Germany, and to ask her to inform his patients he would be back in a year.

Why Germany? Because at that time German science was justly considered the most creative in the world.

He stayed in Germany about a year and a half, and for most of that time was in Berlin, where he attended some chemistry and philosophy lectures, and supported himself by giving English lessons and becoming the sales representative of an American stove manufacturer.

He returned to Philadelphia on a tanker, but he did not resume the practise of medicine. Instead he got two jobs, which he held simultaneously. One was writing advertisements for Gray's Glycerine Tonic, which required frequent visits to New York. The other was as a quasi-consulting chemist for the H. K. Mulford Co., a Philadelphia pharmaceutical house that is now part of Merck and Co.

Both jobs paid well and enabled him to take the biggest chance of his life.

Around the turn of the century major discoveries in fundamental and applied science were occurring so often that almost every young scientist of ability and ambition was inspired by the hope that he would be a discoverer of something of importance.

One discovery quite a few men had struggled toward, for more than a decade, was a silver compound that would be as antiseptic as silver nitrate but not so irritating to the mucous membranes. The need for such a medicine was, and is, constant and world-wide.

Barnes became fascinated by the problem, and intoxicated by thoughts of what such a discovery would mean to him personally, and when an idea came to him that he thought might work, he decided to take a chance and risk everything on its development.

As a first step he took a leave of absence from both jobs and returned to Germany and enrolled at Heidelberg for Rudolf

35

Gottlieb's course of lectures on therapeutics, and for a laboratory course at the Pharmacological Institute. He also attended the lectures in philosophy of Kuno Fischer, but gave them up when he found they were diverting him from his main purpose, to wit, learning how to go about the experimentation that would clarify, concretize, and test his idea of how sliver ions could be set loose on infected mucous membranes and cure infections without damaging the living tissues.

In the summer of 1900, confident he was on the right track, he returned to the United States.

 X

Shortly after his return to this country Barnes paid a visit to his doctor cousin, who was then practising in Milford, the peaceful seat on the Delaware River of Pennsylvania's Pike County, which is in the northeastern corner of the State and contains the northern reaches of the Pocono Mountains.

He had been there only a day or two when he met the woman he married eleven months later, and the woman who gave his life a stability and dignity his particular kind of temperament very much required. Her devotion enabled him to escape many of the effects of his worst qualities, which so easily could have given his destiny a different and downward turn. For as long as he lived he had a perfectly managed house and home.

One morning in the summer of 1900 Barnes' cousin, with a twinkle in his eye, asked him if he would like a dog for a patient and introduced him to a Miss Laura Leggett of Brooklyn, a summer sojourner in Milford, who had brought her sister's fox terrier to be bandaged. The little dog had been spayed, the wound had reopened, and Edith Leggett, disliking blood, had prevailed on her sister Laura to find a veterinarian. There were none in Milford.

Laura Leggett was a petite blonde with blue eyes and was faultlessly dressed in the summer femininities that were so bewitching at the turn of the century. Thereafter Barnes' cousin saw very little of him and Miss Laura Leggett and her sister and mother, and the hotel in which they were staying, saw a great deal. So did the lanes and byways of Milford over which Barnes and Laura Leggett bicycled in the first weeks of their acquaintance.

She was three years younger than Barnes and had been born in the five-story brownstone house at 281 Adelphi Street, not far from downtown Brooklyn, in which she had lived all her life. She was the fifth of the six children—three boys and three girls—born to Richard Lee and Clara Cox Leggett.

Her father, whose ancestors had emigrated from Essex, England, to New York's Westchester County early in the seventeenth century, had been a captain in New York City's famous 7th Regiment in the Civil War. When he was demobilized he entered the wholesale grocery business established by his father, Abram Leggett. The present firm of Francis H. Leggett & Co. was founded by Richard and his brother Francis.

Richard's wife, whom he married on October 9, 1862, while on leave from his regiment, which was stationed in Washington, was of French as well as English ancestry. Her father, one of ten children, had been a silversmith in Birmingham, and her mother's people had emigrated from France during the Revolution and settled in San Domingo, from which they were forced, also by revolution, to flee to the United States.

In addition to having the germ of Argyrol in his head that summer, Barnes also had the Mulford and Gray's Glycerine Tonic jobs, and could not protract his stay in Milford indefinitely. When he said good-bye to Laura Leggett she gave him permission to call on her in Brooklyn. One of their friends in the hotel, observing Barnes' face as he took his departure, warned Mrs. Leggett: "That young man means business."

They became engaged the following October and were married on June 4, 1901, in St. James Protestant Episcopal Church not far from the Leggetts' Brooklyn home. After a few days in Atlantic City they sailed from Philadelphia on the "Waesland" for Bremerhaven, and went from there to Heidelberg, where Dr. Gottlieb and others at the University entertained them, and Barnes ran experiments to test some of the ideas that had accumulated in his mind since he had left the University a year before.

The Barneses then resumed their honeymoon. They went through the Black Forest and Switzerland, had a few days in Rome, and sailed for home from Genoa.

They arrived in the United States early in September and spent a few days with Barnes' parents on Tasker Street. They then stayed in a hotel while house-hunting. In a few weeks they found a pleasant house at 6374 Drexel Road in Overbrook, the first of the chain of Philadelphia suburbs that lie along the Pennsylvania Railroad's "Main Line."

Barnes and his wife lived in that house for five years—the years in which Barnes brought his ideas to fruition and successfully launched Argyrol.

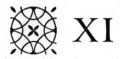 XI

Barnes' two jobs paid him approximately $10,000 a year, in dollars worth three or four times as much today, and he used much of it to finance his experiments. He at first paid members of the University of Pennsylvania's chemistry department to run routine experiments for him. But the instructors were not always free to work when he wanted to disprove a hypothesis or prove a fact.

While studying at Heidelberg he had become friends with a German student named Herman Hille who enjoyed laboratory work and had developed quite a knack for it. Barnes wrote to him and asked if he would care to come to the United States and help him with experiments which he, Barnes, thought might lead to the discovery of a silver protein compound that would be more antiseptic, and less caustic, than silver nitrate.

Hille was the son of a shopkeeper in a small Prussian village whose native ability had enabled him to become, first, a licensed pharmacist, and then an instructor of physiological chemistry at the University of Wurzburg. When Barnes met him he was a candidate for a doctorate at Heidelberg.

Hille accepted Barnes' proposal at once.

Whereupon Barnes rented a small stable in Philadelphia on Thirteenth Street near Spruce, installed a laboratory of sorts on the ground floor, and converted the room above into living quarters for Hille.

When Hille arrived Barnes got him a job at Mulford's, with the understanding that Hille would work for Mulford during the day, and on Barnes' ideas at night. Hille spoke no English.

By that time Barnes' basic ideas were well advanced. He believed that by combining silver with a protein he could overcome the disadvantages of silver nitrate. The protein he had in mind was vitellin, the substance which gives egg yolk its color. His idea was to combine a salt solution of vitellin with a concentrated (30%) solution of silver nitrate so that silver vitellin would precipitate out. The resulting dark brown crystals, Barnes believed, could be economically packaged and sold to druggists who would furnish them to the public in an aqueous solution. Barnes did not get his vitellin from egg yolk but from something much cheaper and easier to handle, i.e., from gliadin, one of the proteins in wheat and rye.

Early in 1902 he was so sure his silver vitellin was more antiseptic and less caustic than silver nitrate that he asked Dr. Edward Martin, with whom he had studied clinical surgery at the University of Pennsylvania, to test it. Dr. H. M. Christian, chief surgeon of the University Hospital's genito-urinary department, also tried it in the treatment of gonorrhea and cystitis, as did Dr. G. K. Swinburne, in New York, and Dr. M. Wassidlo, in Berlin. A favorable verdict was unanimous—and enthusiastic.

It was in the successful marketing of Argyrol that Barnes first put James' pragmatic principles to the test. Also what he had learned from advertising Gray's Glycerine Tonic.

First, he did not patent it, since doing so might reveal how Argyrol was produced, and the patent would run out in twenty years. But he registered the name Argyrol—from the Greek word for silver—as a trade mark. Second, his sales approach was to doctors, not druggists, and he sent circulars —many of them addressed by Mrs. Barnes—to physicians throughout the United States and the world. The circulars contained the endorsements of the doctors mentioned above, and of additional doctors from whom Barnes obtained endorsements at subsequent strategic moments.

The circulars and samples he so carefully spotted around the globe soon created more of a demand for Argyrol than Barnes and Hille were able to produce in their make-shift laboratory in the stable on Thirteenth Street. Late in the Fall of 1902 the newly created partnership of Barnes and Hille rented eight rooms in what had once been a hotel at 24 North Fortieth Street.

The partnership's capital was $1600, all of which was supplied by Barnes. The partners made $40,000 the first year, and $100,000 the second.

 # XII

Those were golden years for Albert Coombs Barnes, the "testing time" of his maturing manhood, in which his physical and mental aptitudes confronted the universe—and won. Those were the years in which he correctly assayed his environment, perceived a human need, discovered what would satisfy this need, and supplied it in a way which made him rich, and his own master. For the rest of his life he looked back upon those years with justified and nourishing pride.

The enemies he made in later life have endeavored to disparage his achievement by inferring, and even declaring, that Argyrol was Hille's idea and that Barnes had "despoiled the impractical inventor." But a glance at the frontispiece of this book will inform the impartial that such denigration is untrue. The man in that photograph is both a thinker and a do-er (a "chance-taker"). That combination of traits is the basic explanation of Barnes' abilities and achievements. Most people are either reflective *or* active—one or the other. Barnes was both. Not many are.

Those who are constitute an elite of the *effective* members of the human race. They are the realists who perceive, with pellucid objectivity, the unpleasant as well as the pleasant facts about earthly existence. They do not waste time and energy, and their lives, rationalizing and systematizing into delusions things they do not wish to see or admit, or any of their other weaknesses and ignorances, and they do not fear to test, in action in the real world, the ideas their intelligence suggests.

Unlike the selfish members of this efficient and proficient

elite, who, throughout history, have held a low opinion of the bulk of humanity, Barnes not only believed *all* human creatures are capable of leading lives in which thought and action are integrated but that everyone should be constantly alert to possibilities for the reintegration of one's personality. In fact, he believed the *art in living* consists of striving to overcome our limitations by the reorganization of our habits, especially the habit of substituting wish-fulfilling fantasies for intelligence, and the habit of being afraid to act.

Barnes had many failures with people, for he often said and did seemingly outrageous things merely to reach their attention, to overcome their psychical deafness, to shock them into a realization that their personal *Weltansicht* required revision.

I think Hille was one of these failures.

For some time after his arrival in this country Hille's work at Mulford's during the day, and his work for Barnes at night, did not allow him any leisure in which to indulge the personality traits that prevented him from adjusting to American life. After he stopped working for Mulford, and during the first year or two of the partnership, Barnes and his wife had him to dinner three or four times a week. There was much to discuss in the working out of the details of the manufacture of Argyrol, and of a second chemical product they later marketed profitably though it never equalled the success of Argyrol. This was an iron tonic they called Ovoferrin, the virtue of which derived from the fact that its iron content was not compounded with something else in a crystalloid state, but was colloidal. Barnes and Hille also worked on, and subsequently marketed, an intestinal astringent they called Interim, and a dusting powder called Biodol. These two items were ultimately dropped.

The success of Argyrol, and, to a much lesser degree, of Ovoferrin, gave Hille time to nurse his dissatisfactions with American life. He was homesick, he hated the United States, and he refused to learn English. But since there was nothing in his family situation in Germany he wanted to return to, he was chronically frustrated. Barnes' trips to Europe to promote Argyrol, which he began making in 1903, intensified Hille's loneliness.

The partnership ended in 1907, after Hille brought suit to force a dissolution. He was awarded, Barnes said many years later, "several hundreds of thousands of dollars." The A. C. Barnes Co. was incorporated in 1908.

Hille then went to Chicago, where he established a laboratory of his own. He died on April 28, 1962, in his home in Deerfield, Illinois, aged 90.

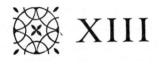 XIII

Barnes was much more successful in transforming the personality of his first employee—Nelle E. Mullen, whom he hired, at the then prevailing rate of $8 a week, soon after he and Hille moved to Fortieth Street.

She came from a large, but poor, family in a modest West Philadelphia neighborhood and was still in her teens when she went to work for Barnes, her first, and, as it turned out, her only, employer. She was a tall girl for those days, and a blonde, with blue eyes and a fair complexion, and a stolid nature which nothing Barnes ever did seemed to faze. She didn't marry, and she gave Barnes a fidelity that was total. She was the only employee to whom he entrusted the making of Argyrol.

Barnes told me once that "after Laura and Dewey, Nelle knows me best." Be that as it may, she certainly served him well, and his lightest word was her willingly obeyed law. She was indefatigable, and the most devoted "gal Friday" I have ever encountered. As the years passed she took on more and more of the administration of the business, until she finally ran it all, and handled all his investments. Barnes gave her books to read, sent her abroad almost every year, and once sent her around the world. But I don't think she had the slightest interest in intellectual things. I once told him the adulation of Nelle and the other women in his office was bad for him. He replied that I was an ignoramus carping at people who helped others while I lolled about helping no one.

Nelle had an older sister, Mary, who was somewhat more intellectual. She came to the A. C. Barnes Co. several years after Nelle and was brought into the company around the time Argyrol began to be counterfeited. She travelled about the country gathering evidence against jobbers and retailers who sold imitations under the Argyrol trademark. The court injunctions Barnes obtained against such defrauders, especially one in New York State, helped to prevent similar infringements in all parts of the world.

In time Mary tired of this work and Barnes put her in charge of the factory's employes, who, at their maximum, consisted of about a half dozen white women and from eight to ten Negro men.

Mary Mullen conducted some of the "classes" in psychology and esthetics at the factory which Barnes inaugurated when he discovered the factory's work could be done in six of the eight hours the employes then worked each day.

Later, under Barnes' urging, instruction and guidance, she worked on *An Approach to Art*, a small book the Foundation published and allowed to go out of print. It espoused the basic theses to which the Barnes Foundation is dedicated: art is the record of experience; the meanings of experience, illumined by an artist's perceptions, are given to us by his integration of the plastic means; learning to see the meanings in a work of art involves education, "which is another name for meeting the practical problems of life."

Later still, Mary Mullen taught at the Foundation, and was

one of its five trustees. Like her sister Nelle, she never married. She died in '56.

The classes in psychology and esthetics at the factory were not all Barnes did for his employes, whom he tried, rather successfully, to treat as individuals.

Not a few of his first Negro employes got into trouble with the police, for disorderly conduct, assault and battery, wife-beating, and such. Barnes at first fired the offenders. But the turnover of this labor was a nuisance and he began to study their lives in order to learn why they behaved as they did.

One, he discovered, was fascinated by machinery and became a peaceable citizen when Barnes let him service his automobile. Another subjected himself to weekly punishment in "battles royal" at a local boxing arena. Barnes got him to see the folly of taking such punishment for 50¢ a night when he could earn more, and suffer less, by learning to box. A white woman who had so much energy she disturbed the women who worked with her labelling and packaging bottles, was put in charge of shipping "where a new motor coordination was needed nearly every minute."

Later, after Barnes had filled the factory's offices with paintings, more systematic efforts were made to release the unused potentialities of the employes, and to encourage them to surmount their limitations and to face, instead of running away from, their life problems.

These "classes" at the factory yielded some of the educational methods Barnes later utilized in the more formal classes at the Foundation, and in an article written for "The New Republic" shortly after the Commonwealth of Pennsylvania chartered the Foundation as an educational institution, Barnes summed up the educational experiments in his factory as follows:

"We do not intend to convey the impression that we have developed a crowd of savants, or art connoisseurs, but we are sure that we have stirred an intelligent interest in spiritual

45

things created by living people, and in the writings of gifted thinkers, which has been the means of stimulating business life and affording a sensible use of leisure in a class of people to whom such doors are usually locked.

"What we believe our experiment indicates is that the great creations in art, literature and thought, can be resolved to fundamentals of human nature, and, in simple form, be so presented that they can be grasped by plain, even illiterate, people—to the point of the particular person's capacity. It is a question of stimulating the individual's interest by a favorable environment, by leaving him free to get his own reaction uninfluenced by external pressure—and here the question becomes one of method. We look upon nothing in our experiment as definitely proved, and we offer no formula and least of all are we interested in reform or edification. We believe that the material we had to work upon was fairly representative of industrial life. We succeeded to a certain extent, at least, in developing an environment which attracted by its own appeal a number of people whose time out of business hours had been a desolate waste. Of course, we encountered the inertia ineradicably fixed in some, but even that was to a considerable extent favorably affected. There has been no attempt at regimentation and no suggestions or criticisms concerning what any of our workers do outside of business hours."

Barnes was a generous as well as an intelligent employer. He bought houses for quite a few of his workers, and provided for many of their other needs. When he sold his business, *in the summer of 1929*, he set up a $250,000 fund that has enabled all of them, and their widows, to enjoy an income down to the present day.

 XIV

By 1905, little more than two years after the launching of Argyrol, Barnes had enough money to build a large home in Merion, the Philadelphia suburb adjacent to, and west of, Overbrook.

The site Barnes chose, of almost three acres, lay along what was then called Union Avenue, only a few hundred yards south of the present location of the Barnes Foundation. The uninteresting name of Union Avenue was later changed by the Lower Merion Township Commissioners to Rose Lane, which neither Barnes nor his wife thought much of an improvement. Mrs. Barnes suggested the road be called Latch's Lane, after the Latch family, which for several generations had owned one of the largest tracts along Union Avenue, on the side across from the property the Barnes had just acquired. The Township Commissioners ultimately agreed.

Mrs. Barnes supervised the erection of the granite, twelve-room home of English architecture which her husband put in her name and called "Lauraston." She also supervised the designing of the furniture of this house, most of which was patterned after pieces in Percy Macquoid's book, and all of which was made for her by the then well-known Philadelphia firm of Hale and Kilburn. And she did the landscaping and planting of the grounds.

Barnes was busy extending the sale of Argyrol, but it was the furnishing of "Lauraston" which first interested him in art. Contrary to what many have written, and he himself said more than once, he did not become a collector of paintings because he discovered at an early age that his talent for painting was merely mediocre. Barnes never painted so much as a sketch.

The first pictures he bought for "Lauraston" were etchings, and the first oil he bought was a Corot, which still hangs in the Foundation.

His first Renoir was "The Torso," which Renoir had painted in 1875. He bought it from a Chicagoan whose wife thought it "improper."

Improper! It is perhaps impossible for the present generation to realize that only fifty years ago a portrait of a woman nude from the waist up was considered improper by a large section of this country's intellectual population, not all of whom were hypocrites by any means. Victorian values dominated our intellectual circles until the outbreak of World War I, even though the vitality of such values had become enfeebled by their success, and men had forgotten the license of the eighteenth century which had caused the reaction that gave rise to the Victorian moralities. By the first decade of this century the creeds and codes which had sustained a century of unrivalled human progress had become mere shibboleths, capable only of delaying, not preventing, a new license. One of the chief reasons Barnes became interested in art, perhaps the major reason, was that in French impressionism he sensed a release from the pointless strictures of obsolete mores, and an opening up of new intellectual vistas the other arts had not yet perceived.

Though Barnes' interest in art began in 1905, it did not grow into an all-dominating passion until five years later. For the acquisition of wealth did not suddenly alter his simple tastes, or those of his wife. His one luxury in those years was keeping a few horses, and, with his wife, taking riding lessons at George McMenamin's academy at nearby Port Kennedy. For a while he belonged to the Rose Tree Fox Hunt, and later to the Pickering Hunt. But he came to the conclusion that the anatomical construction of the human male is damaged by horseback riding. McMenamin tried to disabuse him of that idea, but though Barnes respected McMenamin—he often quoted McMenamin's admonition, "When you come to the jump look up and let the horse do it"—he had made up his mind that being in a saddle was bad for *him*. So, thereafter, instead of getting his exercise riding a horse every day through the lovely countryside around Merion, he got it walking for at least an hour every morning before he went to the office. That meant getting up at six o'clock, which he did for the rest of his life.

In 1910 Barnes bought the Latch property across the road from "Lauraston," remodelled the Latch house, and built four new houses on the spacious grounds. He did this primarily to protect his home, but secondarily to make sure the esthetics of the whole neighborhood would be preserved. He sold all five houses for exactly what they had cost him, neither a penny more nor a penny less.

And he added a port cochere to "Lauraston" and panelled its downstairs rooms and hallways in quartered oak.

 XV

It was also around 1910 that Barnes renewed his friendship with one of his classmates at the Central High School. This was William James Glackens, by that time a well-known illustrator and one of the group of "The Eight," some of whom were later called "The Ashcan School" and included John Sloan, Everett Shinn, Robert Henri and George Luks.

Glackens was an amiable and life-loving painter of Irish descent who had attained a serenity nothing disturbed, not even the feminist opinions and antics of his wife, née Edith Dimock, who had studied with William M. Chase and possessed a large income (Corticelli Silk). She was a not un-talented water-colorist, and two of her productions hang in the Barnes Foundation.

The Glackens began to weekend with the Barnes, and the Barnes to visit the Glackens in New York. While Mrs. Barnes visited her family in Brooklyn, Barnes and Glackens lunched with Glackens' writer and artist friends at Mouquin's, and then at night the two men and their wives united for dinner. In the summer of 1911 the Glackens took a cottage at Bellport, Long Island, and the Barnes saw a good deal of them when they stayed with Mrs. Barnes' mother at Blue Point, not far away.

During the early phases of this developing friendship Barnes bought some of Glackens' best paintings, and the work of some of Glackens' friends, especially Maurice Prendergast, Ernest Lawson, Charles Demuth and Alfred Maurer. Barnes also bought one of John Sloan's oils, the first Sloan ever sold. But though Barnes had Sloan and his wife for occasional weekends in Merion, he did not take to Sloan, whom he came to believe was an artist more in self-promotion than on canvas. But Barnes did take to Prendergast and Demuth, and he and Mrs. Barnes frequently visited the latter in his mother's home in Lancaster, Pennsylvania.

Barnes' liking for artists, and what has been called "the mind of the artist," had several psychological roots. Mrs. Barnes once told me he had wanted to be a lawyer, not a doctor, and he himself once said, when I was mouthing some philosophical pessimism, that one of his most engrossing interests was the "comedie humaine." He added that very few human beings are capable of getting outside of themselves sufficiently to be able to look at their fellow creatures objectively. "Artists can, and do," Barnes said. "They're observers in the true sense, and I like what they see."

He also liked the intuitive and intellectual processes by which genuine artists select the significant elements of a scene, action, or character, discarding all that is irrelevant, in order to give these essential elements the arrangement and form which makes their meaning manifest to others. These were the same thought processes Barnes himself employed in his scientific work, and in much of his everyday life. They are, he believed, the only mental processes capable of bringing order out of chaos in *any* human activity. In short, he came to believe that artists practise, par excellence, what William James preached.

Barnes also enjoyed the extroverted and gregarious bonhomie of artists, though he was always glad to get back to his own non-gregarious and almost solitary routines. It is true that Glackens introduced Barnes to some of the gemutlich aspects of artists' lives, but it is not true, as Ira Glackens intimates in his *William Glackens and the Ashcan School of Art*, that Glackens told Barnes what pictures to buy or bought for him modern paintings he was unable to appreciate.

It is true that, early in 1912, Glackens bought for Barnes, at a Paris auction, a Renoir, Van Gogh's "The Postman," and other canvases. But Barnes had designated the pictures he wanted Glackens to bid on, and had stipulated the maximum prices Glackens was to pay. However, as soon as it became known in Paris that Glackens was bidding for "the millionaire Barnes," the dealers besieged Glackens with their wares. Some of the pictures offered were such bargains Glackens cabled Barnes for instructions, and Barnes authorized Glackens to buy several of them.

The legend that Glackens is responsible for the Barnes collection is a canard not only of the enemies of Barnes, who also deny he discovered Argyrol, and of the dealers he exposed, but is also an ego-soothing fantasy of all the artists I have ever met, who, naively, are certain a non-professional could not possibly, by himself, assemble so great a collection of art.

There are also those who believe Gertrude and Leo Stein and their lesser known brother, Michael, are responsible for Barnes becoming a collector of modern art. It's true the

Steins were the loudest of the early tub-thumpers for Picasso and Matisse, but it is also true that in the summer of 1912, when Barnes first met them, he was being importuned every day he was in Paris by dealers who were equally as eager as the Steins "to make a market" for Matisse and Picasso, and many other French artists. Barnes regarded Michael Stein, the patron of Matisse, as a very skillful promoter, and he had no respect for Gertrude, who, he said, "merely knows how to make blague pay." He did, however, respect Leo, whom he helped financially at several critical junctures, and to whom he dedicated *The Art of Henri-Matisee*.

The truth is that by the summer of 1912 Barnes not only had a large collection of pictures, but had decided, since his business practically ran itself, his major interest henceforth would be the study of art, and its significance for man.

 XVI

The Armory Show of 1913 in New York is usually cited as one of the "Great Divides" of American culture. And with reason, for it revealed intellectual and social changes in Western Christendom which World War I confirmed and intensified.

To Barnes the International Exhibition of Modern Art, as the Armory Show was officially called, was not the novelty it was to many American intellectuals. He had seen, in Europe, many examples of the "modern art" which made the Armory Show the propaganda success it was. Furthermore, through Glackens, who headed the Committee which selected the American art in the Academy Show, Barnes was au courant with much of what went on behind the scenes.

Nevertheless, the Armory Show deepened and solidified his convictions about the significance of French Impressionism and post-Impressionism. I was often surprised, twenty or more years later, by the number of times he alluded to it.

According to Walt Kuhn, the executive secretary of the exhibition, in his *The Story of the Armory Show*, a brochure he prepared in '38 to celebrate the 25th anniversary of that exhibition, the Armory Show grew out of a discussion on December 14, 1911, in the gallery which Mrs. Clara Potter Davidge maintained at 305 Madison Avenue, between Henry Fitch Taylor, a painter who directed that gallery for Mrs. Davidge, Elmer MacRae, Jerome Myers and Kuhn. Those four painters thought the American public should be *made* to take an interest in American artists and they decided to form the Association of American Painters and Sculptors and hold a show of a scope that would attract national attention. Within a few days they had rounded up twelve other artists eager to participate in such an advertising campaign.

Kuhn claimed that the original purpose of the show changed when Arthur B. Davies, who soon replaced Alden Weir as president of the Association, sent him a catalog of the Sonderbund Exhibition in Cologne on which he had scribbled: "Wish we could have a show like this." Kuhn decided they could, and set off for Europe to collect examples of the sort of thing which had attracted attention in Cologne. He was welcomed by all of the European dealers who were promoting "modern art."

The International Exhibition of Modern Art opened on the evening of February 17, 1913, in the armory on Lexington Avenue at Twenty-fifth Street of the 69th Regiment of the New York National Guard. The catalog declared that the show had two purposes: to inform the American people of "activities abroad" and to "break down the stifling and smug condition of local art affairs." The catalog also stated that the Association of American Painters and Sculptors "took no stand" on the merit of the works exhibited, but that the Association was "against cowardice even when it takes the form of amiable self-satisfaction." The show's "emblem" was the pine tree flag of the American Revolution.

Brilliantly publicized by Frederick James Gregg, a former editorial writer of the New York "Sun," and by Guy Pene du Bois, the Armory Show, comprising more than a thousand examples of the work of 300 artists, became *the* conversation piece of intellectuals throughout the United States. Marcel Duchamp's "Nude Descending a Staircase" was only one of the pictures called "insane" or "revolutionary," according to the conservative or liberal temperament of the beholder, and the resulting controversies were so maneuvered and publicized that the Armory Show became fashionable. One of the Astor women went every day, and even Theodore Roosevelt visited it (on March 4, the day Woodrow Wilson was inaugurated). John Quinn was prevailed upon to buy $6000 worth of paintings, and after the show closed the foreign portion of it was sent to Chicago and Boston.

In his 25th anniversary brochure Kuhn says the Armory Show "affected the entire culture of America. Business caught on immediately, even if the artists did not at once do so . . . The decorative elements of Matisse and the Cubists were immediately taken on as models for the creation of a brighter, more lively America. The decorative side of Brancusi went into everything from milliner's dummies to streamlined trains. The exhibition affected every phase of American life—the apparel of men and women, the stage, automobiles, airplanes, furniture, interior decoration, beauty parlors, advertising and printing in its various departments, plumbing, hardware— everything from the modernistic designs of gas pumps and added color of beach umbrellas and bathing suits, down to the merchandise of the dime store."

Barnes smiled at some of Kuhn's claims, when I read them to him at the time, but he pointed out that most of the European painters who were seriously talked about in '38 had been exhibited in the Armory Show. And he agreed that the

Show had profoundly affected the intellectual climate of the United States. He once said its total effect was probably greater than that of the exhibition at the Salon des Refuses in Paris in 1864. When I inquired whether he might not be attributing to the Armory Show effects which were more the result of World War I, he replied: "The war came from the social malaise expressed in the paintings."

Barnes also believed that the continuing vogue of modern art in Europe was largely the result of the sale for it in the United States, which the Armory Show had stimulated.

One effect of the Armory Show, however, he never tired of denouncing. This was the servile and superficial imitation of modern European painting by American artists.

 XVII

The first published formulation of Barnes' organized ideas about art was his article in the April 1915 issue of "Arts and Decoration" entitled "How to Judge a Painting."

It begins with the assertion that a textbook on art "is an impossibility." He had spent months, he explained, with a book by Meier-Graeffe on his lap "and a Cézanne, Van Gogh or Bonnard propped on a chair in front of me," wading through "verbosity and froth," hoping a ray from the book would "reflect from the painting" and "carry the artist's message to my mind." What messages he received, he said, came from the paintings, not Meier-Graeffe. Nor was Bernard Berenson any better. Day after day, Barnes said, for several summers in succession, he had "carried a volume of Berenson's to the Louvre, the National Gallery, the Kaiser Friedrich Museum," trying to learn "the message of the really great in Italian art." The chief result was a development in Barnes of a strong liking for Italian primitives, "with which Berenson's book had little to do."

In another section of the article, however, Barnes admitted that though he had come to regard Meier-Graeffe's books as "wordy foam," they had been of use to him five years earlier largely because "he writes so enthusiastically he makes the reader want to learn." Barnes also admitted that Clive Bell's *Art*, which had been published a year before and had been helpful, "would have been so much Greek to me in the state of my experience five years ago." And he declared that George Moore's books "will give a man more insight into art essence than all other books on art ever written."

If art appreciation cannot be learned from books—and Barnes quoted Degas' dictum that "literature has only done harm to art"—even less is to be obtained from the art criticism in newspapers, which, Barnes declared, is almost always "word juggling at the expense of ideas." Nor are the painters who write about art in magazines helpful.

Barnes singled out for special condemnation Kenyon Cox, who at the time of the Armory Show had said "Matisse makes insanity pay." Cox, Barnes charged, "is a painter of the lifeless, a writer of sophisms about art, a thoroughly conventional, respectable man, but an artistic cripple hobbling through the present on the tottering crutches of the dead artistic past. He does not have the eyes that see." And William Merritt Chase was "a lovable personality" but as a painter, and artist, he unfortunately stood for "the traditional in art rather than good art." Barnes quoted Chase's remark that "Matisse does the best he knows how, but Cézanne never knew how," and declared: "It is my opinion, based upon the fourteen Cézannes in my collection, that Cézanne knew almost exactly how."

Nor are current exhibitions a help since the "normal, annual academy exhibition" purveys "the dregs of once great art movements attentuated to the petered-out state."

The sincere seeker after knowledge about *quality* in painting should go, Barnes suggested, to the great private collections and study the paintings to be found in them. He characterized the Havemeyer, Widener, Johnson, Frick and Altman collections as "superb," and said that in the Havemeyer collection "one could study art and its relation to life to better advantage than in any other single gallery in the world."

But "the single most valuable factor" in his own pursuit of knowledge about art, he confessed, was "my frequent association with a life-long friend who combines greatness as an artist with a big man's mind."

This was a tribute to Glackens, and there was another one in the article. Barnes said that Manet, Monet, Renoir and Degas would all have approved of the painting, drawing, color, composition and "evidence of joy in creating" in Glackens' landscapes with figures.

Some of Barnes' opinions of other artists, in 1915, are also worth citing.

He said that Picasso was a great artist and a great painter and that Matisse was "a greater artist than painter." He said the Picassos in his collection, "painted before Picasso took to having fun with the public with cubes," showed "a masterly welding of the essences of Greco and Cézanne" in a technique that "Manet and Velasquez would have looked at a second time." Matisse, at his best, has individuality, Barnes thought, despite such facts as that his "reversion to the primeval vision" derived from Gauguin, his "fervour" from Van Gogh, his quest for form from Cézanne, and his sense of design and decoration from India.

But it was Renoir who, in '15, and throughout his life, pleased Barnes most. "He paints according to no school, no formula, no technique," Barnes wrote, "the vision of the great artists of the past in the terms I can understand." In Renoir's paintings Barnes was always able to discover "the spirit of perpetual youth in a garden of perennial June loveliness."

The "Arts and Decoration" article also contains some revelations of Barnes as a collector.

Every collector who studies his paintings, he wrote, soon learns to regard the pictures he acquires and subsequently discards as "the necessary milestones on his way to the destination." Buying wrong pictures is not so great a mistake as "keeping them on view" after the collector has developed beyond them. Discarding an expensive but bad picture by a famous artist, he avowed, "hurts me less than putting in the attic a picture by an unknown painter that I thought was good when I bought it." Mistakes are inevitable, he admitted, but "that makes for interest." However, as the years go by mistakes occur less often and "sooner or later one gets a collection that is as personal as its owner's face."

"Then, and before then," Barnes confided, "comes the pleasure one gets from living with pictures as friends, children, objects of worship, diversions, serious mental occupations"— whichever fits the collector's mood.

The least of the pleasures of owning a collection of paintings, Barnes declared, is "the mere possession," and the best is a joy one feels but cannot express. Between these two extremes are pleasures which, like the keys of a piano, are limited only by "the performer's skill and knowledge." Good paintings are more satisfying companions, he believed, than the best of books, and infinitely more so "than most very nice people."

"I can talk, without speaking, to Cézanne, Prendergast, Daumier, Renoir," Barnes said, "and they can talk to me in kind. I can criticize them and take, without offense, the refutation which comes silently but powerfully when I learn, months later, what they mean and not what I thought they meant. That is one of the joys of a collection—'the elasticity with which paintings stretch to the beholder's personal vision,' which they have helped to develop."

The enthusiastic collector, Barnes said, believes that living with and studying good paintings offers greater interest, variety and satisfaction than any other pleasure or work known to man. For "it is more difficult to get a personally chosen good collection than it is to make a big fortune." He who has a home full of good paintings, he continued, "needs no subterfuge of excessive heat or cold to drive him north or south, to get away from his own wearying self." And he who surrounds himself with quality in painting, bought with his blood, "is a King."

This was not rhetoric. As the years passed his paintings became boon companions in a literal sense. He often went to the gallery to commune with them, sometimes in the dead of night.

 # XVIII

"My lifetime," says Arnold Toynbee in his *Reconstructions*, "is still divided into a pre-1914 and a post-1914 period as sharply as the traditional Western scheme of chronology divides all history into B.C. and A.D. At the moment of the outbreak, in 1914, of a great and evidently fateful war in the society into which I happened to have been born, I felt myself suddenly understanding what—it seemed to me—Thucydides must have felt at the moment of the outbreak of the Athens-Peloponnesian War in his society in 431 B.C."

Barnes was 42 when the First World War broke out and his youth and early maturity had been lived in the "pre-1914" world. But he had never identified with that world, and in fact was in rebellion against many of its values, and lack of values.

The war itself interested him very little. The psychical residue of his years in Germany, and his debt to German science, had been counter-balanced by a dislike of German arrogance, and later were overshadowed by a liking for France that developed out of his love for French painting. He assumed the Allies would win, but he did not think his country should help them do so. By financial donations he helped "The Masses" raise a voice against our entry into the war, as well as against the war itself, and when the editors of "The Masses" were prosecuted for their anti-war articles and editorials, he contributed to their legal defense. He never forgave Max Eastman for "caving in."

Once we were in the war, of course, Barnes did what he could to help win it. Army requirements obliged him to step up the production of Argyrol, but not to such a degree that he had to enlarge his plant, and he did not raise its price. He also served as a consultant on the War Department's gas mask program.

Barnes missed his visits to Europe's art galleries and dealers, and he spent the wartime summers motoring through New England with his wife. Then suddenly, in the very middle of the war, a whole new area of experience opened out for him, and brought him a friend he cherished for the rest of his life.

This happened through the publication, in 1916, of John Dewey's *Democracy and Education*. That now neglected book unleashed a horde of new trends in education, some of which Dewey himself did not approve.

Democracy and Education is one of Dewey's least well written books and it is a tribute to Barnes' intellectual zest that he dug out of its careless and obfuscating phrases the ideas which have affected a generation of pedagogues. The book has still something to say, despite the traduction of much of it by so-called "progressive education-ists."

It begins with the assertion that what nutrition and reproduction are to physical life, education is to social life, i.e., the means of renewal. As societies become complex, Dewey continues, the need for formal, intentional, teaching and learning, increases. With the arrival of *institutions* that provide formal instruction, pupils are almost always separated from direct contact with life, and with living social situations. These last are always "the best educators."

Therefore, schools should be miniature communities, in which are pre-sorted and pre-arranged those aspects of contemporary living which it is necessary for the young most fully to understand. A wider and better balanced environment should be created by the school than any environment the young "would be influenced by if left to themselves." And school activities should be "conjoint," i.e., the pupils should actively participate in them in order to acquire a *social* sense.

The prime purpose of helping the young to learn from experience, that is, to learn by *doing*, is the creation of the kind of habits which give an individual a greater measure of control over the environment. *Active* habits are the opposite of routinized conduct, since they involve thought, initiative and invention, and make intellectual growth possible, either by excluding actions which are self-defeating, or by nourishing, fortifying and inspiring actions which lead an individual *more directly* to his goals.

The true function of education, Dewey maintained, is so to equip an individual that he is able to learn from everything that befalls him. This dynamic concept of education, Dewey contended, should supersede those philosophies which hold that education should be a preparation for some future duty or privilege; should abet an individual's own unfolding from within; should train an individual's latent powers; or should furnish the student a recapitulation of the human past. The failing common to all four of these philosophies, Dewey pointed out, is their alienation from, and neglect of, the external, contemporary environment.

True education is a *social* process, Dewey insisted, a continuous interaction between the individual and his environment. The *worth* of the environment, or the society, in which an individual finds himself, can be measured by the extent to which the interests of that environment, of that society, are shared by *all* its members, and the freedom with which that environment, that society, interacts with other environments and other societies.

Barriers to the free communication of experience are stultifying, Dewey warned. The flaw in Plato's philosophy of education was in making a class, rather than the individual, the social unit. The notion of the eighteenth century Enlightenment that a regenerated humanity would ensure the education of the individual was not accompanied by any description of the practical means for achieving the desired end. The idealistic philosophies of the nineteenth century remedied this lack by exalting the national state, but that "reintroduced the idea of the subordination of the individual to the institution."

According to Dewey, the goals of education should be determined by specific social situations and should never be imposed by fiat, rote, or tradition. The great desideratum is the arousal of *interest*, which is defined as "identification with the objects that make up an activity and furnish the means for attaining a goal." Interest is sustained by Will ("continuity of attention and endurance"), and both interest and will best train the mind when the environment gives social approval to intelligent and significant pursuits.

The prime purpose of instruction, Dewey believed, is the creation in an individual of good habits of thinking. Thinking is the perception of "connections between an act and its consequences." Good thinking habits result when a student is continuously active in dealing with a genuine problem and is given an opportunity to test the solutions he himself evolves. The supervision given him should not only provide access to relevant information, but should foster in the student the acceptance of responsibility for the consequences of the solutions he thinks may be efficacious.

Finally, in any *truly* educational process, naturalistic and humanistic subject matter are inter-related, not separate. Nor are the utilitarian and the cultural separated, for such separation perpetuates "the traditional liberal or cultural education for the few economically able to enjoy it, and would give to the masses a narrow technical trade education for specialized callings, carried on under the control of others." The "socially obnoxious features of the present and industrial order" would be modified by an intelligent integration of utilitarian and cultural subject matter. Such an integration would "give those who engage in industrial callings the desire and ability to share in social control, and the ability to become masters of their industrial fate. It would enable them to saturate with meaning the technical and mechanical features which are so marked a feature of our machine system of production and distribution . . . With the representatives of the more privileged portion of the community, it would increase sympathy for labor, create a disposition of mind which can discover the cultural elements in useful activity, and increase a sense of social responsibility."

There has rarely been a more pat example of the right book read at the right time by the right man. Barnes was in the flood tide of maturity when he read it, economically secure and able to devote his life to whatever he chose, confident he had found in art not only an esthetic pleasure but a practical philosophy, if not a religion (the artist's vision increases man's awareness and knowledge of his plight). Certain he had something to give, Barnes found in *Democracy and Education* the *way* to give it.

The first thing he did after reading *Democracy and Education* was to enroll, at the age of forty-five, in Dewey's 1917–18 seminar at Columbia University.

 # XIX

Barnes told me more than once that some of the happiest days of his life were those on which he made the first trips to New York to attend Dewey's seminar. He existed in a kind of euphoria, he said, invigorated and strengthened by the belief that he had come into contact with a man capable of changing American educational institutions in ways that would be conducive to the effective dissemination of Barnes' own ideas about art.

Equally important, and in human terms even more important, Barnes had found a friend to whom he gave a life-long loyalty.

Dewey, of course, was at first flattered that a man of Barnes' years, wealth and accomplishments should become a disciple and apostle. Dewey was then almost sixty and sensed at once that, with this ally of consequence, who had appeared out of the blue, many of the things he still wanted to accomplish might still be achieved. He also realized that Barnes' hopes and intentions could be aligned with his own. Furthermore, there was room, and a need, in Dewey's personal life for a friend. His children were grown, and his wife, if not exactly like Socrates', had one or two resemblances. Dewey needed the sort of friend Barnes became as much as Barnes needed him.

Barnes' trips to New York for Dewey's seminar that first year became fused in his memory, into a lovely golden haze, not only because of the euphoria of awakening friendship. They were pleasant and interesting occasions per se. He usually arrived in New York in time to lunch with Glackens, either alone or with Glackens' friends. In the late afternoon, after the seminar, he would have an hour or two with Dewey and Dewey's friends, and sometimes dine with them. Otherwise he had dinner on the train that returned him to Philadelphia.

In the spring of 1918, as the seminar drew toward its close, Dewey asked Barnes if he would care to finance a field study of some sociological problem that would give members of the seminar a summer job and an opportunity to test, in an actual social situation, the ideas they had been discussing that year. Barnes agreed at once and suggested what the field study might be. He said the Polish immigrants who had settled in great numbers in the Kensington district of Philadelphia, in which he had been born, were not adopting American ways, and it might be of value to find out why.

The members of Dewey's seminar selected for this prototype of today's "research grant" included the Blanshard twins, Brand and Paul; Frances Bradshaw, who married Brand Blanshard later that year; Irwin Edman, then twenty-one and working for his PhD; and an immigrant from the Warsaw ghetto, Anzia Yezierska, whom Dewey had allowed into his seminar for humanitarian reasons. Brand Blanshard, then twenty-six, had been a Rhodes scholar (he later became head of Yale's philosophy department). Paul Blanshard had already been ordained a Congregationalist minister (he later wrote *American Freedom and Catholic Power*). Edman had just obtained, with Dewey's help, an instructorship at Columbia (he later became head of Columbia's philosophy department and turned against Dewey).

Barnes paid each of the "social researchers" $100 a month (multiply by three for today's equivalent). He rented a house for them to use as headquarters, and to live in, on Richmond Street, one of the boundaries of Philadelphia's Polish district, and he supplied desks, typewriters, living equipment and a few amenities, including several copies each of Dewey's *Democracy and Education*, Trotter's *Instincts of the Herd in Peace and War*, and F. M. Alexander's *Man's Supreme Inheri-*

tance. The last had a foreword by Dewey, who was quite taken at that time with Alexander's contention that posture determines not only bodily fitness but also mental acuity. Barnes took lessons and treatments from Alexander for several years—at $50 each.

The "field study" was sub-divided into four major areas of inquiry. Brand Blanshard undertook to discover the role of the Catholic Church in the lives of the Polish immigrants. Miss Bradshaw studied the education of Polish children, which at that time was almost exclusively in parochial schools, and in the Polish language. Edman drew the easiest task—studying the Polish press, with Miss Yezierska doing the translating. The latter, when not translating for Edman, or accompanying Blanshard and Miss Bradshaw in order to translate for them "in the field," investigated the role of the women in the perpetuation of the Polish enclave. Paul Blanshard returned to New York. Barnes thought he wasn't interested.

Barnes visited the little band of researchers at least once a day, and soon realized that no more than the surface of the problem could be scratched in three months by four individuals who were total strangers to the milieu they were investigating. When Dewey arrived on the scene, toward the end of June, he agreed that Barnes' diagnosis of this particular "field study" was only too accurate. He was staying at Barnes' house and he and Barnes decided *they* would do some research on the researchers, i.e., tacitly observe what they did, how they did it, what they didn't do (and their rationalizations therefor), and what effect, if any, they had on the Poles they were investigating.

It was wartime and the Poles were prosperous. Many of the men worked in war plants, including Cramp's Shipyard, which was not far from the Richmond Street house. On several evenings Barnes and Dewey took Blanshard and Edman to the saloons and social clubs in which the Polish males congregated after work. They were neither welcomed nor repulsed. The same sort of uninterested tolerance greeted Miss

Bradshaw and Miss Yezierska when they tried to talk to the women, at their homes or in the stores.

The "field study" began to peter out in August and was wound up well before the end of that month. The conclusions reached by the researchers were obvious ones. The language barrier was the prime retardant in the assimilation process, and the Polish consulate, the Catholic Church, the proprietors of the Polish-language press in the United States, and some Polish merchants, were the chief proponents of non-assimilation. Arrayed against them were the wartime dynamics of American life, which were shattering most of the customs that would have made total assimilation a lengthier process.

Dewey was more tolerant than Barnes of the meagerness of the results. Whenever Barnes alluded to it in later years he gave one the impression that he considered it an example of the fatuity of foundation or government sponsored "projects," which he characterized as nothing but "vacations with pay." Dewey said the mere fact that a group of people had *tried* to investigate such a problem left a residue which had a small effect upon sociology, and possibly upon those investigated. Barnes was unconvinced. Nonetheless, throughout their lifelong friendship he rarely refused a request of Dewey's for financial help for a "project."

 XX

It was through Dewey that Barnes met the sort of writers who were the counterparts of the sort of painters he had met through Glackens. Dewey introduced him at the "New Republic," where Herbert Croly welcomed him, as well he might, for Barnes helped that periodical financially on many occasions (he read it every week and occasionally wrote for it). Dewey also took Barnes down to the Provincetown Players, which Barnes assisted financially more than once.

Barnes liked George Cram ("Jig") Cook, who, with his wife, Susan Glaspell, had organized the Provincetown Players. Cook wrote the first play—*Suppressed Desires*—put on in the studio which Mrs. Wilbur Daniel Steele had fashioned "at the end of Mary Heaton Vorse's wharf" in Provincetown, Mass. Cook was the kind of romantic Barnes liked—to visit, and fondly recollect. Also to help.

Susan Glaspell's *Road to the Temple,* a subjective but nevertheless discerning biography of Cook, was published shortly before I met Barnes and I had only known him a week or two when he told me to read it. After I had done so he questioned me about it and my answers made him conclude newspapering had made me substitute a superficial cynicism for native intelligence and had rendered me incapable of perceiving the deeper truths about a man like Cook.

Barnes said Cook was the best kind of rebel against the status quo because "he knew something about the past" and "his desire to make life better wasn't the whine of an inadequate." In the copy of *The Road to the Temple* he lent me he had marked Cook's description of the group from which the Provincetown Players had come: "Writers, critics, adventurers, painters, having in common a feeling that it would be better to be destroyed than not to create one's own beauty."

Barnes said he had been sorry, in 1921, when Cook forsook the Playwrights' Theatre on MacDougall Street in New York and went to live in Greece. He sympathized, in a way, with Cook's feeling that the Playwrights' Theatre had become "too successful," but he thought Cook should engage the "betrayers" in an all-out fight. Cook, Barnes said, had "the old American thing," i.e., simple honesty and a straight-forward, disinterested desire for life to be better for all. "His

68

idealization of the Greeks was moonshine," Barnes added, "he should have cleaned things up here in his own backyard." A dozen years later, when Cook's daughter, Nilla, who became a disciple of Gandhi, published her autobiography, I asked Barnes if he intended to read it. He replied: "No. She's so far away from her roots she's in a dream world."

Barnes often cited Cook as an example of a man who lacked the self-confidence he was entitled to possess, and who, instead of creating significant works himself, helped others to do it. By this Barnes referred to Eugene O'Neill, who, but for the Provincetown Players, Barnes believed, might never have become our day's foremost dramatist. Barnes had little sympathy for O'Neill's preoccupation with despair, but he had enormous admiration for O'Neill's ability to manipulate ideas in visual and dramatic terms.

Indeed, I often thought Cook's support of O'Neill was the chief reason Barnes supported the Provincetown Players and the Playwrights' Theatre. For Barnes thought little or nothing of the other playwrights—John Reed, Floyd Dell, Susan Glaspell, Edna St. Vincent Millay, Sherwood Anderson, Paul Green and e. e. cummings (especially the last). He liked some of Millay's poems but he thought her plays, and most of the plays of most of the others I have just mentioned, mere attitudinizing. He had no sympathy whatever for John Reed, whom he regarded as a publicity-seeking opportunist.

I once argued with him about Reed, and suggested that a certain amount of self-exploitation is necessary in anyone who attempts to lead large groups of people in times of dynamic social change. Barnes acknowledged this but added: "It's a second-rate game."

I surmised then, and I think now, that his dislike of Reed derived from his devotion to democracy. He thought Reed had renounced the highest social achievement of man, democracy, for a regressive form of tyranny, which it might take centuries to get rid of. Although Barnes had helped "The Masses" when it was suppressed for anti-war agitation, he never, to my knowledge, read the "New Masses," and he never wittingly contributed to a Communist cause, though he did contribute to things in which Communists had injected themselves, as, for example, the Sacco-Vanzetti case.

I once asked him if he didn't think that Stalin's tyrannies were necessary, that without the use of force the counter-revolution would win. Barnes said contemptuously: "Every tyrant has used that excuse." In the '30s, when the Russian revolution was devouring its children, Barnes took pleasure in saying: "I told you so." And he financially helped Trotsky's campaign for vindication, especially the international committee that investigated Stalin's charges of Trotsky's involvement with "Old Bolsheviks" and Soviet generals in an international anti-Soviet conspiracy.

All this had nothing to do with opposition to communism per se, although Barnes did oppose the Russian form of it, and its intellectual baggage, especially dialectical materialism, which he considered mechanical and fallacious, and economic determinism, which he called a meaningless catch-phrase. "Men do not live by bread alone," he said, *and meant it*, for he devoted his life, his fortune, and most of his waking hours, to proving that art, not economics, makes men a little lower than the angels.

Barnes' economic views were not conservative, however. He believed a certain amount of government control over business was necessary, and he thought Roosevelt and his New Deal had prevented totalitarianism here. He believed in a mixed economy—some socialism, democratically arrived at, and some private enterprise. Complete communism—"from each according to his ability, to each according to his need" —he thought unrealistic and contrary to nature. He did not believe environment is all-controlling, but that character traits, inherited and acquired, decide an individual's destiny.

I was always surprised at how well informed he was about contemporary events and personalities. In addition to reading everything of any consequence that had to do with painting and general aesthetics, and any current book or novel of genuine significance, he regularly read, except when he was traveling abroad, "The New Republic," "The Nation," "Time," "The New Leader," "The New Yorker," the "Mercure de France," and the Philadelphia newspapers, including their society sections.

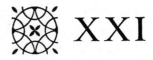 XXI

Barnes' international reputation as a collector and art authority was established in the decade after World War I.

By the time that disaster to Western civilization was over he had decided on the immediate goals to which he would devote his life and his fortune, and had laid down most of the guide lines which determined and delimited his future.

The goals were chiefly three. First, to make his collection as representative of *all* the traditions of painting as he could. Second, to build a gallery for the collection in which it could be studied systematically in accordance with Dewey's educational principles. Third, to write and disseminate books which would make available to the general public the fruits of his own studies and reflections, and those of the teachers and students of the Foundation he would create.

Within a few months after the armistice of November 11, 1918, Barnes was in Europe on a campaign of acquisition which, in its intensive phase, extended over several years. Needless to say, he was waited upon by all the important dealers, and especially by Paul Guillaume, who, as has been said, became Barnes' European representative and the dealer through whom Barnes cleared most of his purchases in the ensuing decade.

Guillaume was then just coming into his own, and his gallery was considered very avant garde. He had been one of the earliest proponents of African sculpture, and the first dealer of any pretensions to rescue examples of it from the curio shops and junkyards of Paris. He had written extensively about it, and had even declared Western painting would have come to a dead end but for its influence upon post-impressionist painters! Guillaume and his wife* knew everyone, and were sedulous in getting interesting people to their gallery for Barnes to meet.

Renoir, whom Barnes never met, died in 1919 and Barnes visited his studio shortly thereafter and bought quite a few things. The following year Leo Stein sold Barnes some of the better pictures he then possessed. From a Greek collector Barnes obtained more than a score of Greek and Egyptian figurines. Through Durand-Ruel, Hodebert and others he obtained examples of Italian, French and Dutch primitives. He acquired an El Greco. And a large assortment of the work of Pascin, Derain, Laurencin, Chirico (who painted Barnes' portrait), Gritchenko, Lotiron, Perdriat, and many others, most of which he later traded off, especially in the 1930s and '40s. Barnes also bought a large assortment of Guillaume's African sculpture.

It was Guillaume who put Soutine over with Barnes, and it was Barnes who put Soutine over with the public. Guillaume put the canvas called "La Patissiere" in his window on a day he expected a visit from Barnes, and when Barnes expressed surprise, and interest, insisted he see the rest of Soutine's paintings at the Zborowski Gallery, where Barnes bought about sixty canvases for $50 each. Zborowski also offered Barnes some Modiglianis, none of which he had been able to sell. Barnes' purchase of them put Modigliani over, too.

Guillaume was also responsible for interesting Barnes in the sculpture of Jacques Lipchitz, who, like Soutine and Modigliani, was also catapulted to fame by Barnes' purchases.

* After Guillaume's death she married Jean Walter.

Barnes at first liked Lipchitz, took him along when he visited dealers and museums, commissioned him to do bas-reliefs for the façade of the Foundation's gallery, and paid for the visit to the United States of Lipchitz and his wife. Later on he came to the conclusion that Lipchitz was using their friendship to promote himself and some of his artist friends.

In January '23 Guillaume put on an exhibition of some of Barnes' "furtherest out" acquisitions, as the current saying is. Soutine and Modigliani were emphasized, of course, and the show created quite a stir. Some of the publicity ruses Guillaume employed to put it over made a lasting impression on Barnes, and not a few of the things Barnes did in later years, which the public misunderstood, were patterned upon Guillaume's publicity techniques.

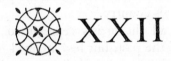 XXII

A month or so before the Guillaume show in Paris, the Commonwealth of Pennsylvania had granted the about-to-be-born Barnes Foundation a charter as an educational institution, and in Philadelphia art circles there was considerable excitement over what Barnes intended to do. When news of the Guillaume show reached Philadelphia, Henry McCarter and Arthur Carles, two of the painters then teaching at the Pennsylvania Academy of Fine Arts, both of whom Barnes knew and liked, asked him to let the Academy put on the same exhibition Guillaume had, and Barnes agreed.

In the foreword he wrote for this Academy show, which opened on April 11, 1923, Barnes acknowledged that "both the paintings and sculpture will probably seem strange to most people." However, he continued, that was usually the case

73

with the new, and he recalled the violently negative reaction in Philadelphia to a piece of Schönberg's when it had been first performed by the Philadelphia Orchestra, and the applause for the same piece when it was repeated some years later.

After remarking that "all the artists represented here, except Modigliani, are living, and all are under thirty-five years of age except Picasso, Matisse and Derain," Barnes asserted that "these young artists speak a language which has come to them from the reaction between their own traits, the circumstances of the world we all live in, and the experience they themselves have had." They all lived in Paris, he continued, but had been born and spent their youth in such diverse places as Russia, Poland, Italy, Spain, Bulgaria, Lithuania and Belgium. "Their work," he declared, "is a product of the influence of the French environment upon cultures and endowments racially and radically foreign to France. Perhaps that explains why the exhibit differs in certain significant phases from any held previously in this country."

Barnes then averred that all the artists represented had studied the great paintings of the past, but had attained to as individualized expressions "of what they believe constitute the essentials of the plastic art" as had any of their predecessors.

"To quarrel with them for being different from the great masters," Barnes warned, "is about as rational as to find fault with the size of a person's shoes or the shape of his ears. If one will accord to these artists the simple justice of educated and unbiased attention, one will see the truth of what experienced students of painting all assert: that old art and new art are the same in fundamental principles. The difference lies only in the degree of greatness, and time alone can gauge that with accuracy."

The review of this exhibition in the "Public Ledger," then Philadelphia's most prestigious newspaper, was written by Edith W. Powell, who knew Barnes and had seen many of

74

his earlier acquisitions. She declared that "Soutine represents the falling to pieces of old concepts." He may "present life as he sees it," she conceded, but what Soutine saw, and the way he saw it, was "diseased and degenerate."

Dorothy Grafly, the daughter of the sculptor, reviewed the exhibition for the "North American," and quoted a remark Arthur Carles had made when he had conducted a sort of briefing for the critics' benefit. He had said that any sort of subject matter can be transformed into a work of art and that he himself could find beauty in a jumbled mass of wrecked freight cars.

"The modernists," observed Miss Grafly, "appreciate a wreck, human or otherwise. It is the 'modernist' in us which will draw us to see blood stream into the gutters after an accident, or watch the parts of a mangled human being gathered into a basket. We may not go home and paint our sensations. It requires courage or bravado for a man to exhibit his depravity in public."

The modernists, Miss Grafly continued, lack subtlety, delicacy and finesse, and their "fevered passion" is only "for unclean things." To her the room in which Barnes' paintings and sculpture were being exhibited seemed "infested with infectious scourge."

The critic for the "Inquirer," C. H. Bonte, attempted to be cute, in an androgynous sort of way. He characterized most of the things shown as "often indescribable curiosities," and Soutine's canvases as "seemingly incomprehensible masses of paint." Matisse's "Joie de Vivre," however, in Bonte's eyes, had certain resemblances to Botticelli, and Picasso's "Peasants and Oxen" had good color and design. He also had ambiguous things to say about some of the canvases of Derain, Pascin, Kisling and Utrillo. And he simply loved Perdriat's "Idyll."

The public's reaction was much like the critics'. One of the fashionable psychiatrists of the day, Dr. Francis X. Dercum, said the insane had produced pictures "superior to the alleged works of art I saw at the exhibition," which he considered "ghastly lesions of the mind and of the body" painted by people who were "either crazy or moral degenerates."

Barnes at once offered to give $100,000 to the Philadelphia Orchestra if Dercum could prove that his comments about the exhibition were free of the mental aberrations he thought he saw in the paintings. This was tantamount to asking the psychiatrist to prove his own sanity, and Dercum refrained.

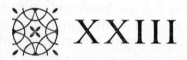 XXIII

Two days after the Commonwealth of Pennsylvania, on December 4, 1922, granted the Barnes Foundation its charter as an educational institution, Barnes turned over to the newly created corporation his entire collection of paintings and sculpture, then conservatively valued at $5,000,000; endowed the Foundation with 900 shares of the common stock of the A. C. Barnes Co., which was to yield an annual income that varied between $250,000 and $450,000, and brought $6,000,000 when the shares were sold in the summer of 1929; and deeded to the Foundation the eleven and a half acre tract north of his home on which was being erected a gallery and administration building.

The indenture committing him irrevocably to this gift was made part of a set of by-laws which stated that "the objects for which this corporation is formed are as follows: To promote the advancement of education and the appreciation of the fine arts; and for this purpose to erect, found and maintain, in the Township of Lower Merion, County of Montgomery, and State of Pennsylvania, an art gallery and other necessary buildings for the exhibition of works of ancient and modern art, and the maintenance in connection therewith of an arboretum, wherein shall be cultivated and maintained trees and shrubs for the study and for the encouragement of arboriculture and forestry, together with a laboratory of arboriculture, if the same shall be found necessary, said arboretum and laboratory to be conducted independently, or in connection with the department of forestry of any university founded and conducted under the laws of the Commonwealth of Pennsylvania."

The original trustees were five in number—Barnes, his wife, Nelle Mullen and her sister, Mary, and Joseph Lapsley Wilson, who had sold Barnes the tract upon which the gallery now stands, and on which Wilson had lived for more than 40 years. Barnes had a road constructed along the northern border of the property, which Mrs. Barnes named Lapsley Road, and built a modern house on it for the old gentleman and his wife, for which the Wilsons paid Barnes a rent of one dollar a year.

Barnes' scheme for replacing trustees was originally this: while he and his wife lived individuals would be nominated and elected by the trustees to fill vacancies, but thereafter to fill the first vacancy the trustees must elect a person who would be nominated by the financial institution which "may then be the treasurer of the corporation." To fill the next vacancy a person nominated by the Board of Trustees of the University of Pennsylvania must be elected, and to fill the vacancy after that a person nominated by the Board of Trustees of the Pennsylvania Academy of Fine Arts. The University and the Academy would nominate alternately thereafter, save when the trustee nominated by the financial institution had to be replaced, in which case a new nominee of that institution had to be elected.

Barnes changed this all important provision several times. The last time he did so was less than a year before his death.

The indenture and by-laws, and their revisions, contain important provisions revelatory of his psychology.

A 1946 amendment provided that after his death "the collection shall be closed, and thereafter no change therein shall be made by the purchase, bequest or otherwise obtaining of additional pictures, or other works of art, or other objects of whatever description. Furthermore, after the death of the Donor and his wife no buildings, for any purpose whatsoever, shall be built or erected on any part of the property of the Donee," i.e., the Barnes Foundation.

Other stipulations:

After Barnes' death no picture belonging to the collection shall ever be loaned, sold or otherwise disposed of except "if any picture passes into a state of actual decay so that it no longer is of any value, it may be removed from the collection for that reason only."

If the collection is ever destroyed, or "it should for any other reason become impossible to administer the trust hereby created concerning the said collection of pictures, then the property and funds contributed by the Donor to the Donee shall be applied to an object as nearly within the scope herein indicated and laid down as shall be possible, such application to be in connection with an existing and organized institution then in being and functioning in Philadelphia or its suburbs."

After the deaths of the Donor and his wife no one but a caretaker may ever live on the Foundation's property.

During the lives of the Donor and his wife the gallery shall be open to the public on not more than two days a week, except during July, August and September, and then only by cards of admission. After the deaths of the Donor and his wife the gallery will be open two days a week, except during July and August, to students and instructors of the Pennsylvania Academy of Fine Arts "and similar institutions," and shall be open three days a week, one of which shall be Sunday, to the public under such regulations "as the Board of Trustees may make."

Barnes then explicitly stipulated that it should "be incumbent on the Board of Trustees to make such regulations as will ensure that it is the plain people, that is, men and women who gain their livelihood by daily toil in shops, factories, schools, stores and similar places, who shall have free access to the art gallery upon those days when the gallery is open to the public."

This admission policy, but not the stricture upon the trustees to guarantee access to the gallery to the "plain people," was also revised several times.

Barnes expressly forbade, after his death, the use of Foundation property for "any social functions commonly designated receptions, tea parties, dinners, banquets, dances, musicales or similar affairs, whether such functions be given by officials, trustees or employes of the Barnes Foundation, or any other person or persons whatsoever, or whether such functions be private or public. Any citizen of Pennsylvania who petitions the Courts for an injunction, based on what reputable legal counsel consider sufficient evidence that the above-mentioned stipulation has been violated, shall have his total legal expense paid by the Barnes Foundation."

The gallery was never to be used for the exhibition of works of art "or of any works whatsoever" that do not belong to the Foundation. This was later amended to prohibit the use of the gallery for painting, drawing, sculpturing "by anybody, whether students, instructors, or whatever. This means specifically that the Barnes Foundation is to be maintained perpetually for education in the appreciation of the fine arts and not as a school for instruction in painting, drawing, sculpturing or any other branch of art or craftsmanship. This restriction also prohibits the copying of any of the art of the Barnes Foundation by any person whatsoever."

Finally, no "painter, sculptor or other artist of any description whatsoever will ever be permitted to use any of the buildings, or the contents of those buildings, for the instruction of pupils who pay or ever paid a fee to that artist, sculptor, etc., for private instruction in art or other form of education."

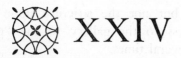 XXIV

The architect who designed the Foundation's gallery and administration building was Paul Philippe Cret, at the time professor of architectural design at the University of Pennsylvania. Barnes never regretted having chosen Cret, though he did come to regard him as "a man with only one string to his bow."

There were intangible reasons, as well as Cret's abilities, for Barnes' choice. He and Cret were about the same age, Cret was French, and had done so well at the Ecole des Beaux Arts in Paris that as soon as he received his diploma, in 1903, the University of Pennsylvania, Barnes' alma mater, had made him an assistant professor. He had quickly adjusted to American life and was liked at Penn and in Philadelphia, especially by architects, some of the best of whom used him as a designer and consultant.

Basically, Cret's taste was classical, in the best sense of that abused word, i.e., he knew the traditions and had assimilated them. The word "assimilated" is important in this connection, for it was one of Barnes' touchstones for judging artistic ability. And although Cret eschewed arid extremes of functionalism, he never wandered, in his designs, from the purposes his buildings were intended to serve.

Some of Cret's best work was done after he designed the gallery of the Barnes Foundation, a commission which undoubtedly advanced his career. Today the Cret touch is to be seen in many other important architectural creations, notably the Detroit Institute of Art; the Folger Shakespearean Library and the Federal Reserve Board building in Washington; the lovely Delaware River Bridge at Philadelphia (now called the Benjamin Franklin Bridge); the American memorial at Chateau-Thierry; the library of the University of Texas; and some of the new buildings at West Point and Annapolis.

Barnes had never learned to read a blueprint and his liaison with Cret and the builders, while the gallery was going up, was Mrs. Barnes. But he had had very thorough discussions with Cret when the architect was thinking out the principles on which he would base his designs.

Cret felt the gallery should provide "conditions the painters themselves would approve." By this he meant there should be no crowding, and that the lighting should be similar to that in which the pictures had been painted. Therefore, Cret reasoned, the rooms should be small, but, to avoid monotony, of varying proportions. The light should not come from the ceiling, and the windows should be high up from the floor.

Cret knew, of course, that corridors in an art gallery are unnecessary, and he avoided them by having two series of interconnecting rooms branch off from a large central hall. He also knew that architectural decoration inside a gallery diverts attention from the paintings, and eschewed it.

Cret's exterior design was an adaptation of the chateau styles of the French Renaissance and was executed in a buff-colored limestone from Coutaineau, France. The roof was faced with red, vaulted tiles.

The final result, which cost about half a million dollars, proved to be an aesthetic as well as a utilitarian success. Close up, as well as from a distance, the exterior of the Barnes Foundation's gallery is as much a visual pleasure today as when it was built. Inside, Cret's lay-out of the rooms enables the pictures and other art objects to be seen with an intimacy museums rarely achieve, and also enables the Foundation's classes to assemble without classroom-like formality.

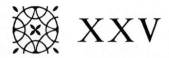 XXV

The formal announcement of Barnes' plans for a gallery and an educational institution was made by Forbes Watson in two issues of "The Arts"—those of January and February 1923.

In his letter authorizing the announcement Barnes said "the hope is that every person, of whatever station in life, will be allowed to get his own reactions to whatever the Foundation has to offer. That means academicism, conformity to outworn conditions, and counterfeits in art, living and thinking, can have no place in the intended scope of the Foundation."

Barnes was serious about the study of art, Watson said, and was beholden to nobody, neither for the wherewithal to buy paintings nor for the judgment to select them. Rumors about Barnes' collection, he continued, had been circulating among artists for a decade, and he predicted that the kind of museum Barnes had in mind "would have no rivals," since its main function would be "to show the work of the men who have changed the course of art since impressionism."

"What if a large part of the public is not yet prepared to enjoy this art?" Watson asked, and answered his question by saying: "The country is not lost if they do not instantly enjoy it. Its value is very great whether regarded as giving an opportunity to amateurs for enjoyment, pure and simple, of works of art, or in giving richer opportunities of study to the young American artist."

Watson characterized Barnes' collection, "of which the cornerstones are Renoir and Cézanne" as a structure into which "nothing drifted for no reason—everything is related to everything else." He said the collection contained, in addition to 150 Renoirs and 50 Cézannes, representations of all the best contemporary French and American painters, and outstanding examples of African sculpture.

Watson's articles were illustrated with thirty photographs of the Foundation's paintings, and it was these which gave the American public at large its first adequate idea of the collection which the Barnes Foundation would use in its educational work. The illustrations included a portrait by Goya; two canvases by Daumier; two portraits of Mme. Cézanne and five other Cézanne canvases; Renoir's "Torso," "Woman and Child," "After the Bath," "Young Girls," and a nude; Picasso's "Young Acrobat"; two portraits by Van Gogh, and his "Postman"; Eakins' portrait of Dr. Agnew; Pascin's "Woman in Dishabille"; Demuth's "Vaudeville"; and paintings by Manet, Monet, Laurencin, Ernest Lawson and the two Prendergasts. But nothing by Glackens, since, Watson explained, he was preparing a separate article on Glackens that would be illustrated by reproductions of a half dozen of the Foundation's examples of that artist's work.

In addition to paintings and sculpture, Watson pointed out, the Foundation also had an arboretum, and he quoted Barnes' hope that the arboretum would be used by the University of Pennsylvania to educate "those who believe better effects can be obtained in American landscape by the study and use of such knowledge as an arboretum affords."

A "fearless" collector of contemporary art such as Dr. Barnes, Watson said in conclusion, "has it in his power to bestow a quite unique benefit upon the public."

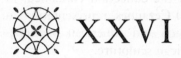 XXVI

While all this was going forward Barnes began work on the book that was to have so primary a place in the educational work to which he devoted so much of his subsequent life.

The impulse to write *The Art in Painting*, he once told me, came to him from reading Percy Moore Turner's *Appreciation of Painting*, which, incidentally, he reviewed in "The Arts." It had been published in England and Scribners had distributed a few copies of it here.

Appreciation of Painting is an able book and still worth reading. It contains many ideas that Barnes wanted his Foundation to disseminate, including the all-important truism that anyone, by effort, can develop the ability to understand and enjoy art.

As Barnes indicated in his review of the book, his admiration for Turner was not only because Turner was "one of the few men whose opinions were free of God-like pomposity" and whose writing was free of the jargon and "ipse dixits" which vitiate so many books about art, but because Turner believed the joy to be found in the contemplation of art is as real as the joy of its creation, and that the emotional capacity required for intelligent contemplation can be attained by genuine, and sustained, effort.

An artist, Turner thought, is he "who by means of some instrument, such as a picture, transmits emotions to a responsive person, or, at least, evokes some aesthetic feeling in him, though the wish to transmit such emotion need not be present." A work of art, according to Turner, is "the vehicle of this transmission." He further defined art as "the quality which enables the producer to tear out a bit of the soul of nature, and so to present it as to excite every artistic emotion within us by an appeal which derives its cogency from its universality."

The praise with which Barnes concluded his review of Turner's book defines the kind of book he resolved to write himself.

Turner, Barnes said, had "traversed the whole field of painting from the primitives to the futurists in a single volume of 236 pages. It shows no signs of forced labor, of padding, or of over-condensation, of prejudices or over-enthusiasm, of egotism, or inaccuracies of statement, of psychological sophistry, or of preciosity. Therein it differs from all other books available to people who feel something when they look at a picture, and desire to know more about what they feel and what they see, or fail to see."

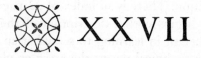 XXVII

The Art in Painting is a unique personal achievement, as well as a contribution to the culture of our time. Now almost forty years old, it still provides a means by which the uninformed can learn what art is, and a method by which the initiated can deepen their understanding of art's meaning to man.

Barnes wrote it during the years in which the Foundation's gallery was being built, and its publication, by the Foundation, was practically simultaneous with the formal dedication of the gallery.

He was helped in assembling the data on which analyses of individual paintings are based, and in formulating philosophical statements about aesthetics, by Laurence Buermeyer. Barnes never forgot the pleasure they had together studying systematically the work of Santayana, Bosanquet, Rignano and many other thinkers who have tried to sift the philosophical and psychological wheat and chaff of aesthetics. The ruin that Buermeyer brought upon his career a few years later was also a tragedy for Barnes, who never again found a mind so akin to his own, and never again found anyone else he could consider a successor to himself.

The Art in Painting was dedicated "To John Dewey, whose conceptions of experience, of method, of education, inspired the work of which this book is a part."

It has been published in three editions, and the last, prepared in 1937, changes nothing that was basic in the original one. As now published it is a volume of 525 pages, of which 301 deal with Barnes' method for the study of art and the traditions of painting; 89 contain analyses of individual paintings; 25 inform the reader in what museums or collections the pictures discussed are to be found; and 104 present illustrations of 122 examples of paintings and sculpture, 62 of which were not in the first edition. There is an index of 22 pages.

The Art in Painting begins with a description of the psychological problems inherent in learning to see what an artist intended; perceiving the technical means the artist employed; *understanding* the human, social or symbolical meaning of a picture; and linking this meaning to the main stream of one's own experience, and to the human experience in general. There is no short cut, Barnes warned, in learning how to do this. You must be interested sufficiently to expend time and energy, and to expend them in a *systematic* way. "Art is as little a plaything, a matter of caprice or uncontrolled subjectivity," he said, "as is physics or chemistry. What has made the study of science valuable and fruitful is *method*."

After making the point that there is art *in* everything—the preposition "in" was incorporated into the title of his book—Barnes explained why art appeals to all sorts and conditions of men: it is one of the ways in which the instincts find satisfaction. All too often our instincts, and the emotions which express them, are mutually antithetical, and the art of life consists in organizing our instinctual drives into harmonious "interests." When we succeed in this we have introduced art into our lives. When an artist succeeds in doing it, in a painting or a poem or a play, he enables us to perceive the deeper meanings of our individual plight, the human situation, the universe itself, or otherwise to obtain instinctual satisfactions. An artist, Barnes declared in his early pages, is he who perceives "the qualities of things which heighten their human significance."

This ability to perceive what many men never notice distinguishes an artist from a craftsman, no matter how great the latter's dexterity in putting paint on canvas, chiseling stone, using words, or combining musical sounds.

What Manet and others meant when they said the subject of a painting did not matter, Barnes then explained, was that the things which interested them can be found in *any* subject whatever. But there is a difference between subject and subject-matter. Many painters have painted their conceptions of the Crucifixion. The *subject* of these pictures is the Crucifixion, but their subject-*matter* consists of the objects, and the arrangement thereof, wherewith they presented the *subject*. Barnes did not believe subject-matter is unimportant, though he always acknowledged that "forms may be charged with aesthetic feeling even when they represent nothing definite in the real world."

A good painting, Barnes believed, is one in which the plastic ingredients—color, line, light and space—are so utilized that "the essence, the reality of a situation" are revealed in a way characteristic of the painter's personality, without the aid of any sentimental, topical, propagandistic or other associational ideas. The artist's personality, however, is not of primary interest. The true artist reveals more of reality than ordinary men apprehend. His personality is revealed in the *way* in which he shows us this greater reality.

The most important of the plastic means, Barnes believed, is color. Light, line, drawing, modeling, composition, design (in the sense not of pattern but of an overall conception)—all have their function, but color is the one plastic means which most effectively organizes and vivifies all the others. However, color must be used *structurally*, for otherwise it is an emphasis of a plastic means for its own sake, which is pedantry. Finally, in deploying the plastic means, contrast and rhythm are essential if unity *through variety* is to be achieved, which is one of the goals of art.

The traditions of painting start, Barnes thought, with the evolution of painting out of mosaics. By the time of the Pompeian frescoes (first century B.C.), he said, painting was relatively highly developed.

The Florentine tradition began with Giotto, to whom Barnes credits four innovations: perspective, three-dimensional modeling, naturalism, and a new use of color. Masaccio greatly extended the naturalism Giotto introduced. Botticelli, a master of line, succeeded more in illustration than in the artistic integration of all the plastic means. Leonardo "was more scientist than artist," and in the paintings of Michelangelo "the claims of the sculptor and the literary poet conflict with the proper function of the painter." Raphael "was a first-rate virtuoso who was far from being a first-rate artist."

The Florentine form at its best, Barnes thought, had a strong sense of design "executed in delicate, harmonious, but not structurally used color, with expressive line, convincing modeling, effective lighting, and rhythmic, spacious composition." Also: "The step taken by Masaccio toward naturalism was enormously influential in the process of bringing art from preoccupation with another world to an interest in this world as it actually is."

The Venetian tradition, he said, began with Giovanni Bellini, who made color "seem to enter into the solid substances of objects." Carpaccio's greatest contribution to the Venetian tradition was a "very expressive use of space" which helped him to create "a circumambient atmosphere by which the effect of color in unifying composition was greatly increased in power." Giorgione's facility with color and line enabled him to further develop this "Venetian glow."

Barnes thought Giorgione's style "probably the most poetic in all painting," and Titian's influence upon later artists "perhaps unsurpassed." Tintoretto's importance, he said, is plain when "we recall that El Greco derived from Tintoretto and that much of what is best in modern painting comes from El Greco."

And he was sure that Venetian painting is "the high-water mark of pictorial art."

The Spanish tradition seemed to him to consist of the personal reactions to the contributions of the Venetians of three great painters—El Greco, Velasquez and Goya.

He thought El Greco used the plastic means for mystical ends, that is, made them intimate more than they visibly represented, just as the words a poet uses suggest more than the words themselves mean. Barnes never tired of citing the distortion in El Greco's paintings when he was justifying the distortions that abound in modern painting.

His praise for Velasquez was based on the fact that Velasquez' painting unified the plastic means so completely no one of them stood out, but there also lurked in his appreciation an admiration for the realism which Velasquez, a Court painter, introduced into his portraits. Barnes once suggested that I write a short story which would dramatize the facts that explain "how Velasquez was able to get away with it."

He thought Goya the greatest illustrator there has ever been.

The German tradition, in Barnes' opinion, has few glories. The greatest of them, of course, is Durer, whose work was free of the heaviness which disfigures so much German art, and whose portraits exhibit "so profound a knowledge of character—realized plastically to the full." Holbein's portraits seemed to Barnes to be more photographic than plastic.

He regarded the Flemish tradition, before Rubens, "with its characteristic color-scheme, clear-cut drawing, and miniature-like painting of detail in features, objects, stuffs, and landscape," as largely an outgrowth of the work of Jan van Eyck, whose portraits he called "supreme examples of an artist's legitimate use of the plastic means to convey the reality of human character with dignity, strength and power." The influence of van Eyck on other painters was enormous, Barnes said, and he specifically ascribed much that is best in Durer to van Eyck. He thought van der Weyden and Memling were van Eyck's inferiors. Hieronymus Bosch seemed to him to be an illustrator and caricaturist whose "importance as a colorist is likely to be overlooked." A greater colorist, the elder Pieter Brueghel, in Barnes' opinion, added "vivacity to the usually rather static Flemish form."

But it was Rubens, Barnes said, who "grafted upon the Flemish tradition the contributions of the Italian Renaissance," and, "more than anyone else, determined the development of later Italian, Spanish and English painting." Rubens' influence, Barnes believed, has been greater than that of Rembrandt and Velasquez "probably because their work, being more individual, subtle, and unapproachable, lent itself less to use by other men." As for Rubens' own paintings, Barnes thought them "grandiose rather than noble or elevated, noisy rather than perfectly convincing, and his means obvious rather than subtle." Nevertheless, he insisted, it was through Rubens that "the Renaissance traditions descended to modern art."

The influence of the seventeenth century Dutch, apart from Rembrandt, was confined to landscape and still-life, Barnes explained. He thought Salomon van Ruysdael had "a rare gift for putting quality into paint" and combined "a fine intelligence with an extraordinarily skillful technique." He acknowledged Franz Hals' technical skill, but thought he simplified too much, did not "grasp deep human values," and was addicted to virtuosity.

Barnes regarded Rembrandt as one of the greatest artists of all time, and said his mastery of chiaroscuro has never been equalled. No other painter "has so combined economy of means with richness and convincing reality," nor evoked so many universal emotions. Rembrandt's colors, Barnes acknowledged, were limited, but "in conjunction with chiaroscuro they assume a great variety" and enable "his expressive forms" to be "so interrelated that decoration is fused with expression in a perfect unity." Furthermore, Rembrandt, "the most mystical and religious of painters, with everything adventitious, remote, or perfunctory left out," represented "the consummation of what Bosanquet calls 'the homecoming of art,' the discovery of the profound meaning in the here and now." In Rembrandt, Barnes believed, the "imaginative interpretation of the actual world" reached its greatest height.

Barnes started his discussion of French painting with a chapter on the French primitives, in which he perceived not only Byzantine and Italian influences, but those of the French manuscript-illuminators and miniaturists.

He gave Poussin a special prominence in *The Art in Painting*, coupling him with Rubens, in the sense that "the whole of the Italian Renaissance in solution" was to be found in Poussin too. The phrase "in solution" was the chemist in Barnes bestowing praise. Poussin's color, delicacy of line, and linear rhythms, delighted Barnes, but he nevertheless felt Poussin "was rather the last of the Renaissance than a constructive factor in post-Renaissance painting."

Barnes thought Watteau academic and repetitive, Boucher superficial and mechanical, and Fragonard a facile eclectic. But for Chardin he could never say enough. Chardin "restored to French painting the dignity of the Venetians," and his mastery of the medium was such that he could give, with seemingly effortless simplicity, and with a grace and delicacy that were functional as well as decorative, "the substance, structure and meaning of things." Chardin's influence, Barnes believed, was incalculable, especially on Goya, Courbet, Corot, Cézanne and Renoir.

David and Ingres were merely very proficient technically, in Barnes' view, and Delacroix was important chiefly because his use of color influenced "such first-rate artists as Renoir and Cézanne." But Corot could use the plastic means so skillfully "his best work represents a balanced creation, containing *in solution* the finest traditions of painting" (my italics).

Courbet, said Barnes, "started the so-called realistic movement which has dominated so much of the important painting since his time." Courbet was not only a masterly painter but "a superb artist in his feeling for the relations of things." His depictions of everyday objects and events provide "a rather subtle abstract of the deeper meanings of the great traditions, stripped of their external appendages and welded in a new and vigorous form, which has had a revolutionary effect."

Daumier's emphasis on design, at the expense of subject matter, Barnes believed, "profoundly influenced the movement in modern art which started about the middle of the nineteenth century." Barnes thought Daumier especially adroit in the use of space, chiaroscuro, and line, and that his greatness as a painter has been obscured by the widespread interest in his cartoons and drawings. Daumier's high place in the history of painting, Barnes declared, is the result not only of his own work but of his influence upon others.

In his chapter on landscape painting Barnes cited Claude le Lorrain for the feeling of place he was able to achieve, and said Rubens' landscapes are too busy. Constable, he thought, had the same feeling for place Claude did, but Constable's was "for the intime, the quietly mystical feeling of the countryside." Constable's composition, Barnes felt, was of the highest order "because it is organized by means of color, as in all the greatest painters."

And he called Constable "the father of impressionism."

Impressionism, Barnes explained, started something new,

something not in the traditions which preceded it, to wit, an interest in the plastic ingredients of a painting rather than in the painting's subject matter. In impressionist painting the drawing is "very broad"; liberties are taken with color, and a single color is sometimes divided into its components; perspective is distorted. The goal is "the realization of pure design."

Barnes had no sympathy, however, with "those ultra-modern writers who contend that plastic form is an absolute creation of the artist, in which no attempt is made to render the quality of anything in nature." Such painting, he declared, results in nothing but decoration, and often not even in that, as in cubism, which, Barnes said, "reduces design to the level of mere pattern."

Despite his predispositions in favor of French impressionists and "post-impressionists," Barnes' appraisals of them were not undiluted eulogies. He thought Monet's experiments with light and color often resulted in "a too literal reproduction of the superficial appearance of things." Pissaro's pointillism seemed to him to be "an obvious over-accentuation of a plastic means." But he thought the pointillism of Seurat effective because of that painter's "mastery of color and space-composition."

Manet's "marvellous ability to apply paint," Barnes declared, enabled him to make color and light the organizing elements of his composition, and his simplified drawing and use of broad areas of flat color, in which detailed representation was avoided, influenced all the impressionists, including Renoir and Cézanne and "most subsequent painters of importance." Unfortunately, Barnes added, "Manet's vanity prompted him to 'show off,' and the frequency of that exhibition of weakness bars him from the class of the highest artists."

Although Barnes admired the fluency of Degas' line, he deplored the deficiencies of his color and thought him superficial intellectually. He thought Gauguin used the plastic

93

means for little but decoration, and that Van Gogh's merit lay chiefly in daring color-contrasts and an astonishing sense of color rhythms. He acknowledged Picasso's technical versatility but said his various "periods" and experiments are the unreflective distractions of an impulsive temperament rather than a "fulfillment of his earlier and more natural interests."

Barnes' relatively brief statements in *The Art in Painting* about Soutine, Modigliani, Pascin, Utrillo, Rouault, Derain and Chirico will be covered in conversations on which I shall report later. His full discussions of Renoir, Cézanne and Matisse in *The Art in Painting* will be dealt with when I describe the thoughtful books Barnes wrote about each of those men. Of his analyses of individual paintings in the concluding portion of *The Art in Painting* I shall say nothing. I lack sufficient knowledge to venture comments about them, and Barnes himself considered them as crude first attempts at analyzing the plastic content of a painting.

I have no illusions about this summary of the contents of *The Art in Painting*. It is cursory, and reeks with my own intellectual and aesthetic preconceptions, predispositions, prejudices and lacks, and omits more than it includes. Do not think you know about this wonderful book because you have read what I have written about it here. It is a pioneering work, and after almost forty years it can still be read, with profit, by anyone who is seriously interested in art and art's meaning for man.

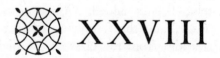 XXVIII

Barnes once told me that in the early years of Argyrol's great success, when it was clear he would soon be very rich, he sometimes paused on his morning walk at a spot from which he could observe the trains on the Pennsylvania Railroad's Main Line.

"I would note the numbers on the freight cars," he recalled, with obvious self-amusement, "and say to myself, 'I have that many dollars,' or 'I have more than that,' or 'I wonder if I'll ever have that many.'"

He related this incident for a purpose. He was urging me to abandon newspaper work and discover my actual potentialities and how to realize them, and he wanted to illustrate the crude, naïve ways in which the human mind accustoms itself to new facts and new relationships.

He further illustrated this subtle psychological mechanism by telling me the thought which had skipped in and out of his mind on the day the Foundation's beautiful gallery was dedicated. "My feelings put together a curious phrase in my subconscious," he said, "It was a variation of the one Morse sent over his telegraph line: 'What hath my parents wrought.'"

But Barnes' sentimentality rarely so overshadowed his basic realism. He was certainly never sentimental about his parents as persons. But he was always mindful of the myriad ways in which the past affects the present, as is evident from his emphasis upon the role of the traditions in a creative painter's style. As a matter of fact, he had first thought of calling the Foundation the Lydia S. Barnes Foundation, his mother's name, and might have done so had not Mrs. Barnes convinced him he had had considerably more to do with the existence of the Foundation than had his mother, and that the name "Barnes Foundation" adequately set reverberating the allusions to his parents that were echoing in his sub-conscious.

The gallery was dedicated on March 19, 1925, in the presence of several hundred people and the dedicatory address, of course, was made by the "director of education of the Barnes Foundation," John Dewey.

In dedicating the gallery, and the Foundation, to "the cause of education," Dewey said, "we are really celebrating here today one of the most significant steps taken in this country for freedom of pictorial or plastic art, for art in education, and for what is genuine and forward-moving throughout the whole field of education."

"This enterprise," he continued, "is not simply a building for the collection of pictures and the dissemination of knowledge about pictures. It is, rather, the expression of a profound belief that all the daily activities of life, the necessary business and commercial activities of life, may be made intrinsically significant, may be made sources of joy to those who engage in them so that they can put their whole beings, not merely their hands and a small section of their brain, but their feelings and emotions, into what they are doing."

Dewey praised "the intelligence, instead of force and mere mechanical efficiency," which had enabled Barnes to build the business that had earned the money which made the Foundation possible, and praised Barnes for rewarding his employes and colleagues "not only by pecuniary renumeration but also by the cultivation and development of their own souls."

He alluded to the arboretum which would be added to the trees planted on the Foundation's property so many years before by Joseph Lapsley Wilson and which "under the especial charge of Mrs. Barnes, the vice-president of the Foundation . . . will be a worthy setting for the beauty within the gallery . . . and part of the educational resources of the Foundation."

He called the examples of African sculpture in the Foundation's collection symbols of the Foundation's interest in "what sometimes seems to be not merely a perplexing but a hopeless problem—that of race relations," and characterized the African sculptures as an evidence of the Negro's artistic capacity that furthers "the cause of bringing all people from all over the world together in greater harmony."

Though it is always dangerous to prophesy, Dewey said in conclusion, "I feel confident we can open our eyes and look into the years ahead, to see radiating from this institution, from

96

the work of this Foundation, influences which are going to affect education in the largest sense of that word: development of the thoughts and emotions of boys and girls, youths, men and women, all over this country, and to an extent and range and depth which makes this, to my mind, one of the most important educational acts, one of the most profound educational deeds, of the age in which we are living."

The Foundation was welcomed into the community of educational institutions by Josiah H. Penniman, Provost of the University of Pennsylvania, and by Dr. John J. Coss, of Columbia University. Leopold Stokowski said a few words on behalf of "the artists of America." Judge John Faber Miller, who had issued the Foundation's charter as an educational institution, spoke for Montgomery County. State Senator Fletcher W. Stites, a resident of Merion, spoke on behalf of the Commonwealth of Pennsylvania "and the neighborhood."

And Dr. Edgar A. Singer, Jr., professor of philosophy at the University of Pennsylvania, read a somewhat involved parable, of his own composition, about how "there is no more sincere and no more generous patron of art than the general public, which is to say, all mankind," and how such a patron "devotes its modest resources" to the encouragement of artists who are no longer living. Therefore, "second only to those who risk their lives for art and science" are those "who give their means" to the end that "issues of right and wrong, of truth and error, may not be left to the arbitrament of average insight."

He was glad to pay tribute, Singer declared, to such a "private patron" as Dr. Barnes, who sought to "use the experience of all humanity in the cultivation of eyes fit to judge a work of art."

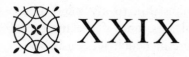 XXIX

At that time Singer was trying to get the University of Pennsylvania to offer a new type of course in which the resources of several of the University's departments would be utilized correlatively. His idea was that a philosopher is no longer one who conceives an explanation of the universe and systematizes facts to fit it, but is now the one who explains, objectively, what it is we do when we think. Since psychology is concerned with *how* we think, and *what* we think touches history, sociology, religion, science and the arts, Singer felt a new type of course should be evolved that would better orient the young philosophically, and be given, perhaps collectively, by specialists in the various branches of learning. These specialists, he thought, would enthusiastically cooperate if the University's trustees could be induced to share his—Singer's—vision of the real function of philosophy in the modern world.

All of which was the sort of thing Barnes thought a university *should* do, and he offered to underwrite the expenses if the University of Pennsylvania undertook the realization of Singer's program.

As a beginning it was agreed that Buermeyer would give a course at the University called "The Aesthetic Experience," in connection with the course then being given by Louis W. Flaccus, the University's professor of aesthetics, and that Thomas Munro would give two courses—one on modern art and one on research in plastic art. The students of all three courses would have access to the Barnes Foundation's paintings. Barnes also authorized the University to offer several scholarships for study in Europe to students who did especially well in these courses.

The results were negligible, and the courses soon abandoned. The University had made no effort to publicize them and the students who enrolled lacked the intellectual background that would have enabled them to appreciate what they were being offered. There were also other institutional rigidities at Penn preventing the realization of Singer's plan.

It was this, and subsequent, experience with the University of Pennsylvania, his alma mater, that account for many of the attacks Barnes made on essentially well-intentioned individuals and institutions throughout his life. He was intelligent enough to know that such attacks, by and of themselves, were not likely to result in the changes he hoped for. Intellectually, but not emotionally, he understood the power of inertia. And he had no illusions that it is possible to attack individuals and institutions, especially those that mean well, without being resented, and being attacked in return. But he thought the warfare a *necessity*, and one not of his choosing. He used to say, with truth, that he never started a fight and never backed away from one. Sometimes the fights had a publicity purpose that did not appear on the surface, and were mere shadow boxing. But some were begun, and carried on, because Barnes believed *it was his duty* to expose intellectual shams.

His rationale for all this was carefully thought out and was set forth in an editorial he wrote for the October '25 issue of the "Journal of the Barnes Foundation." He titled it "Construction and Controversy" and began it by noting that when people used the phrase "constructive criticism" they usually meant that criticism should be merely "comment on matters of detail, a recommendation of patching and tinkering that leaves the essentials untouched." Anything that advocated drastic alteration, or extirpation, of the thing criticized, is labeled "destructive criticism" and explained away as "a love of chaos or ruin for its own sake."

But new ideas, Barnes believed, have to battle old ones merely for a place in which to grow. Occasionally they can be grafted on the old, and, when they can, "a policy of intransigeance is undesirable." But when they can't be grafted on the old, the new ideas must struggle for very existence, "and since everything fights for its life, such a struggle cannot always be kept within the rules of decorum which regulate friendly association between individuals, and to consider decorum as the first necessity of debate *is often to surrender a cause*" (my italics).

This is especially true, he continued, when existing institutions are firmly established and surrounded by a prestige which "prevents an impartial examination of their right to exist." Any attempt to question the performance of such institutions, he believed, "is treated as a piece of presumption, or else simply ignored."

He then pointed out that abstract reasoning *of itself* never changes a deeply rooted habit. An alcoholic, for example, rarely if ever gives real thought to his state until he discovers his job, or his health, or both, are gone. "Social institutions which owe their fixity largely to habit," Barnes declared, "are in no different case. So long as the success of their workings is not challenged in a manner striking enough to arrest attention, the voice of mere reason beats upon deaf ears."

All-out attacks, he continued, are often the only way this psychical deafness of individuals and institutions can be overcome, but all-out attacks are usually countered by the rationalization that they are "in bad taste." They *are* in bad taste, Barnes acknowledged, when they are motivated by malice, by a desire for personal aggrandizement, "or by any motive other than the desire for the general good." But all-out attacks are not in bad taste when, in seeking to "go to the root of a matter," they question "the essential rightness of what is." When such attacks are called bad taste "good taste is nothing but a weapon by which vested interests fight off any penetrating analysis of their prestige and privileges."

It is impossible to attack institutions, Barnes believed, without attacking the individuals responsible for what those institutions do or fail to do. All institutions are directed and utilized by *persons*, "and if the institutions are noxious that fact is apparent in the effect they have on individuals, including the individuals who profit by the operations of the institutions. This is the ground for the legal maxim that all guilt is personal."

Destructive criticism is legitimate, Barnes contended, "if it offers an alternative to what is criticized, and if it is free from animus." For "whoever considers something wholly bad cannot without compromise of his convictions urge less than its total abolition," and if that involves saying "the activities of some individual have no justification for existence . . . the obligation is no less binding. In the long run, it is not even kindness to the individual to do anything else. The piercing of hollow pretensions is a humanitarian as well as an intellectual duty."

There is no more deplorable superstition, Barnes believed, than the feeling that "no one should be subjected to searching criticism if his intentions are good." He did not quote Twain about hell being paved with good intentions but he was convinced "the harm done by ill-intentioned persons is utterly trivial when compared with that done by those whose consciences approve their every act." Since everyone agrees that crime and malice should be wiped out, the only anti-social acts "significant enough to be worth discussing are those of men who are 'doing their best' but whose best springs from demonstrably untenable convictions. The militarist, the religious persecutor, the defender of unintelligent subservience to mere custom and authority, these, who are not considered criminals at all, are the real enemies of humanity." And their guilt "is shared by all who in the presence of unmistakable evils take refuge in inertia or invoke prestige to stifle discussion." Not to expose the harm done by well-intentioned persons "is to resign oneself to futility."

Over the years I had many arguments with Barnes about the tactics of his attacks, which often were poorly calculated to achieve the results he intended. But I, and others, were at a loss when he would contend that the cruder things he said and did were deliberately intended to shatter the psychical deafness which people employ when they don't want to hear something you want them to.

It is easy to say, as many do, that in the course of trying to achieve a working alliance with the University of Pennsylvania Barnes did inept things. He most certainly did. But it should be remembered that he was frustrated in attempts to accomplish things *that were desirable per se*, as well as educationally and sociologically, and that he was eager to defray all the costs, and ultimately to give control of his Foundation, including its buildings, aboretum, pictures and endowment, to the University.

Barnes' good intentions no more excused his tactical errors than the good intentions of the University officials excused their inertia, and since Barnes gave officialdom no quarter he was entitled to none in his dealings with it. But I think the scale tips in Barnes' favor if we take into account just what it was he wanted to do and what he wanted the University to do. Indeed, the following outline of his proposals comprises a program some university ought still to undertake.

Barnes wanted the University of Pennsylvania to use *some* of its resources, and *all* of the Barnes Foundation's resources, to provide:

1. Two courses that would be prerequisites to its courses in the fine arts: a) a survey of intellectual history that would trace man's cultural development—religious, philosophical, scientific, and artistic—of which the plastic arts have been a partial expression; b) a course in psychology or experimental logic "in which the thinking process is explained in relation to impulse, perception, habit, emotion and intelligence."

2. A general course in aesthetics "very different in content and method from the usual present one. It should begin with aesthetic psychology, i.e., with a description "of the aesthetic experience in relation to other activities of life"; emphasize "the need for intelligent reflection and open-minded sensitivity to new experience"; reveal inductively "the principles of form common to all the arts, along with the peculiar functions and limits of each art"; work out hypothetically "certain general standards of artistic value"; and show that art has very practical effects not only upon civilization, but upon the student himself personally.

3. A revised course in the history of art that would emphasize, not biographical facts, subject matter, and the historical associations of particular paintings and other art objects, but "the continuity and variation of traditions in plastic design," which is to say "the distinctive forms of the Egyptian, Greek, Oriental, Renaissance and modern schools, and of great individuals, to show what each has contributed of permanent significance to the artistic heritage of society, how influences were transmitted, and how old forms were adapted to new subjects and interests." Such a course should make use not only of photographs, casts and lantern-slides but also of "visits to galleries where originals are to be seen."

4. In either the course just described, or in a separate course, the work of contemporary artists should be studied, using "original specimens so far as possible," so that the student can acquire "a sense of the vitality of the art of his time" and develop an ability "to break up narrow habits of preference and to work out by intelligent reflection his own standards."

5. A course in which students create something of their own in a medium of their choice, based on subject matter from their own experience, with freedom to experiment, and receive from the teacher chiefly allusions to "traditional works of art that are relevant to the student's particular problem."

6. A course on the applied and industrial arts that would be linked "closely with work in the fine arts" in order to show how "standards of utility may be thoroughly reconciled with those of beauty."

7. A course for prospective teachers of art that would show how the special problems of art can best be handled pedagogically.

8. Small seminar courses that would specialize on specific branches or periods of art, e.g., the Greek period, modern sculpture.

It is a sad, but human, fact that whenever Barnes' relations with the University of Pennsylvania, and other institutions, are discussed *today*, his personal clashes and vituperation are talked about, not the concrete objectives he was trying to attain.

What might Barnes have accomplished had he and the University of Pennsylvania achieved a working relationship in the middle 1920s, and he not had to go it alone? A surprising number of people, including some of his enemies, agree that his life would have been totally different, and more productive, and that the University of Pennsylvania would have profited even more than he.

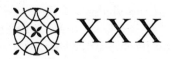 XXX

After the break with Penn, Buermeyer left to teach at New York University, but continued to do research and editorial work for Barnes for a dozen or more years. Thomas Munro, whom I never met, left to teach at Long Island University and Rutgers University, and later became professor of art at Western Reserve, and, since 1931, has been the Cleveland

Museum of Art's curator of education. The book he did for the Foundation in collaboration with Paul Guillaume, *Primitive Negro Sculpture*, has long been out of print.

A few years before I met Barnes in '27 he tried to induce Francis Hackett to join the Foundation's staff. He had admired Hackett's reviews and articles in "The New Republic" and elsewhere and invited him to Merion to discuss joining forces. Unfortunately, Hackett was married to a Danish-born feminist (Signe Toksvig), whom Barnes loathed on sight, as she did him.

As the years passed quite a few promising people joined, and departed from, the Foundation's staff. Some had ability, but could not adapt to Barnes' ways, or get along with other members of his staff. Some were opportunists who had no genuine interest in what he was trying to accomplish.

The member of the Foundation staff who most conspicuously proved the truth of Barnes' contention that we all have latent abilities which art fructifies, was Albert Nulty, whom Mrs. Barnes had hired as a chauffeur before World War I. Barnes quickly became aware of Nulty's native intelligence and exceptional manual dexterity, and, long before the gallery was built, while the Barnes still occupied "Lauraston," he began to entrust the physical care of his paintings to Nulty, whose ability to clean, restore and refinish paintings and antiques proved to be unrivalled, and was so regarded by Barnes. So much so Barnes made him one of the Foundation's trustees.

Today only two members of the Foundation's art teaching staff were at the Foundation while Barnes was alive. One is Angelo Pinto, a Philadelphia-born painter whom Barnes encouraged and helped to develop, and who devotedly tries to teach his classes at the Foundation the method of art appreciation Barnes taught him.

The other is Violette de Mazia, whom Barnes made co-author on four of his books, and who, after his death, became the Foundation's director of art education, and a trustee.

I have always thought of Miss de Mazia as a loner and never felt I understood her, though Barnes told me a great deal about her, and used to analyze her abilities and potentialities in considerable detail. Her father, I believe, was born in Russia, of Italian parents, and educated in France, where he married a French woman. During World War I he removed to London, and it was from England that Miss de Mazia, after the war, sailed to the United States on a temporary visa. With the help of relatives in Philadelphia she found employment as a teacher of French at Miss Sayward's School for Girls in Overbrook, and while so employed earned extra money by giving private lessons in conversational French. While Dr. and Mrs. Barnes were in Europe Miss de Mazia was hired by Nelle Mullen to give such lessons to herself and other members of Barnes' office staff. She quickly perceived what Barnes was trying to do, and her assiduity, and memory, prompted him to appoint her to the Foundation's staff, first as a researcher, and later as a teacher. She never married.

The first work on which she did extensive research for Barnes, and on which he put her name as co-author, is *The French Primitives and Their Forms: From Their Origin to the End of the Fifteenth Century*. It was published, by the Foundation, in 1931, and was the fruit of three years of study, much of it in Europe. Practically all of the paintings listed as French primitives in the world's principal galleries are analyzed or discussed in this book. Their plastic qualities, and styles, are shown to have derived not only from French miniaturists and manuscript illuminators, but also from Italian and Byzantine painting and mosaics. The field is specialized and had not been adequately dealt with before Barnes set to work. The attribution of not a few French primitives has been changed as a result of this book.

Barnes was under no illusions about its appeal to the general reader. I happened to be visiting him the weekend after Roosevelt closed the banks in '33. In anticipation of that action everyone had laid in the amount of cash they thought they would need for the period of the close-down. On the Saturday evening of that weekend, while we were having a pre-dinner Scotch, Barnes asked what sort of hiding place I had picked for my cash. When I told him I had put it in my copy of *The French Primitives and Their Forms* he laughed and exclaimed: "It's safe!"

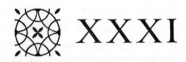 # XXXI

The classes at the Barnes Foundation were, and are, conducted along lines Dewey laid down half a century ago.

The phrase "progressive education" has been used to describe some of them, and though the term is currently in disrepute, connoting in many minds children who have been so permissively treated they can't read and are nincompoops, if not juvenile delinquents, Dewey neither intended, nor sanctioned, the misinterpretations and excesses which have given "progressive education" its bad name.

Nor did Barnes.

The essence of Dewey's educational ideas is still valid. He regarded education as *a form of growth*, and thought it should consist, not of rote or coercion, but of assisting an individual's inborn powers to unfold in harmony with the society in which he or she lives. Education should be pleasurable, and can be made so if thought is given to how a student's *interest* can be aroused. Dewey thought this is most easily achieved when the student is presented with problems to solve that have meaning for him *personally*. In the course of solving such problems, i.e., in the course of *doing*, the student accumulates information he probably would have resisted or ignored had he been made to acquire it under the old methods of rote. And if he did learn it by rote he would not have understood it.

Art education should not deal with facts *about* art, Dewey and Barnes contended, but with an individual's spontaneous reactions to real things, and with the *organization* of these reactions, and the perceptions which result from them, into a coherent body of aesthetic knowledge. After aesthetic self-confidence is established, Dewey and Barnes thought, an individual can more readily, and effectively, be taught the traditions of art, and the significance, or lack thereof, of contemporary experimentation in art.

They believed teachers of art should not lay down dogmatic rules, but should foster a sort of play spirit, an atmosphere that is conducive to the free expression of an individual's reactions, opinions and preferences. The importance of marks and examinations should be minimized (there are *none* at the Barnes Foundation).

But anarchy is not to be allowed, nor are the lazy, and the excessively introverted or extroverted, to be permitted to dissipate the energies, and frustrate the intentions, of the teachers and other students.

Since aesthetic understanding and appreciation enrich every aspect of life, the study of any one art should ramify into all the arts, and, at least theoretically, into all culture, and these interrelationships should be studied in terms that are as close as possible to the student's own experience.

Both Dewey and Barnes felt that the study of art *chronologically* is not always best, since the early forms of art are usually the most remote from the student's experience. The principles common to all great art can be perceived in *any* period, and the connection with antecedent or subsequent periods can be elucidated more meaningfully when and as the student's interest arises. At the outset the distinction between the fine and the applied arts should not be accentuated, and *all* human activity should at first be considered fit subject matter for aesthetic analysis.

Barnes thought art instruction, perhaps more than any other kind of instruction, should encourage intellectual and emotional *groping*, and that a student's interest is greatest when his own reactions and responses to works of art are used by the teacher to lead him, and the class, to new and deeper insights. In aesthetics, which consists of so many intangibles, Barnes contended, systematized educational procedures can stymie the learning process by stifling the student's spontaneity.

Aesthetic appreciation and understanding are not, and should never be allowed to become, a passive business. Their essence is the imaginative apprehension of a set of ideational relationships comprising the experience the artist has endeavored to communicate in a book, play, painting, sculpture, or whatever.

The foregoing is a rough approximation of the pedagogic principles underlying the sort of instruction Barnes wanted the Foundation to provide.

No one knew better than he that such an educational method, to be effective, requires teachers of very exceptional ability.

During the two autumnal months I attended the Foundation's classes they were conducted by Barnes, Mary Mullen, Laura V. Geiger. The two women were devoted to the Foundation and earnestly tried to pass on the things Barnes had taught them.

Needless to say, it was Barnes himself who best demonstrated the efficacies of the Foundation's method of art education. He had studied painting so thoroughly, and loved it so deeply, and his mind was so well stocked in so many different realms, that attending his class was a major intellectual experience. The fact he could not suffer fools gladly, and did not like to be disagreed with, especially by the ignorant young, of whom I was one, was compensated for by the more important fact that he had the desire to impart knowledge.

I was often fascinated by the sheer abundance of his allusiveness when analyzing a canvas, and his subjective and imaginative reactions were as interesting as his objective perceptions. This is an important fact, for a great many small minds have misconceived his emphasis upon the non-subjective aspects of a painting. Barnes believed the subjective and objective each had its place, and he always insisted that his analyses of paintings were not to be taken ex cathedra, but as gropings after what the artist had experienced, and the means he had employed to communicate his experience. Barnes would not hesitate to say such recondite and debatable things as that Picasso's blue period could be traced back to Piero della Francesco's use of blue, if he thought such a train of reasoning would stimulate thought. And his celebrated juxtaposition of Titian's "Entombment" and Cézanne's "Still Life with Gray Jug," to prove that different subject matter can have the same compositional form, is a demonstration of a fundamental fact about painting even I could understand.

Dewey's pedagogical hypotheses and principles may not be suitable for young children, but as practised at the Barnes Foundation they have perhaps had their fairest chance of proving themselves. The Foundation's students are of college age or older, and have enrolled voluntarily, which implies a *genuine* interest.

To be effective, Dewey's ideas require teachers who not only know the subject they teach, but are so intuitively sensitive they can guide students without seeming to. Such teachers are hard to come by. Barnes was such a one, despite his intolerance of the self-deceptions and other weaknesses which stifle the learning process. I can recall moments when even the sorriest opportunists in the class—bohemians who attended only because they thought it gave them prestige— were reached by the richness of his mind and the force of his convictions.

The opportunists, of course, were fired from the class as soon as Barnes, or one of the other teachers, spotted them. And occasionally, alas, an honest but gauche student would be misinterpreted and be fired, too.

I don't think anyone who ever attended Barnes' classes can say he got nothing out of them.

 XXXII

Barnes' dedication to the proposition that the proper appreciation of painting involves serious study of its techniques and traditions, and its psychological, social and philosophical implications and significances, irked quite a few whose place in the art world should have made them allies, but whose indolence or indifference made them enemies.

In the mid-twenties, a fine, public-spirited citizen of Philadelphia, Eli Kirk Price, was creating, almost single-handedly, the Philadelphia Museum of Art, and he brought Fiske Kimball, the head of New York University's fine arts department, to Philadelphia to be director of the gestating institution. Kimball's training had primarily been in architecture, but he was a convivial soul and he proved to be what Price thought he might be—unusually successful in raising money and getting art objects, and even whole collections, donated to the museum. He was its Director for almost thirty years.

Not long after Kimball's arrival in Philadelphia Barnes received a letter from DeWitt H. Parker, then professor of philosophy at the University of Michigan, in which, in the course of praising Barnes' *The Art in Painting*, Parker mentioned that his friend, Fiske Kimball, shared his, Parker's, enthusiasm for that book. Still hopeful of finding men connected with important institutions who would help him to promote his ideas, Barnes visited Kimball in the building in Philadelphia's Fairmount Park called Memorial Hall, which then housed the collections of the Pennsylvania Museum of Art, the basic unit from which Price was evolving the Philadelphia Museum of Art.

Kimball was new to Philadelphia and to his job—in fact he had to create the job de novo. He was under a variety of pressures, and he was a snob. I don't think it ever occurred to him that Barnes could be anything but an addle-pated eccentric, even though Barnes went out of his way to elicit his interest and told him that if the trustees of the museum regarded him, Barnes, as a wild man, he would keep in the background if that would help the museum to spread throughout Philadelphia the kind of art appreciation which enriches individual lives and raises a community's cultural level.

To get things started Barnes offered to pay for Munro to lecture at the Museum, and to admit the students in the Museum's art school to courses at the Barnes Foundation. These offers were not exactly turned down, but neither were they adopted. Kimball merely did nothing about them. Some years later, when I was interviewing Kimball on another matter, I asked him why. He gave me the impression that he considered Barnes' ideas poppycock. When I asked Barnes for his opinion of why Kimball had been so obtuse, Barnes said he thought Kimball "had been afraid I'd show him up intellectually."

Be this as it may, Kimball did not hesitate to ask Barnes to let his friends see the Foundation's paintings. He asked so frequently Barnes finally wrote him and said the requests "to have your friends and acquaintances use the Foundation as a diversion" indicated Kimball shared "a very prevalent idea that the Foundation is a place for more or less conspicuous Philadelphians to entertain their friends." Were Barnes to accede to all of Kimball's requests it would "make you or your institution a passport to the Foundation—which is about the limit of exploitative absurdity." Barnes then alluded to his hope, at the time of Kimball's arrival in Philadelphia, for co-operation between the Museum and the Barnes Foundation "in any move that could be intelligently interpreted as educational," and added bitterly: "All that came of it was these requests."

Kimball was not the self-confident extrovert he seemed and he worked up delusions of grandeur as a protective covering in his dealings with the rich, whom he patronized whenever he felt he could get away with it. In his early days at the Philadelphia Museum his insensitivity to the feelings of others was accepted as an occupational disease of the museum director who has to extract money and/or art objects from not always willing donors. But as the years slipped away Kimball's delusions became systematized and so dominated his personality he had to be relieved from his post, and his last days were tragic.

Not long after Barnes told Kimball to stop using the Foundation as a means of self-aggrandizement, and just before the Philadelphia Museum of Art was to open, Kimball asked Barnes to lend the Museum some of the Foundation's paintings as "the first step in a cooperation which could go much further when we secure additional gallery space and the floor specifically devoted to educational work is finished and put into operation."

Barnes was so little impressed by this ulterior offer of co-operation, in a vaguely indicated future, that he didn't deign to reply. Nelle Mullen wrote Kimball that his proposal "would make a horse laugh" and "would be offensive to the intelligence" were it not "so provincial and embedded in the matrix of the stereotyped blah which comes to us so often from performers who would like to annex us as a sideshow to their circuses."

Barnes was not just working off hurt feelings. Nor did he refuse because he was aware that museums ask collectors to *lend* what they hope to induce the collectors ultimately to *donate*. Barnes refused Kimball's request, and similar requests from museums all over the world, primarily because the paintings were in constant use in the study courses at the Foundation.

Kimball never asked again, but others connected with the Museum did.

While Barnes was doing the research for *The French Primitives and Their Forms* he had visited, with some of his assistants, the John G. Johnson Collection, which had not yet been transferred to the Philadelphia Museum, but was crammed into the rooms and corridors of Johnson's old home at 510 South Broad Street. Henri Marceau, the collection's curator, arranged for Barnes to study the collection's fine primitives with a maximum convenience and Barnes reciprocated by inviting Marceau and his wife to Merion. When the Johnson pictures were transferred to the Philadelphia Museum, Marceau became the Museum's curator of paintings.

A few years later Marceau wrote an article for the Museum's bulletin entitled "The Art of El Greco in Philadelphia" and sent it to Barnes, explaining that the Museum was planning an exhibition of the El Greco works mentioned in the article. Would Barnes lend?

Barnes probably would have sent Marceau a *polite* refusal but for two facts. He had recently attended a lecture by one of Marceau's assistants which consisted chiefly of paraphrasing of an article from the *Encylopaedia Britannica*. As he listened to it, Barnes could not help thinking of the quite different kind of lecture he had hoped to help the Museum to provide. Secondly, in his article Marceau had eulogized "two pictures which every well-informed person knows are fakes." Hence, Barnes said, the exhibition Marceau proposed would merely "entertain an uninformed public" and provide an opportunity for "a pretentious parade of 'society' people and *fonctionnaires*."

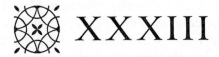 XXXIII

The deeper truths usually have the subtler manifestations, and the way Barnes spoke in later years of his attempts to enlist the cooperation of Kimball and the Philadelphia Museum of Art, in the days when that institution's policies were being formulated, makes me think the experience affected him more than he ever admitted.

In the time of his first negotiations with the University of Pennsylvania, and his wooing of the Philadelphia Museum, I think he was blithely confident that he could win those institutions over to his way of thinking with ease. Penn's resistance gave him pause, but did not extinguish his naïve hopes. The experience with Kimball did. He never stopped trying, as we shall see, but his subsequent efforts were in the resigned spirit of half a loaf being better than none.

These rebuffs from Penn and the Philadelphia Museum turned him inward, but they also made him more determined than ever that the Foundation should be capable of achieving, by and of itself, all he had hoped to do in cooperation with other institutions.

Accordingly, in the spring of 1929 he entered into negotiations for the sale of the A. C. Barnes Co. to Zonite Products Corporation, and in the summer of '29 that company bought, for six million in cash, the shares of the A. C. Barnes Co. which Barnes had given to the Foundation.

This money, like all of Barnes' own money, and the money he had given the Foundation previously, was invested in tax-exempt bonds, a fact people should bear in mind when they think, or say, the Barnes Foundation was created to avoid the payment of taxes.

I moved to New York in the summer of '28 and did not see Barnes with any regularity until about a year after he had sold his business. However, I did lunch with him in New York not long after the great crash of the stock market in October '29 and he laughingly told me his friends, and foes, were saying he was "wiser than the wizards of Wall Street." But, he said, the truth was quite different. Had he not wanted to devote all his time to the Foundation, he said, he wouldn't have sold his business when he did, and hence wouldn't have acquired "this reputation of being a financial wiseacre."

"A reputation you'll soon be ascribing to your study of James, Santayana and Dewey," I said with a smile.

"Who knows?" he murmured thoughtfully. "There wouldn't have been a Foundation but for them. So maybe I *did* sell my business in the summer of '29 because of James, Santayana and Dewey."

Several years before his death in '51 some of his detractors began alleging that he had learned of Fleming's isolation of penicillin, which occurred in 1928, and, realizing that much of the efficacy of Argyrol would be supplanted by antibiotics, had hastened to sell out before that happened.

"It's the sort of story that's sure to be believed," Barnes said. "Despite the fact that Fleming didn't publish his findings until many years later, and the fact that I wasn't au courant with what was going on in chemistry in '28 and '29 and didn't know about antibiotics. As for the implication that the buyer got stung, Zonite's done quite well with Argyrol for twenty years."

And the Chemway Corp., into which Zonite evolved, is still doing quite well with it.

 XXXIV

The sale of his business meant he had to acquire new quarters for the office staff which handled the affairs of the Foundation and helped him with the research that went into his books. Since the gallery at Merion did not have room for offices, Barnes bought a 27-year-old three-story brick house at 4525 Spruce Street in Philadelphia, about a mile from his old factory, and remodeled it to suit his office needs.

Desks, typewriters, files and other paraphernalia were no sooner installed than the City of Philadelphia presented him with a bill for $756 worth of taxes. He returned it with a brief note which stated that the property was used for offices by the Barnes Foundation, an educational institution that is exempt from taxation.

A bureaucrat in the tax bureau sent the bill back with a rubber stamped notice that it must be paid by such and such a date.

Barnes sent it to his current lawyer, Robert T. McCracken, of Montgomery, McCracken, Walker and Rhoades, and told him to inform the tax bureau the case would be fought with every resource Barnes could command. Barnes' former lawyer, Owen J. Roberts, who had obtained the Foundation's charter as an educational institution, had just been appointed an associate justice of the United States Supreme Court and was no longer available.

When the case came to trial Barnes made it plain that he was refusing to pay the tax because of a principle, and he offered to donate $756 to any charity the prosecuting attorney cared to designate. Paying the tax, he explained, would be tantamount to admitting the Barnes Foundation is not an educational institution.

John Dewey testified that it most certainly *is* an educational institution, and gave the reasons why. Mrs. Barnes described the arboretum she was creating on the Foundation's property. Barnes told of the Foundation's classes and books.

In doing so he provided a glimpse into the way he did the research for his books. He told the Court that while working on the forthcoming *The French Primitives and Their Forms* he had made six trips to Europe and spent $50,000. He said he always traveled with at least two stenographers, who took notes in relays as he dictated in museums and private collections *in front of the paintings*. As soon as their notes were transcribed, he said, he went over them, arranging, rearranging, deleting and emphasizing his ideas. The following day he retraced his steps and checked with the paintings what he had written the day before.

When he got back to Merion, he continued, he worked the notes up into a text, and the following summer checked all the paintings again to make sure that what he had written withstood the test of time and re-examination. "We try to corroborate everything," he said, and added that often there were unforeseen ramifications to check out and that "this year I thought the book was all done . . . and we found a lot of new material and I came back with 500 typewritten pages," which he had had to digest and incorporate into his manuscript.

Three years later the Pennsylvania Supreme Court ruled the house at 4525 Spruce Street *was* used for offices by an institution which was properly exempt from taxation. The City of Philadelphia did not take appeal to the United States Supreme Court, where, of course, Justice Roberts would have had to disqualify himself.

 XXXV

A year or two before *The French Primitives and Their Forms* was published, by the Barnes Foundation in '31, Barnes had begun work on a book about Matisse, whom he regarded as the greatest living painter.

Matisse first visited the United States in 1930 on his way to Tahiti and in the fall of that year he returned here to serve on the jury of the Carnegie International Exhibition, which had given him a first prize in '27. He and his fellow jurors—Bernard Karfiol and Glyn Philpot—gave the 1930 first prize to Picasso for "Portrait of Mme. Picasso." When he visited Merion Barnes invited him to do a mural above the three windows in the main room of the Foundation's gallery. Matisse thanked Barnes for the honor but said he'd have to think it over, and he returned to France without giving a definite answer. In January '31 he came back to Merion and said he would undertake the commission.

Barnes did not then, or later, dictate to Matisse about the mural in any way whatsover. The spaces over the windows were meticulously measured by Albert Nulty and the measurements were given to Matisse. So were paper cut-outs that were the exact shape of the three lunettes the mural was to occupy.

Since the total width of the mural was to be a few inches over 45 feet, Matisse hired an abandoned film studio in Nice to house the canvas on which he worked for a year.

His basic plan derived from a painting he had done twenty years before which the Russian collector, Sergei Shchukin, had acquired, and which, after the Bolshevik Revolution, found its way into the Museum of Modern Western Art in Moscow. The background colors were to be a light sky blue, a rose pink, and black, and the dancing figures would be merely silhouettes in very light gray. Their postures would indicate human movement rather than any particular sort of dance.

Matisse finished it in the winter of '32 and *then* realized he had not followed Nulty's dimensions and had not allowed for spaces between the lunettes. Rather than patch out what he had done, he decided to start over again and so informed Barnes, to whom, on February 22, 1932, he cabled: "Mille excuses comme nouvelle composition est necessaire je termine panneaux actuels presque finis et recommence sur nouvelles toiles envoyez gabarit inutile venir merci lettre suit." The letter, sent the next day, admitted the mistake was his and apologized for it.

Typical of many of the denigrations of Barnes is the allegation that he, and not Matisse, was to blame for Matisse's mistake. Alfred H. Barr, Jr., in his *Matisse: His Art and His Public,* so states and although he corrected his error in an errata slip issued after his book was published, few of Barnes' detractors pay any attention to the correction.

Matisse's second version of the mural was finished in April '33 and installed by Albert Nulty, with Matisse's help, in May.

Barnes was never completely satisfied with it, but he never told the artist so. Instead, he valorously wrote Matisse: "One would like to call the place a cathedral now. Your painting is like the rose window of a cathedral." But in his book on Matisse Barnes did not discuss the mural.

Matisse's own comments about it are curious. He said his aim had been "to translate paint into architecture, to make of the fresco the equivalent of stone or cement." After he saw it in place he said he "felt it was detached absolutely from myself, and that it took on a meaning quite different from what it had had in my studio, when it was only a painted canvas.

There in the Barnes Foundation it became a rigid thing, heavy as stone, and one that seemed to have been spontaneously created at the same time as the building."

Some of the Foundation's finest paintings hang in the main gallery which this mural was intended to adorn—an entire wall of Renoirs, Cézanne's best "Card Players," Suerat's "Poseuses," and many other famous paintings. Below the mural itself are Matisse's "Riffian" and Picasso's "Composition" (a 1906 painting of a peasant with a basket of flowers). Matisse himself was aware that his mural should not try to compete with such pictures. "From the floor of the gallery," he said, "one will feel it rather than see it, as it gives the sense of the sky above the green seen through the windows . . . It is a room for paintings: to treat my decoration like another picture would be out of place."

It is the only Matisse mural in the United States. Matisse sold the first version of it to the Musee de l'Art Moderne de la Ville de Paris.

 XXXVI

About a month after Matisse agreed to do the mural, that is, in February of '31, Barnes received a telegram from R. Sturgis Ingersoll, who had recently been elected a trustee of the Philadelphia Museum of Art, soliciting his advice "with respect to certain matters in connection with the Museum's Committee of Modern Art, of which I am chairman."

Ingersoll, who is now president of the Museum, was then thirty-nine and the Museum's youngest trustee, an honor he owed to the influence, and tradition of public service, of his family. After St. Paul's and Princeton he had worked for several years in the editorial department of Lippincott's and it was not until '21—he was a first lieutenant in World War I—that he joined the Philadelphia law firm of Ballard, Spahr, Andrews and Ingersoll and began assuming his share of the public service which the Ingersolls have performed for three or more generations.

Several years before he sent the telegram just mentioned Ingersoll had given Barnes reason to hope his interest in art was a personal and serious one and not a mere part of the social repertoire of a cultivated Philadelphian, and Barnes had invited him to Merion. Ingersoll had thanked him as follows: "Sunday afternoon was a glorious experience. *The Art in Painting* comes so close to being the only intelligent book on the subject that it should have a wide and useful scope. Your contribution to life here is immense."

The advice which Ingersoll wanted from Barnes concerned a Matisse canvas, "Trois Soeurs," which a New York dealer, Valentine Dudensing, had offered to sell to Ingersoll for the Museum. Barnes knew the picture and agreed to look at it again and tell Ingersoll what he thought. After doing so he advised Ingersoll to buy it. Barnes said it could be had for $15,000.

Ingersoll then said he would have to raise the money himself since the Museum trustees would not meet for some time. Barnes offered to take an option on it and asked Ingersoll to fix a date by which the money could be raised. Ingersoll thought a week would be enough. But it wasn't, and he so informed Barnes, who thereupon bought the picture for himself. But after telling Barnes he couldn't raise the money, Ingersoll induced Fiske Kimball and Carroll Tyson, a Philadelphia collector who was also interested in modern art, to co-sign with him a note at the Provident Trust Co. for $15,000. When Ingersoll told Barnes he now had the money, Barnes of course told him it was too late.

The episode created bad blood, which rankled for years. Ingersoll, Tyson and Kimball told the story in such a way that Barnes was made to seem like a vulgar Maecenas, who, bloated with Matisses, deprived the museum of his native city of one he did not really want and did not need in his collection. Barnes told it quite differently. He said Ingersoll's request for advice had been a dodge and that its real purpose, which Ingersoll revealed only later, had been to get him, Barnes, to buy the picture for the Museum. In New York Dudensing's competitors spread the story that Dudensing had used Ingersoll as a catspaw and that since he, Dudensing, was well aware that the Philadelphia Musem of Art, in the Depression year of '31, had no money, and the Barnes Foundation had plenty, Dudensing had stage-managed the whole contretemps in order to effect a sale.

Barnes also said that when he had telephoned to Dudensing and asked that Ingersoll be allowed more time, Dudensing replied that he was buying a villa in France and needed the money at once and that if Barnes and Ingersoll didn't want the painting he'd sell it to someone else.

Fiske Kimball returned the $15,000 to the Provident Trust and sent the cancelled co-signed note to Carroll Tyson as a souvenir, saying: "We always knew Barnes was a son of a bitch and now we can prove it." Tyson returned Kimball's letter with the notation: "Approved. Please return for framing."

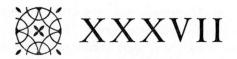 # XXXVII

Barnes wrote his book on Matisse during the years in which the Great Economic Depression forever altered Western Civilization.

Except intellectually, and sympathetically, the Depression

did not touch him. He had never invested in common stocks, so the stock market crash affected neither him nor the Foundation. And even at the bottom of the Depression only an inconsiderable number of his and the Foundation's bonds suspended interest payments. As prices fell, including the prices of paintings, Barnes' economic position, and that of the Foundation, improved.

His benefactions to individuals during those terrible years were many, and one of his institutional benefactions did an inestimable amount of good. This was the gift of thousands of dollars to the Tindley Temple, the largest Negro Church in Philadelphia, and one of the principal agencies through which assistance passed to Negroes in the days before such aid was organized governmentally.

I did not see much of Barnes until the Depression was approaching its nadir. I had gone to work for Charles Scribner's Sons at the beginning of '30 and was unable to get to Merion with any regularity, but in '31 I resumed weekending there with some frequency. Scribner's was then at the height of its renown and working there was a delight. To British authors like Galsworthy, Barrie and Winston Churchill, they had added, under the impetus of its great editor, Maxwell Evarts Perkins, such American ones as F. Scott Fitzgerald, Ernest Hemingway and Thomas Wolfe. Barnes took pleasure in my intellectual growth.

I used to send him new Scribner books, and those of other publishers, to learn his reactions. For example, he was amused by, and agreed with, Hemingway's pillorying of Waldo Frank in *Death in the Afternoon*, and he said an interesting thing about Hemingway's celebrated style. He thought the emotion-laden Zeitgeist *of the readers* accounted for the effect, more than Hemingway's selection and arrangement of words. "His craft is with the unconscious, not the conscious," Barnes said.

We had quite an argument about that, in the course of which Barnes predicted time would not be kind to *The Sun*

Also Rises, A Farewell to Arms and *Death in the Afternoon.*
Some years later, however, he went out of his way to assure
me he thought Hemingway's short stories would live. As for
the hoop-la about bullfighting in *Death in the Afternoon,*
Barnes said he didn't intend to check on Hemingway's enthusiasm since "the last time I went to a bullfight in Madrid
I came away with the feeling the whole thing is a vicarious
expression of sadism."

Barnes admired Thomas Wolfe's vitality, and, like everybody else, deplored his lack of form. He did so when we were
lunching with Perkins, who defended Wolfe on the ground
that striving for form would extinguish Wolfe's creative élan.
Barnes conceded that it might, but declared it needn't necessarily have that result, and conceivably might equip Wolfe
for greater things. He enjoyed hearing stories about Wolfe
and asked me several times to bring him to Merion. I tried
on and off over the years but the three of us never happened
to be free at the same time.

Faulkner's *Sanctuary*, which was published by Harrison
Smith, not by Scribner's, engrossed but also irritated Barnes.
"I'd like to kick him all over the lot," he wrote. "A fellow of
such rare talent should not affect an ideal of obscurity and
so mess up his matter that he befuddles and leaves one up in
the air about the essentials." He agreed that Faulkner had
written *Sanctuary* for the sole purpose of getting talked
about.

Although Barnes held Max Eastman in low esteem, he
liked his *The Literary Mind*, which Scribner's published in
'31, and we spent several weekends analyzing the ideas in
it. Barnes was, of course, delighted with Santayana's *The
Genteel Tradition at Bay*, and he was fascinated by Edmund
Wilson's *Axel's Castle.* So much so he wrote Wilson a long
letter of praise, which ended with strictures because Wilson
detected symbolism in Douanier Rousseau. Barnes wrote so
little about Rousseau I shall quote some of the things he wrote
to Wilson:

"I have had Rousseau's work for twenty years and I think the symbolism in him is about five per cent and the naturalism ninety-five. His estrangement from the world was a forced one—his daily efforts were directed to trying to put himself in the real world of ordinary people and events. He was not an exotic, a hot-house plant, as were the rest of the group you treat. Nor had he the ultra sophistication which is the backbone of the symbolist. He was a primitive in the same sense in which certain painters have been primitives from time immemorial, as could be seen in the pictures recently exhibited by the Newark Art Museum.

"That is, he was untrained in academic technique and totally lacks the school tricks which most great painters, from Giotto to Picasso and Matisse, retain the traces of even after they have been emancipated from their early training. Because of this Rousseau's expression is all the more natural and naïve. The great difference between him and the French *peintres paysans* of 1840, and similar early American painters, is that he had extraordinary skill in the use of his plastic means. A careful study of his work shows that though naïve and simple, he was wise without being sophisticated. The proof of this is that he assimilated the contributions of the Florentine tradition and converted them to his own ends without resorting to stock stunts or tricks. It was his misfortune that fairies like C———, and more respectable people like Guillaume Apollinaire, put him on a pedestal and befogged him with their own myasmatic emanations. You can hang him alongside a Cézanne or a Renoir, but you can't do that with Degas. All I have said savors of an *ipse dixit*, but if you will come over some Sunday before noon and look with me at the pictures in our gallery, I think you will agree with what I have said. One thing is sure: no painter, however skilled, could fake a Rousseau that would fool anybody, except, possibly, critics like Clive Bell and Henry McBride."

Barnes read very little fiction, but he would read a contemporary novel if its subject matter, or style, was well above the average. The "sets" in the living room of his home included the fiction of Henry James, Joseph Conrad, George Moore, Anatole France, Flaubert, de Maupassant, Romain Rolland, Tolstoy, Dostoievski, Turgenev and Chekov. He read quite a few detective stories, and enjoyed some of the S. S. Van Dine ones I sent him.

I remember sending him *Tobacco Road* when Scribner's published it and he told Perkins that Caldwell had talent but no integrity and showed signs of becoming a pornographer. When Perkins commended Caldwell's naturalism, Barnes let the conversation dribble off inconclusively.

Barnes and Perkins were too profoundly unlike to become friends. Barnes said Perkins was "too inarticulate" but granted "he may be one of the few who repay cultivation." Perkins thought Barnes had a brilliant mind which he was "boxing in," by which he meant Barnes was too engrossed in creating an aesthetical theory. I once cited *ideational* things Barnes had said about particular paintings, but Perkins gave me one of his quizzical looks and ambled off.

When I proposed that Scribner's publish Barnes' *The Art of Henri-Matisse* Perkins, of course, was all for it.

 # XXXVIII

The Art of Henri-Matisse—the hyphen is one of those neurotic preciosities Matisse then insisted on because he wanted to distinguish himself from a painter in Paris called August Matisse—is a brilliant intellectual performance and established a pattern for Barnes' later, and more important, books on Renoir and Cézanne.

I was Scribner's liaison with the author while that work was being prepared for publication. Two years intervened between the signing of the contract and publication, and I saw a great deal of Barnes during them and communicated with him constantly, and thereby obtained first hand knowledge of how he wrote a book.

The philosophical and aesthetical sections represented his own thinking, carefully checked by Buermeyer, and okayed by Dewey. The detailed analyses of individual examples of Matisse's work were the result of his own reactions and the research of Miss de Mazia. Punctuation and grammar were the province of Mary Mullen. And her sister, Nelle, was in charge of all the correspondence, which was extensive and world-wide, and of the photographs and all administrative and business details.

There were an unusual number of publishing problems, for Barnes' office staff was meticulous about dotting every "i" and Barnes spared no expense to get even the smallest points absolutely right. His books would not be what they are had he not had practically unlimited financial resources.

The Art of Henri-Matisse is a work of 464 pages, of which 223 comprise the text; 135 contain the 151 black-and-white illustrations; and the rest present a biographical sketch of Matisse, analyses of a score of his most important paintings, catalog data on *all* the works of art mentioned, and a detailed index.

The text begins with a restatement of the method of art appreciation outlined in *The Art in Painting*. The more difficult points are made with greater lucidity, and greater pains are taken to explain why "fear of the new" so often engenders mental "paralysis." The discussion of "design" is more extensive, as it should be in an evaluation of such a painter as Matisse.

The chapter on plastic form and design is more readable than comparable material in the first edition of *The Art in Painting*. The two kinds of design—expressive and decorative —are carefully differentiated, and the result of emphasizing one at the expense of the other is weighed psychologically as well as aesthetically. Of the primacy of decoration in Matisse's design Barnes says:

"He is, however, a real and great artist and there is therefore in his work a uniform and successful execution of as much essential reality as is needed to give his forms standing in the real world. His design, at its best, shows a precise coordination of all the plastic means and their execution is perfectly adapted to whatever decorative purpose animates the picture in question. Because of his wide experience with all the traditions of painting he is able to borrow from the most diverse sources, and because of his artistic integrity these borrowings are always judicious, neither merely imitative nor speciously plastered upon the surface of his forms. His intelligence is shown by the fact that, lacking a command of the profounder sources of inspiration, he selects subjects which call only for the means which are completely within his power."

Though Matisse's range is strictly limited, Barnes explained, he painted fluently and exuberantly and reflected the wide variety of forms possible if a painter has "an open and flexible mind, great erudition, adventurousness of spirit, unflagging interest in the contemporary scene, and an admirable command of his medium." His effects, though essentially decorative, are consciously planned and executed, and their appeal is to the intellect, and only rarely to the emotions. It is Matisse's "encyclopaedic knowledge of all the plastic traditions," Barnes said, that enables him to paint "a wealth of decorative forms unparalleled in range in the whole history of painting."

In the chapter on decoration and decorative design Barnes explains the psychological basis for the human liking of decoration. At the root of it, he says, is the human eye, which is so constituted that whenever it perceives light, line, color and space in harmonious relationships, *it* engenders a sensation the brain deems pleasurable. Decoration, Barnes acknowledges, is one of the lesser aesthetic forms since "mere pattern, from which every interpretative quality has been banished, is so devoid of meaning that it becomes cloying."

Matisse's preoccupation with decoration often obliges him, Barnes pointed out, to discard "precise realism altogether" and even to resort to the "bizarre." But "his distortions are incidental to his decorative design and his procedure is always orderly, intelligent and resourceful, and the audacity that academicians feel and dislike indicates not eccentricity but vitality."

The most original chapter in *The Art of Henri-Matisse* is called "Transferred Values."

In it Barnes shows how the "hushed reverberations" of past experience—Santayana's phrase—are inchoate and "in solution" in our minds, and how, "deeper, fuller and richer than in the mind of the ordinary man, they constitute an artist's capital. What is called the magic of the artist resides in his ability to transfer these values from one field of experience to another, to attach them to the objects of our common life, and, by his imaginative insight, make these objects poignant and momentous."

Matisse did this, Barnes says, by giving to a picture, *whatever* the literal character of its subject matter, the *effect* of one or another of the following eight things: 1) a bouquet of flowers; 2) a poster; 3) a piece of cretonne; 4) an Oriental rug; 5) a Persian tile; 6) a mosaic 7) a tapestry; 8) a map. This means that a Matisse nude directs the mind more to the "transferred value" of a mosaic, for example, than to sex.

In addition to the above eight *effects*, Barnes says, Matisse exploited various subsidiary motifs, such as "rosette-patterns," by which the effect "of flowers, wheels, or conventionalized stars" is secured; "tiles," which set off, in the beholder, associations of "hard surface-qualities like those of porcelain, mosaic or stone"; and "stripes and bands."

The sources of Matisse's ideas and styles, Barnes believed, are, first, the Venetians, "as are those of every painter who works primarily and systematically with color." From Manet he got his emphasis on flat color, and from Gauguin the juxtaposition of sizable areas of different colors. From Cézanne he borrowed "simplification of planes and diminution of their number." From Oriental art—Chinese, Japanese, Persian and Arabic—he derived not merely his preoccupation with decoration, but also such devices as the distortion of perspective (from the Persian), the freely flowing line (Chinese), and *linear* patterns and space-composition and the use of black (Japanese prints). Barnes also noted borrowings from Byzantine mosaics and African sculpture.

Matisse's drawing, as was natural in a man who was primarily a colorist, Barnes thought, was done by "color and color relations, especially those of contrast, movement and rhythm." Matisse's constant resort to linear contours—"actual lines, sometimes black, sometimes colored, sometimes bare canvas"—was a device to emphasize pattern or aid space-composition. Matisse eschewed these linear contours, Barnes said, whenever he wanted an effect "of lightness and delicacy."

Matisse's color, "which makes his pictures what they are," was the result of an exceptionally large palette which included, for example, two tones of violet and three of green. Matisse's success with color, Barnes thought, was largely due to the originality of his color contrasts ("contrast is the essence of all drama"). Matisse contrasted not only hue and tone, but would put thick pigment next to areas in which paint was thinly applied. His use of black to accentuate contrasts sometimes seemed to Barnes to be too facile a ruse.

Barnes acknowledged that Matisse's modeling was scant and that solidity in his paintings "is usually slight." And Matisse's line, "like the other plastic means, is subordinated to the requirements of Matisse's decorative designs." He used light chiefly to heighten color, and whenever a Matisse painting "fails in plastic integration the fault is usually to be found in the over-accentuation of light." Space, Barnes noted, is rarely used realistically and space relations are "either compressed, with a very considerable reduction in the number of planes, or radically distorted, as when all the objects seem to be projected upon a single flat surface."

To the charge that Matisse's themes are repetitive, Barnes replied that Matisse varied every odalisque, every still life, every "goldfish." As for Matisse's portraits, he granted that the "realization of the character or personality of the sitter is so rare as to be negligible," and he proffered, in Matisse's defense, Matisse's oft-quoted remark, "It is not a woman—it is a picture." Barnes thought Matisse's black-and-white work "inferior in plastic quality and technical resourcefulness," and Matisse's attempts at sculpture a mistake.

Despite all this, Barnes maintained that Matisse was "the greatest living painter," a remark which made Perkins murmur, "Alas."

Barnes admired Matisse's "marvellous versatility, intellect, intelligence, curiosity about the contemporary world," and his "ability to put down on canvas what his lively imagination has seen, without faltering or stumbling." Matisse's conscious craftsmanship, Barnes thought, makes us feel he "is interested less in objects for what they really are than in the ways in which they can be woven into decorative designs. His imagination, though never sinking into mere adroit ingenuity . . . rarely rises to the level of profound inspiration." And, in the corpus of his work, "a whole realm of values remains unevoked."

The Art of Henri-Matisse did not receive the critical attention it deserved, and almost all of the reviews were lazy evasions of the mental effort the book requires. "What concern I have about the lack of sale," Barnes wrote me, "is for the sake of the publisher, not my own. I am sure the book will live, and I am equally sure the world is not yet ready for that kind of study. That the time will come when the world *is* ready is no more to be doubted than that the sun will rise tomorrow."

One review, however, irked him. It was by Thomas Craven* and appeared in "Books," the Sunday book review section of the New York "Herald Tribune." In the course of it Craven minimized Matisse's importance—"what artistic virtue can atone for the poverty of his human significance"— and asserted that Barnes' method of analyzing a painting led to art being considered "as a dead thing." Barnes wanted to work up a campaign that would "put the final kibosh on this four-flusher" and asked Dewey, myself and others to lend a hand. Dewey was too busy. Since art was *the* thing Barnes did *not* regard as dead, I wrote a letter saying so which Irita Van Doren was kind enough to print, and Barnes cooled off.

 # XXXIX

To almost everyone's surprise Barnes dedicated *The Art of Henri-Matisse* to Leo Stein, whose review of *The Art in Painting* had prompted Barnes to do a devastating analysis of him.

Entitled "Day-Dreaming in Art Education," and pub-

* A decade or so before Barnes had hoped to make Craven a member of the Foundation's staff. But an article of Craven's in "The Dial" entitled "The Progress in Painting" seemed to Barnes so full of errors and untruths that he asked Craven to demonstrate, in front of paintings, the statements made in the article. When Craven could not do so, Barnes insisted on "The Dial" publishing an article by Buermeyer adversely analyzing the ideas of Roger Fry "and his disciple Craven." Craven replied caustically to it, and Buermeyer replied to Craven's reply. Not long afterward the editor of the "The Dial," Scofield Thayer, had a nervous breakdown and developed the delusion that Barnes was persecuting him. Barnes lost several friends because of Thayer's delusion, notably Charles Demuth, until Georgia O'Keefe took up the cudgels for Barnes and pointed out the real causes of Thayer's illness.

lished in the April '26 issue of "The Journal of the Barnes Foundation," the analysis begins gently with an explanation of why a leisured elite is not the best arbiter of a society's culture. Immunity from physical toil, Barnes pointed out, isolates a human being from experience with reality.

Those who do not come into contact with reality, he continued, compensate by "entertaining ideas, forming theories, weaving a mental fabric" which all too often are the "phantasies of the day-dreamer and the delusions of the paranoiac." Cleverness, ingenuity, or even ably articulated systems of ideas, are no proof that genuine thought has occurred. Unchecked by reality, the human mind "tends to get away altogether from the solid earth of facts, to build castles in the clouds—to dream dreams. It must be periodically brought back to earth by the brute force of events, and compelled to face a reality unsoftened by illusions."

Ideals *can* be hiding places for ineffectuals, and "the idealism which is merely day-dreaming takes the form of disparaging what *is* in favor of what *was* or what *might* be, without offering any definite guidance" in the practical matter of how change is to be brought about. To espouse an ideal without bothering about the means for attaining it "is the very essence of day-dreaming," and "when to this is added an impatience with the only approximations to the ideal at present available, the day-dreaming becomes not only idle but petulant and pernicious."

Which brought Barnes to the subject of Leo Stein's review of *The Art in Painting* (in "The New Republic").

The fact that Stein had had no experience with educational practises, Barnes declared, did not deter Stein from promulgating "the *ipse dixits* of his dream world. His ideal system of aesthetics is one from which the personal factor is to be rigidly excluded. He says it is permissible to point out the use made by a painter of color, light, line and space, but not to say that such use is good or bad. He asserts that statements of the former sort belong to science, and have general validity, and that statements of the latter sort reveal something not about the picture but only about the person who is looking at it."

Such "sublime aloofness," Barnes continued, is not a *sine qua non* of critical acumen but "a psychological impossibility." Any critic who pretends he has surmounted preferences is trying "to impose them without avowing them or subjecting them to the give-and-take of contact with the preferences of others." Even if it were possible for Stein to point out the objective factors in a picture without passing any judgment on them he would be uttering nothing but a bald statement of fact that is "destitute of any aesthetic significance whatever—here is a patch of red, here is a patch of blue."

Barnes then quoted William James to show that all thought, however scientific and impersonal, is conditioned by personal desire, has a subjective basis, and is "judged true or false according as it satisfies our whole nature, including our feelings." Stein's "ideal" of objectivity is therefore impossible of attainment and is merely a rationalization of his disinclination, and inability, "to approach the relative objectivity which *is* possible." Stein, said Barnes, is like the skeptic who, because all thought may err, refuses to think at all, and his withdrawal from reality is the result of "a dread of accepting the responsibilities of action" and not of "a highly sensitive intellectual conscience."

The purpose of education, Barnes declared, is to enable a man "to distinguish better from worse," and a statement of a quality judgment "is not dogmatism if warning is given that method is one thing and specific application another." Such a warning, Barnes said, was given in the preface to *The Art in Painting* and whenever errors due to subjective bias can be corrected by someone else using the same method, the method is valid and useful to human beings. The primary purpose of *The Art in Painting*, he said, is to present a method whereby art may be understood, and the evaluations of particular painters and paintings in *The Art in Painting* "are chiefly incidental and illustrative" and are offered "not as finalities but as challenges, and that fact is repeatedly stated in the text. If anyone's individuality is so feeble he gives assent to every debatable assertion, little is to be hoped from him in any event."

The vast majority of those who profess an interest in art, Barnes reiterated, "are dilletantes, sentimentalists and antiquarians" who are "prepared to amass information about the history of art, or to go into irrelevant raptures before a particular painting" but are "unprepared or very reluctant to make any serious effort to understand what makes a picture a work of plastic art" and "do not wish to admit that any such effort is necessary. *The Art in Painting* is an emphatic challenge to the sentimental as well as to the academic habit of mind. Mr. Stein's demands would leave the field entirely in the possession of those who are really benighted."

Stein's basic error was "the aged one" of mistaking "meaningless impulse for true freedom," an intellectual folly which leads to "the aesthetics of the ivory tower." Stein's contention that qualitative judgments should not be expressed was merely the yelp of one who "with no conception of the problems to be met, insists on ideal solutions that emerge from confused dreams. The compensatory character of his 'ideals,' and their function as a justification for sterility, is only too evident. It is hot-house preciosity passing for distinction, and is based on the delusion that whatever inhabits a rarefied atmosphere is therefore elevated. It shows that life, freed from responsibilities, is not richer but more attenuated, because it is nourished not by thought but by reverie. It is inefficacious practically, not because it is too fine for the real world, but because it is too feeble, and its sterility is an indication of its inner emptiness. It explains why the book on aesthetics which fifteen years ago Mr. Stein announced as forthcoming, has never materialized."

Stein didn't speak to Barnes for six years.

Then, one day in '32, in an art gallery in Paris, he went up to Barnes and offered his hand. They began corresponding again and when Stein wrote that he was hard up, Barnes several times sent him several thousand dollars.

And when *The Art of Henri-Matisse* came out the dedication read:

"To Leo Stein, who was the first to recognize the genius of Matisse, and who, more than twenty years ago, inspired the study which has culminated in this book."

 XL

It was also in '32 that Paul Guillaume died, from peritonitis, I believe, resulting from a burst appendix, although this has been questioned.

He had gone out of Barnes' life several years before when he had tried, on learning that Barnes had bought a picture through another dealer, to get part of the commission, though he had performed no service in connection with that particular sale.

With Guillaume's passing Barnes was freed from an influence that had not been altogether for his good. Guillaume's enthusiasm for, and promotion of, Derain, Kisling, Laurencin, Pascin, Soutine, Modigliani and others, had occasionally led Barnes to buy pictures he later had to repudiate, and sell or trade off. I don't think Barnes ever liked anyone less akin to him intellectually, or more intellectually irresponsible.

A quite different sort of person succeeded to the valid functions which Guillaume had performed for Barnes. This was Georges Keller, a Swiss who had spent his youth in South America and had later learned the ropes of the Parisian art world from the head of the Barbizon Gallery, a character out of Balzac named Hodebert. Barnes first met Keller at the Barbizon Gallery and sensed at once that he was far more interested in painting per se, and much less interested in promoting novelties, than Guillaume. After Hodebert's death Keller went with Etienne Bignou, and it was this gallery which Barnes used until Bignou's death. Thereafter he used the Carstairs Gallery, of which Keller was sole owner.

Keller was exactly the kind of dealer Barnes needed and over the years he devoted time, energy, ingenuity and intelligence to helping the Foundation and Barnes' research for his books. Keller was especially helpful in locating the paintings which enabled Barnes to increase the Foundation's representation of all the traditions, and he introduced Barnes to Port Manech, the fishing village in Brittany where Barnes so often relaxed in summer, and where he once almost bought the Tante Jeanne Hotel, when he thought the Parisian lawyer who owned it might not continue to operate it in a way that would keep Port Manech "unspoiled."

Keller often introduced people he thought would interest Barnes and one such was Nicolas Nabokoff, a Russian composer who had recently had a symphony played by Monteux in Paris and Koussevitsky in Boston, and whose ballet-oratorio, "Meditations at Night on the Majesty of God as Revealed by the Aurora Borealis," had been produced by Diaghilev in '28. Nabokoff and his wife spent several weekends in Merion and Barnes arranged for him to give a weekly lecture at the Foundation, which he did for about a year. He also tried to induce the University of Pennsylvania to use Nabokoff, and offered to pay his salary there, but nothing came of it.

Barnes had begun work on his Renoir book while the Matisse manuscript was in the course of publication, and it was more or less assumed Scribners would publish it. But I left Scribners in the spring of '33 and wrote *The Great One*, a novel about Boies Penrose, a Philadelphia aristocrat who became a United States Senator and the boss of Pennsylvania's corrupt Republican "machine." I dedicated it to Barnes and he wrote me a kindly, but honest, letter, in which he noted the book's merits as carefully as its flaws, which, he said, "I would tell to no one but yourself."

After it was published I became editor-in-chief of G. P. Putnam's Sons, which had been bought, not long before, by Melville Minton and Earle H. Balch, who merged their own firm, Minton, Balch and Co., into it. A month or so before my advent they had published John Dewey's *Art as Experience*, and when I proposed that Putnams publish Barnes' book on Renoir the suggestion was adopted at once.

Dewey's *Art as Experience*, incidentally, was dedicated "To Albert C. Barnes in gratitude," and in his preface Dewey declared:

"My greatest indebtedness is to Dr. A. C. Barnes. The chapters have been gone over one by one with him, and yet what I owe to his comments and suggestions on this account is but a small measure of my debt. I have had the benefit of conversations with him through a period of years, many of which occurred in the presence of the unrivaled collection of pictures he has assembled. The influence of these conversations, together with that of his books, has been a chief factor in shaping my own thinking about the philosophy of aesthetics. Whatever is sound in this volume is due more than I can say to the great educational work carried on in the Barnes Foundation. That work is of a pioneer quality comparable to the best that has been done in any field during the present generation, that of science not excepted. I should be glad to think of this volume as one phase of the widespread influence the Foundation is exercising."

 XLI

Dewey also wrote a foreword for Barnes' *The Art of Renoir*, a work which Dewey said "leaves nothing for me to add, and contains nothing I would wish to change."

Toward the end of his foreword Dewey declared he knew "of no statement of the relation of scientific method to intelligent living—the real meaning of science—equal to that found in the early pages of the first chapter of the present volume," and added, a bit bitterly: "I take profound, if somewhat melancholy, ironic, satisfaction in the fact that the most thorough-going embodiment of what I have tried to say about education, is, as far as I am aware, found in an educational institution that is concerned with art."

In his own preface to *The Art of Renoir* Barnes noted that Renoir had probably painted more pictures than any other important artist and said the Barnes Foundation had (early 1930s) 175 examples of Renoir's work. He also said his study of Renoir, brought to fruition in *The Art of Renoir*, had extended over twenty years.

In the entire history of painting there is no painter who so completely fulfills as does Renoir Barnes' conception of what a painter should be. Renoir's integration of *all* the plastic means was enriched, Barnes believed, by an assimiliation of *all* the traditions, with the result that Renoir was able to express effortlessly his individuality, and to attain to an artist's highest achievement, i.e., the revelation of aspects of the universe *seen and provided by no one else.*

The Art of Renoir is a paean of thanksgiving to the artist who had provided Barnes with more pleasure than had any other single painter. But the book contains thoughtful, as well as deeply felt, appreciation, and contains some of Barnes' most ably reasoned thoughts about aesthetics and the nature of painting.

It begins, as do all of Barnes' books, with a statement of the *method* he employed to arrive at the ideas he presents. There is repetition of things first stated in *The Art in Painting*, but new insights as well, and new, and more felicitous, formulations.

The purpose of the method Barnes spent his life refining and re-formulating was the elimination of "the idiosyncrasies of the particular observer" so that the observations and interpretations of a painting by one individual can be verified by another. It is an ideal only to be approximated by imperfect human beings, and Barnes' enemies have scorned his attempts to use it in such inaccessible realms as the unconscious of the creative artist. Barnes' reply was that the scientific method was similarly scorned in the past when scientists first applied it to natural phenomena which were subsequently brought under human control.

Barnes begins his discussion of Renoir with some incisive definitions of perception, a psychological process which is much more, he says, than a mere matter of light rays stimulating our retinas to stir images in our brains. Those are merely the mechanics, and the more important part of perception occurs when, because of the past experiences stored in the warehouse of our minds, we sort out the new images, discarding some, emphasizing others, and integrating what has newly come in to us from the external world, or up from the internal world of the imagination, with the totality of our past experiences, to the end that the universe, and all it contains, is more fully comprehended.

Our sensitivity, Barnes continues, and the *kind* of things we are spontaneously sensitive to—either because of necessity or temperament—"determine what we shall notice, how we shall interpret it, and what we shall do about it." These *ways* of seeing, interpreting and doing, become habitual, and it is these habits which constitute, for the overwhelming majority of mankind, perception. But not for the artist.

An architect walking down Park Avenue perceives things to which a heart specialist is blind; the latter notes things a dressmaker never dreams of; and she observes subtleties a porter might not understand even after they are explained to him. But a *genuine* artist—i.e., not a pretender or a dilletante—will be sensitive not only to aspects of reality which ordinary men recognize, but to aspects of reality few if any other men are aware of. If the artist be a dramatist or novelist, his medium is language and his essential material is the cause-and-effect nexus of human affairs. If the artist be a painter his medium is sight and his essential material is the *appearance* of the world, animate or inanimate. The *meanings* beneath the appearances will be implicit, not explicit, and are determined by how rich the artist's "funded experience" is.

The funded experience of a *genuine* artist is rich in two ways—technically and culturally. Mastery of technique is necessary for the proper formulation and expression of an idea, an insight, or an imaginative intuition, especially of a new one. Mastery of technique entails an assimilation of the traditions, i.e., of what painters "have in the past discovered and revealed as significant," of the "ways of seeing" and the ways of organizing insights which earlier artists discovered and used.

Traditions are "the working capital of every artist," and the richer an artist's funded experience the more sentient and capable he is, but "mere acquiescence in a tradition" leads a painter only to academicism. Aesthetic perception requires two things: the qualities of an object, or situation, must be visible to our senses, and the perceiving of them must be done by a mind sufficiently well stocked to interpret them in more than a superficial way. Barnes therefore defined perception as "an organic blending of data furnished by the alert senses of a live animal" with the store of meanings the animal has accumulated from past experience. If the blend is intelligent there will be "a continuous reorganization of the motor-energies of the perceiver, and an ever-changing series of read-justments between the new material and the background of accumulated meanings which constitute mind."

An artist's perceptions "are never an inventory of objective facts" but a *qualification* of facts and a re-presentation of them. Hence, a painting is not only an end result but also a record of how the artist attained that end result, and, when we analyze a painting, we are analyzing not only an artist's technique, but also his psyche.

Analysis in aesthetics should not be denigrated as "dissection," for it is "the indispensable first step toward discrimination" and "an ultimate re-synthesis." Moreover, a creative artist engages in a similar analysis when he selects from Nature the items he intends to interpret. He also "analyzes" before he can alter a trait, or device of technique, of a previous painter in order to bring off a novel effect. A non-painter's analysis of a painting is no different psychologically, despite the fact that its purpose differs intellectually. It is this intelligent analysis of a work of art that brings "the familiar warmth and glow" that prevades "the whole self when a new experience is born." This "warmth and glow" cannot be simulated and is "as positive and real as when they are experienced in front of a fire on a cold day. In any case, it is the expenditure of energy which makes perception effective. Effortless, automatic recognition is easy, but it doesn't generate the warmth of being alive."

This psycho-physio nexus, Barnes said, constitutes *genuine* aesthetic experience. He believed we can all have aesthetic experiences whenever we are sufficiently free from care or other preoccupations. One of the prime concerns of an artist is keeping free of the preoccupations which blind. We could all keep free of them if we wished, for, as Barnes never tired of explaining, art-potential is in us all, and there is no "fundamental difference between the perception of the artist as he creates and the beholders' perception" of what is created.

But an artist's perceptions and his interpretations thereof are only half the story. To make his insights and interpretations accessible to others an artist must have mastery in a particular medium, i.e., technique. Technique is secondary, *not* primary, and the mere recognition of technical skill "is as far removed from genuine understanding of painting, and quite as irrelevant to it, as sentimentalism." Whenever technique is predominant the artist's achievement is mere virtuosity. Technique is "strictly subordinate" to "aesthetic perception." It is aesthetic perception, not technique, which is the *sine qua non* of the creative artist.

Although technique is not primary, it is very necessary, and lack of it accounts for more "mute Miltons" than do callous and unappreciative environments. Whenever an artist "is impelled to extricate, to draw out, from the object of his emotion the particular set of qualities and relationships that called for this response, and to reincorporate them into a form of their own," he expresses something not only out of his personality but also out of the clay, paint, musical tones or words and it is his knowledge about these materials and his proficiency in handling them, which enables him to evolve a personal style, or *form*.

What is form? The inter-dependence, and inter-determination, of disparate parts, says Barnes, "constitutes form in a work of art as it does in a machine or an organism." In a painting "form is the harmonious merging of the plastic means—color, light, line and space—through which the artist gives expression to his experiences." Whenever an artist's form is truly distinctive it is so permeated with the artist's personality that it is "a book or record of the artist's mind and soul, and the medium through which he publishes his experiences and communicates them to the world." An artist's form is his hallmark.

Because artists see the world in different ways their form

varies, but in all form there are some common ingredients—e.g., movement, contrast, rhythm, symmetry, coherence of parts, unity of form and meaning, and individuality of purpose. The great unifier of these disparate ingredients is rhythm,* for there are rhythms in everything—in color, lighting, line, shape, mass, space, and even in "such general qualities as grace, charm or power."

Genuine art can be detected and be differentiated from "its simulacrum," Barnes declared, by observing whether rhythm, contrast, symmetry and balance inhere "as an organic unity" in all the parts of an artist's form or whether they are factitiously superimposed. In Renoir, Barnes said, they inhere as an organic unity to a degree equalled by no other painter.

And not only that. Renoir's triumph was a greater one than achieving a form suited to the things he wanted to express. "The basic reason for his greatness," Barnes declared, "was an enormous innate capacity to learn continuously as he grew in years and practised his art. From the very beginning of his career his endowment enabled him to grasp what was significant in the life about him, and in the traditions of the past, and to incorporate the findings in a form of expression that was his own. The successive stages of his painting reveal an ever-expanding personality embodied in new and highly individual forms." Renoir, Barnes believed, "challenges comparison with the profoundest and most astute thinkers."

* Says Barnes of rhythm: "The regular recurrence of night and day, of the seasons of the year, the systole and diastole of the heart, are natural rhythms to which we are all subject and which profoundly affect our lives. The alternation of these rhythms in nature lends contrast and movement to life, as their repetition, and interdependence, their interweaving and dovetailing, lend unity; they thus provide both variety and unity, the indispensable conditions of satisfactory living."

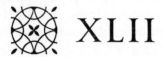 XLII

In his biographical sketch of Renoir Barnes was careful to make a point of the fact that Renoir began earning his living at the age of thirteen, in a porcelain factory as a painter of ornamental designs, and that "the clear and transparent tones of all his mature work were probably a survival of his porcelain-painting." Barnes took equal pains to point out that Renoir subsequently made his living "painting fans and window shades," on which he often reproduced "pictures by the old masters, especially by the French painters of the eighteenth century."

Thus, in the pristine time of life, Renoir learned: 1) the habit of work; 2) the handling of paint and brush; and 3) something of painting's past, and of how earlier painters approached or solved technical problems. Renoir was almost a fulfilled personality at an age when many youths still flounder, and he never deviated from his course. "The dearth of incident in Renoir's actual existence," Barnes observed, "is in striking contrast to the wealth, variety and audacity of his inner life . . . He had no need to wander afield for material. It is typical of him that when told of Gauguin's departure for Tahiti, his comment was 'one can paint so well at Batignolles.' His surroundings were those of a petit bourgeois . . . but in the most commonplace scene he could find an inexhaustible source of interest and delight. Even when his success enabled him to live in greater comfort he was satisfied with the barest of rooms and the simplest of furnishings; the color and light, the grouping of objects, which he cared for above everything, could be found everywhere. When he went to a reception, it is said, he was so absorbed in a burst of color in a flower, the light playing across a face, that he forgot to listen to what was said to him . . . Except under compulsion he never missed a day's painting in his whole life; in the hospital, awaiting an operation, he propped up a canvas on the bed before him and painted the flowers which had been sent him . . . He even said, 'C'est avec mon pinceau que . . . j'aime.' He called himself a painter, not an artist, and despised the need for unusual conditions or emotional 'inspiration' which condemned other painters to long periods of inactivity. Though he enjoyed music and literature he gave them up when they threatened to compete with his own work, and though he took pleasure in the companionship of other painters, he had not the slightest interest in theories about art . . . Joie de vivre never left him, and survived the infirmity [arthritis] of his later years, and the canvases painted when he could not hold a brush unaided were as filled with it as those of his early youth. His life and art were completely one; there was nothing in himself which he could not put on canvas, and nothing on his canvases which was not completely himself."

One of the best sections in *The Art of Renoir* is that in which Barnes traces the evolutionary development of Renoir's form.

In the 1860s, when Renoir's career began, Barnes says, the rebellion against the "pseudo-classicism" of David and Ingres, who still controlled academic circles, was led by Delacroix, Daumier, the painters of the Barbizon school, Courbet, Manet and Monet.

Delacroix had "borrowed Constable's method of color-division"; Daumier had "revived Rembrandt's use of chiarascuro"; the Barbizon school "had taken painting out of doors"; Courbet had "resuscitated the naturalism of the Dutch and Spanish masters" and had "formulated a style of painting adapted to the emphasis of the unadorned reality of familiar things"; Manet had "simplified and generalized draw-

147

ing"; Monet had concentrated on "the effects of actual sunlight falling upon colored surfaces."

Courbet's influence, Barnes says, was the strongest on Renoir in the 1860s; Delacroix's in the early '70s; then Manet and Monet's; and always "the dull silver-gray circumambient atmosphere common to Corot." In the late '70s Renoir experimented with the techniques of Pissarro, Sisley and Monet; and then, toward the end of '83, he reached an impasse. "I had travelled as far as impressionism could take me," Renoir wrote Vollard, "and I realized the fact that I could neither paint nor draw."

So he went to Brittany and the Isles of Guernsey and Jersey, and to Italy and Africa, and was soon painting again. It was in the semi-tropical sunlight of Algiers that Renoir discovered the color-effects which were to be the interest that engrossed the rest of his life.

Barnes contends in *The Art of Renoir* that Cézanne influenced some of Renoir's work in the early '80s and one of our major disagreements occurred over this point, as will presently be related. I didn't think Barnes proved it in *The Art of Renoir*, and I still don't think he did.

But Barnes certainly proved that the years 1885–87 were the years in which Renoir changed his drawing and modeling and began using fluid contours instead of "a hard, tight line," and began drawing, and modeling, *by means of color*, and evolving the form in which color played a more comprehensive role "than it had at any other time in the history of painting."

Renoir made color "the very substance of volumes and spatial settings" and "the agent of coordination of all the plastic means," Barnes explained. Indeed, Renoir's "color-suffusion" was so integrated with the other plastic means that it was not decorative only but also compositional and expressive. At the apogee of his career—after 1910—color-suffusion was responsible for most, if not all, of the Renoir "magic."

Renoir's apotheosis, Barnes thought, is the "Bathing Group"

of 1916, painted three years before his death. In it "color attains to the highest levels of sensuous quality and active movements: every object is constructed of deep, rich, luscious, voluptuous color, and the richly variegated organization is resplendent with shimmering color-chords, and has the exuberance and the glamour of a glorified bouquet, studded with sparkling jewels. A delicate, many toned rose-red dominates the ensemble and its areas interlocked with large areas of green and blue to form a three-colored general pattern which is interspersed with areas of iridescent light and color . . . Color is in supreme command everywhere: line, space and light have no independent identity except as aspects of color; hence, the indissoluble one-ness of all the individual plastic units in a single, highly decorative and expressive form . . . The technical means by which the suffusion is achieved are likewise condensations of devices previously employed . . . Any one of the individual units may be selected as a focal point and corresponding units will be found elsewhere in the picture to balance it and establish equilibrium.

"Moreover, these subsidiary groupings flow into one another in a continuous movement that embraces every plastic factor in the entire composition. The unity thus established is of more plastic relationships than in any of Renoir's previous paintings, and the technical skill of Renoir's execution represents the climax of his powers."

Renoir's triumph, Barnes says in conclusion, was that "his painting represents in the highest degree the discovery of human and mystical values in the world we actually live in. There is not the slightest smack of other-worldiness in his painting; he transfigures the world without ever abandoning it. It is in finding the supreme values of experience in the particular scenes and events of everyday life that he shows his unparalleled power of insight and imagination."

 XLIII

There is a curious chapter in *The Art of Renoir* entitled
"Renoir and Cézanne" and in it Barnes attacks the "Cézanne
cult" for regarding Cézanne "as the greatest, if not the only
great, artist of modern times." Barnes acknowledged that
"Cézanne's influence has been deservedly very great" and
that when it was exercised "upon artists capable of grasping
and assimilating it "Cézanne's influence had borne fruit." But
upon "lesser men" it has been "a blight."

Barnes thought Cézanne and Renoir were both "artists of
the first rank," since both "enriched the great traditions of
art," and that to choose between them is "to confess to an
essential shortcoming in one's personality." The contrast between them is like that between "a massive, firmly founded
and solidly built cathedral and a bouquet of bright, glowing
flowers, arranged by a person of exquisitely sensitive taste.
No normal person wishes to live exclusively either in cathe-
drals or in flower-gardens. Cézanne and Renoir, discriminately
grasped, do not compete with each other . . . and to laud one
at the expense of the other is a disservice to both."

Cézanne's interests, Barnes explained, "were very much
narrower in range than Renoir's and Cézanne never displayed
any comparable capacity for growth. Furthermore, they
never "had at their service a comparable command of the
medium of paint . . . Cézanne struggled his whole life long to
get what he had in mind upon canvas, and the marks of the
struggle appear in nearly every picture; the efforts were, as
he himself felt and said, rarely altogether successful, and the
percentage of pictures left unfinished or abandoned as fail-

ures is immensely larger in his work than in Renoir's.* So much of his energy went into the work of execution that he seems to have had little or none left to expend in broadening his interests."

What Cézanne had to say in 1906, Barnes continued, "was essentially what he had had to say in 1877," and "the same absence of essential variety" characterizes Cézanne's plastic means and technical devices as well as what he has to say. All his pictures consist essentially of "a dynamic organization of solid color-masses constructed of planes and set in three-dimensional colorful space." Notwithstanding all this, "Cézanne was a supreme artist in his ability to make color the fundamental means of all his plastic effects." But "what does wear thin" is "intellectual interest," and "after the observer's feelings have felt the force of the impact, he inevitably wishes, if he is an intelligent being, to analyze it, to understand its objective content," and, after doing so, Barnes said, one all too often agrees with Leo Stein that Cézanne is "more completely the squeezed lemon than any other painter of anything like equal importance."

Cézanne, Barnes shrewdly pointed out in conclusion, is easy to imitate, but Renoir is inimitable.

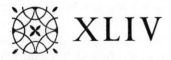 XLIV

It so happened that a few days after Barnes sent me a rough draft of this chapter I was weekending with my sister, who then lived in Narberth, a Philadelphia suburb adjoining

---

* Barnes observed in a footnote that "many of these abandoned pictures were completed by inferior painters, and, ironically enough, are lauded by critics as important and representative Cézannes."

Merion on the west. At seven-thirty on Sunday morning the bell was rung by Barnes, whom I had promised to visit that afternoon. He followed my incommoded brother-in-law, whom he had never met, upstairs and awakened me with the cry: "It's too wonderful a morning to sleep, and I want to discuss that chapter with you!" I fixed him with a baleful eye, and stumbled out of bed.

It *was* a beautiful morning and we took one of our longest walks and had one of our frankest talks.

As soon as we were out of my sister's house he revealed the reason for his precipitancy: "How did the chapter strike you? Did you think I was carrying water on both shoulders?"

"You have broad shoulders," I said warily.

"Don't give me any damned publisher finesse! What did you think of it? Look at the swoop of that bird."

I followed his glance and saw a bird's flight trace arcs against the sky as graceful as the most felicitous line in any of his canvases. As soon as Barnes saw that I saw, he said: "Well?"

"Don't let's break our truce," I murmured. I referred to a tacit understanding we had at that particular time whereby I did not attack what I regarded as his excesses in the application of his method of analyzing pictures and painters, and he did not attack the Marxian opinions I had recently embraced, much to his disgust.

"I'm not asking for the Party Line on Cézanne and Renoir," he said with scorn and loathing for my having associated myself with such intellectual tyranny. "What impression will that chapter make on readers?"

"You want a publisher's opinion after all," I said, to pay him back for his contempt for my Marxian illusions. "What can I do but finesse your question? Authors never think publishers know *anything*."

"I'm not asking you as a publisher, but as a friend," he said with a shyness that took me by surprise.

I said at once that I thought there was too much in the

chapter for intelligent people to fix on the thing which made him fear he'd be charged with carrying water on both shoulders. He asked what these over-riding things were. I replied that his attack on the Cézanne cult was justified and a definite contribution; that his acknowledgment of Cézanne's limitations was also a contribution; and that the biggest contribution of all was his contention that Cézanne was being touted over Renoir because Cézanne's one architectonic theme and technique was easily understood by critics and easily imitated by painters, whereas Renoir's effects were mystical and his technique inimitable.

Barnes brushed this aside and said belligerantly: "Let's have the *but*."

I said the "but" had to do with his claims, explicitly stated elsewhere in *The Art of Renoir*, that Cézanne had influenced Renoir.

"Cézanne *did!*" he asserted with finality.

"You don't prove it," I said softly. "And if Cézanne did, his influence was miniscule, which is really what you're saying in the chapter we're discussing."

This elicited considerable vituperation, in the course of which Barnes said that when I came to his house that afternoon he'd show me, in some of his detailed analyses of Renoir's paintings, just how extensive Cézanne's influence was. I was nettled by his personal cracks and rejoined that some of his analyses of the paintings contained too many *ipse dixits*, and, anyway, were not to be taken ex cathedra as he himself had said in his reply to Leo Stein's review of *The Art in Painting*.

He was silent for perhaps ten seconds and then launched into a defense of his analyses. I made no comments and he finally exclaimed: "You're getting too big for your breeches!"

I laughed, and we were friends again. He clapped me on the back and said: "You've grown! You shouldn't have left Philadelphia! You could've been of use to the Foundation."

"No," I said guilelessly, "I couldn't have gotten on with your female staff."

I was sorry as soon as the words were out of my mouth, for I saw a look of dismay cross his face before he burst out with some of his most unbridled invective. He called me an impudent ignoramus and declared the women on his staff had given him a selfless devotion of which I was incapable. He said they had helped him make the money which had made the collection and the Foundation possible, and that one of them had become a better researcher than he had thought possible and would develop into exactly the kind of teacher the Foundation, and Dewey's educational method, required.

I apologized.

"There's really something wrong with you," he said, quietening down. "You've been prejudiced against them for as long as I've known you. Why, do you know?"

I apologized anew, but it didn't satisfy him and he insisted that I tell him what I had against his office staff. I said I had nothing against them, that I knew they had been of inestimable help to him, and that I was ready to believe all he hoped from them in the future would be fulfilled.

"Then what's eating you?" he demanded.

"I merely said I couldn't have gotten on with them," I replied, as gently as I could.

It didn't satisfy him.

"What have you got against them?" he reiterated.

I said I didn't have anything against them as persons, and made the mistake of adding: "They're everything you say and necessary to you, but you need around you men who're as strong as you are."

"Find me some!" he exclaimed.

I looked into his eyes and saw he was in earnest.

"You have me there," I said honestly, and added with a smile: "I wonder if there are any."

He patted my head and said brusquely: "You've still a lot of growing to do."

"You've had a lot to do with my growth to date," I said in a way that told him I meant it.

"You're a romantic," he said kindly. "Stick around and I'll beat it out of you."

He then launched into a description of the psychological nature of romanticism, and this led us into other facets of Cézanne, and painters, and writers, and cabbages and kings.

 XLV

Not long after *The Art of Renoir* was published I left Putnams in order to devote myself whole-heartedly to the Left causes which were then attracting many American writers to their Communist-controlled ranks.

Barnes told me I was ruining my career and thereby affecting my whole life. He said I was old enough to know that self-interest is instinctive and cannot be eradicated by any political or economic system and that all socialist and communist experiments of the past had floundered because of the primacy, in human conduct, of self-interest. He said dialectical materialism is merely a new philosophical dress "for that old whore called ends-justify-the-means," and that economic determinism is a specious over-simplification and "an *idée fixe* of the mentally lazy." He said Lenin had been able to saddle the Russians with "Soviet tyranny" because the Russian people are several centuries behind the rest of Europe, have never had a non-tyrannical government, and are incapable of appreciating how precious even a faulty democracy is.

My reply was that dialectical materialism might be double-talk, and economic determinism a fallacy, but millions of hard-working, self-respecting Americans had lost their jobs and their homes through no fault of their own and that any system of production and distribution which allows people to starve in the midst of potential plenty is ipso facto obsolete. Barnes acknowledged that unemployment and the other ills of the Depression were unnecessary but he said Roosevelt's New Deal would make the necessary corrections without abolishing democracy, which, he reiterated, "is the best and most advanced governmental form men have yet invented."

When he asked why I had decided to be a political activist, I quoted what he had said about people who entertain ideals without trying to make them effective in everyday life. He replied that working in league, or even in parallel activity, with the American Communist Party, was foredoomed. The Party, he said, had no interest in improving American life since it was financed and dictated to by the Soviet Ministry of Foreign Affairs, which "is interested in nothing but Russia and the clique that grabbed power there." The slogan, "dictatorship of the proletariat," Barnes said, means "dictatorship *over* the proletariat, not dictatorship *by* the proletariat," and the front-organizations run by the American Communist Party are "traps for gullible fools like you."

He was genuinely disappointed in me and we agreed to disagree. He said he hoped it wouldn't take me too long to learn "what a sorry mess of pottage you're trading your birthright for," and he felt similarly about all the American writers who were then lining up on the Left, especially Edmund Wilson, whom he regarded as the country's foremost literary critic. "He'll waste some of the best years of his life," Barnes said.

Late in '36 he sent me a wireless from the boat that was bringing him back from Europe asking me to meet him at the dock "on a matter of importance to you."

I did so and was greeted with: "You're against Franco?"

He then explained that he had met a young Basque in Paris, I have forgotten how, who was in the Spanish Government-in-Exile then quartered in the French capital. The young Basque had convinced Barnes that the Soviet Union did *not* dominate the anti-Franco forces in Spain and that in the Basque country the Catholic Church was opposed to Franco and was active on the side of the Loyalists. "If this were understood in the United States," the young Basque told Barnes, "it would counteract the propaganda that it's only the Reds who are resisting Franco."

"Here's your chance," Barnes said to me with genuine fervor. "Go over, get the facts, publish them in newspapers and magazines here. I'll pay your fare. I'll pay your wife's fare too, if she can't live without you."

I was eager to go and sailed a week later, for, like most American intellectuals, I was convinced the Spanish Loyalists were fighting not only to preserve the Spanish Republic which Franco's revolt sought to overthrow, but also to defeat "international fascism," which Germany and Italy, by supporting Franco with money, materiel and men, sought to impose on the world.

On arriving in Paris I discovered that the young Basque to whom Barnes had talked had returned to Bilbao and it took almost two weeks to set up the clearances for getting into Spain—United States passports were not then good for travel in Spain—which Barnes had expected would be arranged before my arrival. When I reported these contretemps he was miffed and cabled: "Get on with it."

Once I got to Bilbao, the Basques helped in every possible way. I soon learned that everything the young Basque had told Barnes was true. I witnessed the celebration of mass by Catholic priests in the front lines of the Spanish Loyalists, and ascertained that in the Basque country, at least, Communists were not in control of the Loyalist forces.

I had arrived at a time when Franco was mounting a new offensive, and his invasion of the Basque provinces was expected almost hourly. When his forces approached Bilbao the Basques arranged for my wife and me to be taken out on a French destroyer.

On my return to the United States I wrote a series of articles for the New York "Post" about Catholic opposition to Franco in the Basque part of Spain and the role of the Basques in the Civil War in general. I also spoke at meetings to raise money for the Spanish Loyalists that were arranged by a variety of organizations, some of them Communist-dominated.

Barnes gave a sizable sum to a committee in Philadelphia that was raising money for ambulances for the Loyalists. "I do it," he explained at the time, "because of the heroism of the Spanish people and because the Reds are less than a fourth of those opposing Franco." He also said he did it despite a fear that the ambulances would arrive too late and might be captured by Franco.

 # XLVI

In addition to lecturing on the Spanish Civil War, I was soon interpreting other aspects of the international and domestic scenes and Barnes attended several of my meetings in the Philadelphia area, and at one of them, at least, responded when the chairman invited him to speak.

He did not have what is called "platform presence," and had never seriously tried to acquire it. He endeavored to win audiences by "making himself one of them." In doing so, he evolved, over the years, a myth about himself which he felt was useful in helping audiences, and individuals, to overcome their awe of him as an art collector, a scientist, or a millionaire.

The myth consisted of over-emphasis, and even outright exaggeration, of the poverty of his youth in "The Neck," the southernmost, and in the '80s the toughest, part of Philadelphia. Another ingredient of the myth was the fiction that he had wanted to be a painter, but, realizing he could never be more than a dauber, had burned his productions and had resolved to collect the works of his betters. This particular item, borrowed from Maugham's *Of Human Bondage,* had been carefully pondered, and was adopted, Barnes said, because it worked on so many different emotional fronts simultaneously—it provided a reason for collecting paintings even the benighted could understand; elicited the sympathy of the sentimental, who, thinking he had a secret sorrow, could feel superior to him; and implied a certain amount of nobility, since his renunciation of his ambition to paint had been self-imposed.

I always felt audiences were subliminally aware of Barnes' myth-making, and once told him so. He said nothing was ever one hundred per cent efficient, and that those who were aware of what he was doing would understand why he did it, and those who took what he said at face value would react to "the one touch of nature that makes the whole world kin," which his myths provided. He was psychically deaf when I suggested that fictions of rhetoric are not exactly "touches of nature."

His most successful speeches, I think, were impromptu ones delivered before the audiences he assembled in the Foundation's gallery for the annual concerts of the chorus of the Bordentown (New Jersey) Manual Training and Industrial School for Negroes. Their rendition of Negro spirituals, under the direction of Frederick J. Work, was, as Barnes rightly reiterated before each concert, a work of art.

He usually began these speeches with a vivid account of how the spirituals came to be as powerfully evocative as they are. This consisted of recounting how African slaves, transported to a civilization they did not comprehend, and totally lacking any means of affecting the environment which controlled their destinies, found in the supernatural religion of their masters a comfort and a hope, and combined their African animism with the simpler and more emotional aspects of Protestant Christianity. As the years passed they changed its hymnody, substituted new words (and new verbal formulations of its ethic and cosmogeny), added to the hymnic melodies the rhythms that were echoes of their erstwhile tribal life and of the physical, as well as psychical, relief from their isolation on the plantations of our Southern states.

Barnes would then explain why Negro spirituals have the power to affect others than the Negroes who created and sang them. The words, he said, were secondary in importance and were never to be considered by themselves, but only in conjunction with the musical rhythms which move the hands and feet, as well as the heart and head, and are a kind of counterpoint that evolved out of the Negro's propensity for artless improvisation. Each different group of Negroes who sang a spiritual would change it, but the versions collected by Frederick Work, Barnes was always careful to state, had not been "refined" or complicated by white musicians or by the kind of Negroes who imitate them.

I heard him go over this ground many times and he always did it with so much feeling that audiences were more appreciative of what they subsequently heard than they would have been had the Bordentown Chorus sung without his commentary. In intervals between groups of spirituals, designed to give the chorus a rest, Barnes would extemporize further remarks, and toward the end of a concert he would usually be singing himself.

But when he spoke in public elsewhere he was not so natural, felicitous and effective. He rarely if ever wrote out in advance what he was going to say, though he did carry in his pocket a set of stock notes which covered his basic points about the understanding of art, to which he would have recourse when other subjects failed, or he was called upon solely as an authority on art and education.

In the spring of '36 the Central High School invited him, as an alumnus, to give the Barnwell lecture for that year. He prepared no formal address and some of the things he said on that occasion were typical of what came out of him when he extemporized. The one that most surprised the audience was his declaration that the greatest artist Philadelphia had ever produced was Connie Mack, the manager of the Philadelphia Athletics baseball team.

"Let me reconcile this apparently wild assertion," he explained, "with the facts of the case. Connie Mack would not accept a recruit who would not rather play baseball than do anything else in the world. He gets team-work out of men who are concerned primarily with their own excellence. When Connie Mack is successful, his team has the attributes which all aestheticians agree are the indispensable requisites of great art—unity, variety, individuality, and the production of aesthetic pleasure in others . . . Connie Mack has given honest aesthetic pleasure to more people than anybody I know of in a lifetime spent in Philadelphia."

He also said Ross B. Davis, chief of Philadelphia's fire department, was an artist. There are firemen, Barnes said, who are artists in the way they fight a fire, and firemen who are artists in the way they later tell how a fire was fought. Chief Davis was an artist "in the way he gets men to work together." There is as much art in getting individual human beings to cooperate, Barnes always said, as there is in "painting, literature, music or any other fine art."

Declarations such as these were good newspaper copy, but Barnes rarely got a good press. He had a shrewd publicity sense *in the abstract,* but none in the actual handling of reporters and editors, and art critics. Some of the last, it is true, alienated him by pretending to knowledge they did not have, or picked fights with him to get publicity for themselves.

There was one occasion, however, when Barnes handled art critics with some *savoir faire*. It happened during the visit to this country of Ambroise Vollard, a French art dealer who stood in relation to impressionists and post-impressionists in the way Duveen did to old masters. Vollard had had some hard sledding during the Depression and had sold Barnes quite a few pictures, including Cézanne's "The Bathers," which Barnes obtained for $70,000 (at one time Vollard had asked $200,000 for it).

Vollard's visit to the United States was more or less under the aegis of Etienne Bignou, and it was Bignou's partner, Georges Keller, who arranged for the New York art critics to cover Vollard's first sight of Barnes' pictures and his address to the students of the Foundation. Among the critics Barnes invited were Henry McBride of the New York "Sun," Edward Alden Jewell of the "Times," Carlyle Burrows of the "Herald Tribune," Margaret Breuning of the "Post," and Alfred M. Frankfurter of "Art News." Barnes sent automobiles to fetch them from the North Philadelphia station and plied them with Scotch and good food.

Barnes liked Vollard and admired the way he had built and manipulated the myth about himself that had not only paid off handsomely but had enabled him to do a great deal of good. Beneath his showmanship, Barnes said, Vollard was a wise man of impeccable taste, and his conduct in the Parisian art jungle had set an example of intelligent and independent behavior which art dealers everywhere should emulate.

Vollard's opinion of Barnes was equally high, and in a radio broadcast shortly before his return to France he said his visit to the Barnes Foundation was the outstanding event of his "very short trip to America." And he added: "With the authority which my age permits me to assume, I assure you that there does not exist, and will never exist, in the world, another collection of masterpieces of the two greatest artists of the nineteenth century, Cézanne and Renoir, comparable to the one assembled by Dr. Barnes."

 XLVII

In 1937 and '38 Barnes made his last serious attempt to arouse the trustees and director of the Philadelphia Museum of Art to an awareness of how much more they should, and could, do for the city and its people. His purpose was to prod the Museum into adopting the kind of educational program he so whole-heartedly believed would make art, and the art spirit, a tool which everyone could use in everyday life, no matter how prosaic the daily round might be. Beneath the objective facts of the specific issues which Barnes raised, and exploited in the press, there always lurked the hope that public pressure, or *something*, would force the Museum to become the dynamic cultural force he thought it could be.

It should be borne in mind that by '37 and '38 he had become practically convinced that the Museum's trustees were so somnolent that a gentle prod was useless. They were, he acknowledged, "well-intentioned citizens of unimpeachable character," but not one of them, he pointed out, "has ever contributed an idea *of his own* to the intellectual, artistic or cultural development of the community." That was the crux of what he thought was wrong. He did not expect the Museum's trustees to devote their lives to art as he had done, but he did think their public service should amount to more than allowing the Museum to be merely "a pedestal upon which a clique of socialites pose as patrons of art and culture." It was the trustees' complacent acceptance of institutional inertia that drove Barnes to challenge them.

It is easy now, after a quarter century has stilled the passions and dulled the cutting edge of events, to say Barnes' tactics could not possibly have accomplished the ends he had in mind, and therefore were megalomania. *At the time* they were not without their logic, nor without a chance of success.

Barnes first took the Museum to task for a bird-brain exhibition it allowed to run for six weeks in the spring of '37. It was called "Forms of Art" and was advertised as "a fresh approach to the understanding of the art of the past and the present" which shows "how time and place become secondary to the creative character of the works themselves." It was the ambition-child of a Museum employe named Emanuel Mervyn Benson, who had convinced Fiske Kimball he could put on a show that would blaze new aesthetic trails.

Benson's idea was that all paintings, sculpture and other objets d'art can be sorted into three categories: 1) formal and humanized values; 2) social comment and social satire; 3) phases of fantasy. A circular handed to the public at the door alleged that the exhibits illustrated basic similarities of "procedure and attitude," "close approximation in form and feeling," and "unanimity of purpose."

In the "Phases of Fantasy" section, for example, Benson grouped some miniature paintings of eyes, an Egyptian rendering of a human eye, and Redon's "An Eye Like a Bizarre Balloon Ascends Toward the Infinite." The only thing they had in common was their subject-matter—the human eye. The plastic means of each, and the traditions affecting their use, were all different. The same was true of a grouping of Persian and Delft ware, a Tournai tapestry, some modern ceramics and a photograph of a Henri Rousseau, which Benson had apparently placed together because they all contained representations of animals. Similarity of subject-matter also accounted for grouping the works of Gropper, Daumier and Ensor together, and those of Steen, Longhi and Knaths.

This exhibition was so half-baked and immature Barnes felt it disgraced the City of Philadelphia as well as the Museum. To make sure he was right in regarding it so he asked

Dewey to take a look at it. After doing so Dewey said it was even more confused, intellectually and aesthetically, than Barnes had said.

"It was bad enough to call it, in the accompanying circular, a 'fresh approach,'" Dewey wrote Barnes, "when the leading idea of the circular is obviously borrowed from *The Art in Painting* without referring to that book. But the exhibition itself not only fails to carry out the borrowed idea, as expressed in the circular, but so completly contradicts it as to show that Mr. Benson never got the idea, but only some verbal expressions of it."

Dewey then pointed out that Benson's separation of artistic productions into three arbitrary classifications "is a flat contradiction of both the idea and statements (supposedly his own) that artists 'speak essentially the same language,' and of his reference to the 'ageless continuity of the basic art forms.' This alone is proof of Mr. Benson's confused state of mind.

"Aesthetically, his groupings of the works exhibited are based on common subject-matter and have nothing to do with the similarity of artistic form. I noted at least three or four instances in which the actual grouping is based on a principle which exactly reverses his announced one. These groupings would have some artistic point if he had said their purpose was to show how common subject-matter receives radically *different* artistic treatment according to the individuality and different environments of the artists who created the works of art. Instead of making this point, which is obvious to anyone with personal aesthetic understanding, the circular says they are grouped together as having a similar 'procedure and attitude' and as 'approximating' one another 'in form and feeling.' Incidentally, the comment one acquainted with paintings would naturally make is that some of the contemporary pictures exhibited 'approximate' the surface appearances of El Greco and Picasso, but only in an imitative sense. Numerous other paintings which Mr. Benson classes as 'creative' are so clearly academic repetitions of ante-cedent painters' forms that they too prove he does not know the difference between imitation and creation.

"That Mr. Benson should be thus confused personally is not a matter of great importance. That a great public in-stitution should lend itself to propagating the confusion is serious. Such exhibits ought to direct the efforts of students, both beginners and those more advanced. The present ex-hibit prevents this education."

Barnes thereupon wrote to the president of the Museum—then J. Stogdell Stokes—and formally complained that public money was wasted on such a pretentious infantilism. Stokes told Benson to reply.

In doing so Benson remarked that he had read, enjoyed and been stimulated by *The Art in Painting*, but that he had also read "Faure, Woelfflin, Ozenfant, Kurt Witt, Fritz Burger and many others—all of whom, in their own way, arrived at analogous conclusions, each through his own experience. These writers, including yourself, have undoubtedly left their mark on the development of my ideas, but nothing could have, or would have come of it if fresh personal experience with art and life over a period of many years had not con-firmed a point of view. We may be walking towards the same goal, but we are traveling different roads."

Barnes then had a detailed analysis made of the works of the writers Benson cited—all of which had been published after *The Art in Painting*—in order to determine whether the ideas in Benson's circular *had* derived from them. He also had all the articles Benson had ever written analyzed to find evidence of "parallel thinking." These researches convinced him that the ideas Benson had misapplied *had* come from *The Art in Painting*.

Stokes did nothing, the Museum's trustees did nothing, Fiske Kimball did nothing, and some years later Benson was promoted to a deanship in the Philadelphia College of Art, which the Museum administers.

 XLVIII

Another example of how the Museum stifled art life in Philadelphia was brought to Barnes' attention when one of the students in the Foundation's classes informed him he would have to withdraw because the rules of the Federal Art Project, set up during the Depression under the Work Progress Administration to give assistance to needy artists, obliged him to be in his studio between nine and twelve o'clock each morning, and one and four each afternoon, Monday through Friday.

This rule struck Barnes as nothing but bureaucratic stupidity, for, as he wrote the student, it forced artists to choose between "two of the necessities of the artist's life—bread for his body and a study of masterpieces as a nutriment for his spirit."

Barnes decided to investigate and see what he could do. He at once discovered that the Federal Arts Project in Philadelphia was administered by a Mary Curran, who had been expelled from the Barnes Foundation some years before because of "incompetence and misconduct." He also discovered that her appointment had been suggested by Fiske Kimball.

After considerable further investigation Barnes wrote the following to Robert L. Johnson, the head of Pennsylvania's Emergency Relief Board, through which the Federal funds then passed:

"Governor Earle's expressed fear of bread riots prompts me to report an incident which indicates that Philadelphia is likely to be the scene of the kind of disorder the Governor warned against last night. A group of writers, badly nourished and poorly dressed, called at my office yesterday and asked my advice as to the advisability of their throwing bricks through the windows of Mr. Fiske Kimball, Miss Mary Curran, and your local administrator, Mr. William H. Connell, the trio who, they claimed, are responsible for the situation revealed by the enclosed photograph clipped from last Saturday's 'Evening Ledger' [it was a photograph of artists picketing the Project office]. The artists, obviously facing despair, claim that Miss Curran, who awards the relief jobs, had dismissed their appeal in a high-handed manner and had refused to accept from them a written statement of their case. The artists told me that when they carried the matter to the two men above mentioned, all they obtained was a demonstration of specious buck-passing, which leaves no doubt that, de facto, Miss Curran controls the situation.

"The persons who called on me have the reputation of being peaceful citizens and competent artists who do not believe in Communism. Under normal circumstances their commission of illegal acts, such as they proposed, would be unthinkable. But they are driven to desperation by dire need, which is exaggerated by the incompetence and injustice which they claim they can prove exists . . . I advised them to throw no bricks, but to lay before you in person their grievances and pray for relief. Last week, when I saw the local trouble developing, I wrote letters to Mr. Kimball and Miss Curran . . . Not any of these letters were acknowledged . . . The complaints have reached me because of my position as president of an educational institution with about 150 students, most of them poor artists, only three of which are on the relief roll . . . I have not given a copy of this letter to the newspapers. I want to help you to solve the problem, not add to its difficulty."

Johnson did not himself reply, but his assistant, Frank Schmitt, wrote that everything was being done for the artists that could be done under the rules and regulations established by the Federal Government. Barnes replied that such a letter was an insult to the intelligence and a "farrago of nonsense, irrelevancies, hot air and issue dodging" which said, in effect, "Oh go away and let me sleep."

Meanwhile, Barnes' investigation of Miss Curran's administration of the Federal Arts Project in Philadelphia had uncovered an assortment of inefficiencies, as well as instances of personal favoritism and bureaucratic despotism.

Miss Curran was a well-meaning woman but a poor choice for administrator of a public relief program during this country's worst depression. At the time Kimball picked her she was running a gallery in which artists could exhibit for a nominal fee of three dollars per picture. In order to keep the gallery open and functioning she sometimes did not take the small salary she allowed herself. But she had no understanding of the economic and sociological forces swirling about her after she became head of the Federal Arts Project in Philadelphia, and no gift for dealing with the anxieties, some of them irrational, of hunger-driven honest people, nor with the lies and duplicities of the lazy or dishonest eager to get Government checks for doing nothing at all. And absolutely none for coping with the Communists, who were very active among all relief workers, whom they organized in the hope of gaining control of the administration of all the Federal work relief projects. Miss Curran never learned how to combat the Communists, either on the project or in the newspapers, and fled from the trouble they caused whenever she could. She took refuge in a clique, rewarded those she thought were on her side, and harassed those who seemed not to be.

For example, when she staged an exhibition of the work done by Project artists, four of her favorites dominated the show, and one of the four had *twenty* canvases exhibited. When artists of New Hope asked for Project jobs, she told one of them that since New Hope artists had never liked her she did not see why they solicited her help. Because A. L. Chanin attended classes at the Barnes Foundation she classified him as a student, thereby making him ineligible for work on the Project, notwithstanding the fact that one of his canvases was accepted for exhibition at the Pennsylvania Academy of Fine Arts. She told one sculptor to stop doing athletic figures and to do female ones; she asked applicants for places on the Project to sign a declaration that they were not members of the Artists' Union and did not want it to represent them (the National WPA office made her stop this); she segregated union leaders in a scenic art project which she then liquidated; and she urged mural painters to take up easel painting because "canvases are more mobile."

When Barnes stirred up as much agitation on the artists' behalf as he could, Kimball came to Miss Curran's defense. His attitude was that administering a works project was a headache, finding someone to do it was not easy, Miss Curran was doing her best in a situation in which it was impossible to please everybody, and he knew of no one who could do the job any better.

Kimball's chronic inertia, more than Miss Curran's personality, was the real menace, Barnes declared, since Kimball's influence, and that of the Museum of which he was the head, should be behind the expansion, not the contraction, of cultural vitality.

 XLIX

Kimball was preoccupied at that time in elaborate, indirect maneuvers to get the great Widener collection for the Philadelphia Museum of Art.* Joseph E. Widener had been made a Museum trustee and was deferred to in the hope that the collection would remain in the city in which he had been born and his father had made his fortune. One of the deferences was empowering him, when in Europe, to buy pictures for the Museum with the income from a fund of $700,000 left to the Museum years before by W. P. Wilstach, a leather manufacturer who had also left the Museum his paintings.

In the fall of '37 the Wildensteins told Widener in Paris that the Pellerins were willing to sell their "largest Cézanne." It was a version of "The Bathers" and Widener said the Philadelphia Museum would pay $110,000 for it, which was $15,-000 less than the unspent income from the Wilstach fund the Museum then had on hand.

Kimball let Widener choose the spot in the Museum in which "The Bathers" would hang, and had Widener approve the text of the press release in which the purchase was announced.

The press release said, among other things: "The acquisition of the Pellerin 'Bathers' gives to Philadelphia and its neighborhood the distinction of owning the two best known versions of the painter's famous subject. The second version, a slightly smaller picture, is in the collection of the Barnes Foundation at Merion."

This was a silly, as well as an indiscreet, thing for Kimball

* The Widener collection ultimately went to the National Gallery in Washington. Widener's father, who had formed the basic collection, stipulated in his will that his son could give it to any museum in Philadelphia, Washington or New York, but while he was alive had often indicated a preference for Washington, should a truly National Gallery ever be established there. The scales were further tipped in favor of Washington when the John G. Johnson collection was left to Philadelphia on the condition that the city pay the Pennsylvania collateral inheritance tax ($500,000). The then mayor of Philadelphia, Thomas B. Smith, said in Widener's hearing: "I hope no one else makes us gifts of this sort." Widener retorted: "You can be sure I won't." Mayor Smith also alienated Widener by asserting that the Widener fortune had been "stolen from the city" (via street car franchises).

to say, for he knew very well that the Cézanne "Bathers" in the Barnes Foundation is an incomparably better picture, despite its smaller size. Barnes asked Stogdell Stokes to have the Museum send a correction to the newspapers. When Stokes did not reply, Barnes wrote again and said that if Kimball did not correct his inaccurate and gratuitous public comparison of the two pictures, he himself would do it.

In the course of the ensuing controversy Barnes pointed out that although much could be said for the Cézanne "Bathers" the Wildensteins had sold the Museum through Widener, it was nevertheless one of the many canvases Cézanne had never finished, and that that was the reason the Pellerins had never been able to sell it, despite the active demand for Cézanne's work. He also said the Pellerins had offered it to him some years before for $85,000, and that a dealer had once told him it could be had for $50,000. And he analyzed the two paintings in order to show how they differed "in drawing, color, kind and quality of pigment, technique, space, composition and modeling."

An attempt to answer Barnes' charge that the Museum's "Bathers" was an unfinished picture which Cézanne had abandoned was undertaken anonymously in a letter to the Philadelphia "Evening Bulletin" signed "Syndic." The writer argued that Cézanne often left portions of a canvas bare intentionally, and that in his later work he sometimes used paint so sparingly his pictures had an "unfinished" appearance. In the course of making these points the anonymous writer went out of his way to call *The Art in Painting* "a masterpiece of dull and pedestrian writing."

Since the non-obsolete meaning of "syndic" is "an officer of government" or "agent of a corporation or other association," Barnes naturally assumed the letter had been written by someone connected with the Museum and he told Stokes, and the public, that if the Museum hoped to obscure its derelictions by throwing dirt he could throw a little too. In doing so he called Widener "an ignoramus" and "an absentee dictator of the local art situation who functions principally at the race tracks of Miami, Saratoga and Deauville," and said that Carroll Tyson, another Museum trustee, had admitted "he was half-drunk when he talked to a reporter about the Museum's 'Bathers.' " Barnes also said the Museum had paid $24,000 more than it need have for *another* canvas, and that "getting stung is a habit with the Museum officials, and nobody knows it better than the Paris picture dealers."

Barnes knew quite well that that sort of eristic disputation leads nowhere and he thereupon organized the "Friends of Art and Education." Dewey was its honorary president; Barnes was president; Robert Gwathmey, an artist, was vice president; De Haven Hinkson, a Negro physician whom Barnes had helped financially, was treasurer; and I was secretary. Several public meetings were held, several pamphlets were issued, but the public's response was slight, and in the spring of '38 Barnes went to Europe to complete the research on his book about Cézanne, which was almost ready for the publisher.

It is an error to consider Barnes' controversies with the Philadelphia Museum merely as evidences of eccentricity. He would sometimes stage a row in public *with an individual* to amuse himself and the public, but he was very much in earnest when he took on a *public institution*. Because he knew that many museum directors and staff workers get increasingly lazy, and arrogant, as the years go by, secure in the conviction that the public's ignorance of art will prevent an exposure of their indolence and incompetence, Barnes felt it was his duty to rouse sleeping dogs. *He* knew about art, and how museums were run, and didn't have to kow-tow to anyone.

"There should be one of me in every large city," he remarked when I informed him of a particularly scurrilous thing one of the Philadelphia Museum people had said about him.

L

Barnes sailed from New York on May 21 and on the following day, a Sunday, Glackens died.

The Glackens had gone on May 21 to Westport, Connecticut, to weekend with Charles Prendergast and his wife. Glackens and Prendergast had had a happy Saturday evening, after one of Eugenie Prendergast's best dinners, tippling and reminiscing. They arose late the next morning, and, after an elaborate breakfast, were conversing in the living room when a cerebral hemorrhage instantaneously flooded Glackens' consciousness away. He died within half an hour. He was sixty-eight.

For some reason I cannot now recall, if I ever knew, Barnes was informed of Glackens' death not by wireless to the boat but by letter to Paris, and he did not learn Glackens was dead until June 3, at which time he wrote to Edith Glackens:

"I feel a deep sorrow, because I loved Butts as I never loved but half a dozen people in my lifetime. He was so *real*, and so gentle, and of a character that I would have given millions to possess. And as an artist, I don't need to tell you I esteemed him: only Maurice Prendergast, among all the American painters I knew, was in his class. He will live forever in the Foundation collection among the great painters of the past, who, could they speak, would say he was of the elect. My heart goes out to you in full measure . . ."

Barnes mentioned Glackens' death several times in the thirteen years which intervened before his own, and always with the admonition: "That's the way to go."

I remember one hauntingly lovely spring afternoon when the flowering dogwood and magnolia on the Foundation lawn made him exclaim: "How Renoir and Butts would have itched to paint this view."

That led to a discussion of whether cosmic pessimism is possible in a personally happy man (Barnes thought not), and that led to Pirandello's "right you are if you think you are." Which led to William James' will-to-believe and to an argument over whether those who believe in a future life are happier than those who do not (Barnes thought it depended on temperament). This led to a discussion of death, its chemistry and physiology and inevitability, and the strange fact that it is death which dictates so much of what human life may be. "It's a very lucky thing," Barnes remarked, "the human consciousness is so constituted it cannot conceive of its own extinction."

From there we got to the Freudians' "death wish," which Barnes thought to be nothing more than a fancy name for the will-to-fail of lazy, incompetent or ignorant people. "The secret of life," he said then, and on many other occasions, "is struggle." He thought of a human being as a gigantic molecule that can disintegrate at any moment and believed "It's our struggle against entropy that gives life its savor—and meaning." What of those who have incurable diseases against which it is impossible to struggle, I asked. "They must struggle to learn how to die well," I was surprised to hear him say. It prompted me to mutter: "Each man gets the death he deserves—our end is in our beginning."

"Butts did—he never knew what hit him," Barnes said brusquely, and added: "That's the best death."

I said Glackens had had headaches, eye trouble and other warning symptoms, for a year or more. Barnes acknowledged this and started to say Glackens would have lived longer had he been less fond of good food and drink. But he broke off that train of thought and exclaimed: "Edith certainly had guts when she told the doctor if he couldn't bring Butts back the way he'd been before the stroke not to bring him back at all."

 LI

Barnes' *The Art of Cézanne*, which Harcourt, Brace and Co. published in '39, is Barnes' poorest book, probably because Cézanne presents some of the most difficult problems in all of aesthetics, and because there is unanimity of opinion on only a few of his canvases.

The sketch of Cézanne's life and personality in *The Art of Cézanne*, however, is the best such essay Barnes ever wrote. It is also the longest—more than three times the length of the one on Matisse and more than six times the length of that on Renoir. And it contains original ideas about romanticism and the psychology of power.

It begins, as it should, with Cézanne's birth in Aix-en-Provence on January 19, 1839, and his classical education there. His father was a local banker, and Emile Zola was one of his schoolmates. Later, Barnes pointed out, Zola was one of those who encouraged Cézanne to abandon the law, which he had studied to please his father, and to devote himself to painting—in Paris.

Barnes then takes note of the interesting psychological fact that though Cézanne responded to the artistic rebellions of Delacroix, Daumier, Pissarro, Manet, Monet and Sisley, in his young manhood and throughout his life, Cézanne remained deeply conservative, religiously and politically.

Barnes also noted Cézanne's morbid fear that people would "get their hooks into me"; his gradually increasing dislike of

Paris and his returns to Provence; and his "constantly recurring fits of uncertainty and depression," and "long periods of retirement." His association with Hortense Fiquet, whom he eventually married, Barnes said, had little or no direct effect upon his work, but indirectly resulted in a protracted relationship with Pissarro. "Since Cézanne was still in complete dependence on his father, who would have refused to sanction either an irregular union or a marriage with a dowerless girl," Barnes wrote, "Cézanne could not visit Aix in the summer of 1872, especially as a son had been born to them the winter before. Accordingly he went to Auvers-sur-Oise, near Pontoise, where Pissarro lived. The two men began to work together constantly, and Cézanne, for the first time doing most of his painting in the open air, really assimilated the impressionistic technique."

Pissarro, said Barnes, was the impressionist "most congenial to Cézanne in the particular bent of his mind," and he helped Cézanne "form the habit of painting his landscapes directly from nature." It was during his stay in Auvers-sur-Oise, Barnes believed, that Cézanne became conscious of "the magnificent colorfulness of nature," and began to modify "the very heavy, lumpy impasto of his first period, and to apply pigment in the smaller regular brushstrokes characteristic of his mature work."

Although Cézanne had pictures in the impressionists' exhibitions of 1874 and '77, Barnes said, his isolation and obscurity steadily increased during those years. In '86 he married Hortense Fiquet and shortly thereafter his father died, leaving him a sizable fortune. In the early '90s Cézanne's health began to decline. He "reverted to a closer communion with the Roman Catholic Church," became a recluse, and "on one visit to Paris, he refused to speak to his oldest friends when he passed them on the street." Nevertheless, it was during this period of loneliness, Barnes thought, that "much of his very best work was done."

Cézanne's isolation began to give way in 1894, Barnes says,

when the Caillebotte bequest of impressionist and post-impressionist paintings to the French Government caused Gustave Geffroy to publish an enthusiastic article about him, Vollard to arrange his first one-man show the following year, and "wealthy collectors, such as de Camondo and Pellerin, to begin to buy his pictures."

Barnes made a point of the fact that Cézanne's grief in 1897 over the death of his mother, "to whom he was deeply attached," was alleviated when his son assumed "the direction of his finances, his negotiations with picture-dealers, and the other practical affairs to which he felt himself unequal. On the whole, the last decade of his life was probably the most peaceful and cheerful that he ever had."

However, after 1904 Cézanne's diabetes, which was of long standing, grew worse, and physical infirmities began to affect his powers as a painter, which were "only then attaining full maturity." In October, 1906, Barnes wrote, "while painting in the open country, he was caught in a heavy storm . . . and was brought home unconscious. The next day he rose early and attempted to go on with his work, but collapsed almost at once, and died before his wife and son could reach him from Paris."

 LII

Cézanne, Barnes believed, was a romantic, which Barnes defined as one who "lives only partly in the world we all share" and whose real interests are in a world of the imagination "from which boredom, defeat and disillusionment have been banished—in brief, a more glamorous world." All too often the romantic's imaginings are "merely a flight from reality,"

and if the romantic's intelligence is crippled "he becomes the dreamer too absorbed in his dreams to make them real; if it is entirely paralyzed, he becomes the lunatic for whom dreams are the only realities."

Romanticism, Barnes continued, can justify itself only in the world of reality. It is not realism that is the opposite of romanticism, but conventionality, since "to conceive a world more rational than that habitually taken for granted, capable of arousing more interests and yielding more profound satisfactions, is not an indulgence in illusion if the dream or vision is used as an instrument for the discovery of realities here and now. Subject to this control, the art of the romanticist becomes analogous to the art of the scientist, a process of exploring the environment and bringing to light in it things to which the conventionally minded are permanently blind."

Cézanne's romantic conceptions, Barnes thought, were accompanied by "an extraordinary degree of integrity and force of character" and "extraordinary potentialities as an artist." Cézanne's "fidelity to his inner vision" was so great he could write to his son that, compared to himself, "all his compatriots were dirt" and to declare to others that he was "the only painter." Despite such declarations, Barnes pointed out, Cézanne was never self-confident, never the master of the medium of paint, and never *conscious* of the magnitude of his achievement, which was, Barnes said, "the interpretation of objects in terms of color planes, and of total situations in terms of dynamically interacting color-volumes."

But Cézanne was *unconsciously* aware of the significance of his insights, Barnes believed, "and it was mainly the systematic push of his unconscious that furnished the drive toward his ultimate goal. This unconscious refused to be deflected, overrode every obstacle . . . It was manifested in his concentration of purpose, his capacity to undergo endless labor and hardship, his self-imposed isolation, his renunciation of every interest that could have detracted from his singleness of mind."

179

It is fixity of purpose, unremitting labor, willing sacrifice, and isolation from all distraction, Barnes asserted, that comprise "psychological power," and it was psychological power that enabled Cézanne to convert his personal romanticism into an artistic expression which spoke to all men everywhere. "Because of the power in himself," Barnes wrote, "he had an incomparable eye for power in nature, for the qualities which can make the simplest material object seem massive, immovable and immutable." When Cézanne called his compatriots "dirt," dressed badly, and secluded himself, other painters thought him strange, "but when he put into painting the psychological equivalent of this social strangeness, they admired it, saw in it a personality doing and revealing something new, individual, fundamentally significant, with the very subject-matter, technique, independent spirit, honesty, and sincerity, which they looked upon as their very own."

 LIII

The "essential and fundamental fact" about Cézanne's painting, Barnes believed, is Cézanne's omnipresent theme of the balance of nature's architectonic forces—in an apple, a landscape, a man. "His figures are human beings only in broadest essentials," Barnes acknowledged. "Psychological characterization, as one finds it in Goya or Rembrandt or even Renoir, is absent, and little or no emphasis is put on the particular thing the subjects happen to be doing. Fundamentally, they are static: not inert or dead, but active as a tower, a pier or buttress, is active. The drama in which they take part is an interplay of abstract tensions and forces, not one of human intellect and personal emotion."

Cézanne's forms, Barnes continued, "are designed and they are *composed*—composed not only in the usual sense of having their parts disposed in an orderly arrangement, but in the sense in which we speak of a person's 'composure' as equivalent to his balance or poise . . . Even the first impression of Cézanne's work, as received by a sensitive observer, is that of a systematically planned architectural structure."

Cézanne's early work, Barnes pointed out, was heavily on the side of "melodrama and literary romanticism," and, because Cézanne was unskilled in craftsmanship, was characterized by "heavy impasto, sharp contrasts of light and dark, very emphatic rhythms extending in varying directions throughout the painting, alteration of patterned and unpatterned areas of canvas, and bizarre and picturesque distribution of subject-matter. The color scheme . . . is for the most part dark, with pure blacks, greenish blacks, deep grayish-greens, and occasional deep reds, related to whites tinged with gray . . . Light at this period is present mainly as chiaroscuro."

Barnes quoted Cézanne's remark about it having taken him "twenty years to learn that painting is not sculpture," and carefully traced the changes in Cézanne's application of paint to canvas from the early "piling-up of impasto to obtain surface-quality and sculpturesque volumes," frequently applied with a pallette knife, to the perceptible brush-strokes with thin paint and bare canvas in his later work.

Rather surprisingly, Barnes was reluctant to cite El Greco as a major influence on Cézanne, and even wrote: "No evidence has yet been found that he had ever seen El Greco's paintings." El Greco's form, Barnes explained, consists of "intricate and very active movement, often of excitement and turmoil," whereas Cézanne's mature form has "the monumental character of a well-ordered and firmly constructed building that symbolizes composure and tranquility." In a subsequent passage, however, Barnes admitted that "El Greco, after centuries of neglect, regained recognition and influence only after Cézanne had reopened the critics' eyes."

Cézanne's paintings are above all else composed, Barnes reiterated, and "the analysis of his form is primarily an account of his composition." The effect which a Cézanne painting produces, Barnes thought, derives from the totality of a Cézanne picture, not from its components. "Particular figures, natural objects, areas of pattern, segments of line, or intervals of space," he said, "have relatively little independent aesthetic importance. Detail is not itemized, and often, as in landscapes, the important compositional divisions cut across individual objects. Through the technique, the color is integrated in the composition as a whole, and the separate units are chiefly stages in the organization."

Cézanne's revelation of the planes which inhere in natural structures, Barnes declared, was largely accomplished by his grouping of his brush-strokes, and these patches, or areas, of strokes, "often impart to the ensemble the patterned character of a patchwork quilt, or the varied effects of mosaics and tapestry," and constitute the "fundamental unit" of Cézanne's composition and Cézanne's distinctive way of drawing, modeling, and organizing space.

Cézanne's canvases, Barnes pointed out, are divided into definite areas that are "almost always precisely shaped, usually bounded by strongly marked linear contours, and further distinguished by contrasts in color . . . illumination." The pyramid was the shape most often employed, and so was the double pyramid, which makes the shape called a diamond, and the variant of the diamond, the oval. Cézanne's most characteristic compositional arrangement Barnes called "table-top composition," because it consists of "a vertical plane, the foreground of the picture; then a roughly horizontal plane, on which the details of the subject matter—plates, fruit and the like—are placed; then a vertical background-plane which brings the recession of deep space to an end and thus shuts in the composition as a whole."

As for Cézanne's favorite colors, they are those of the Provence landscape. When I was in the Gorge du Tarn, not far from Aix, I wrote Barnes that "this is indeed Cézanne country. His buffs, blues and greens are all about me." Barnes replied: "Even the three-quarter blind can see that. Try to see the *planes*."

The real proof of Cézanne's greatness is not his "cult," Barnes declared, but his influence on every contemporary painter of any eminence. The "Cézanne cult," often "buttressed by misinterpretations of Cézanne's own sayings," Barnes thought, has retarded a proper understanding of Cézanne by making "a fetish of the obvious and superficial aspects of Cézanne's design."

Barnes repeated in *The Art of Cézanne* what he had said in *The Art of Renoir* about it being impossible to choose between Renoir and Cézanne because "far from competing with one another, they are both indispensable to a fully rounded contemporary aesthetic experience. Both, in short, are so valuable as to be invaluable." And he quoted Renoir's praise of Cézanne, and cited a dozen or so Renoir paintings in which he discerned Cézanne's influence.

Picasso, Barnes thought, owes more to Cézanne "than to any other preceding artist." Picasso's "blue period," which extended from 1902 to '07, "shows the most numerous and varied derivations from Cézanne as well as the widest range of authentically creative forms."

Cubism, Barnes believed, "would never have existed but for Cézanne, and the theories of art, fabricated to justify it and comparable schools and cults, have usually taken for their point of departure principles for which Cézanne's authority is claimed. The intersection of the angular planes of varied geometrical shapes, and the broad contour lines, which are outstanding features in the framework of Cézanne's mature paintings, form striking patterns that have a unique aesthetic appeal over and above their function as elements in fully expressive form. It was this effect of pattern which intrigues young painters of the first decade of the present century and was one of two source-materials utilized by them in the experimentation which resulted in many types of abstract painting, including cubism."

Matisse's early compositional arrangements, Barnes thought, were based on Cézanne's, and Matisse adapted Cézanne's compartmentalization of color, and even imitated the "levitation of objects frequently seen in Cézanne's still-lifes." Barnes thought Cézanne's planes and "color patches" can be seen in most of Pascin's paintings, and he traced evidences of Cézanne's influence in such disparate painters as Gauguin, Van Gogh, Soutine, Maurice Prendergast, Modigliani, Demuth and Utrillo.

Barnes was particularly pleased by his formulations in *The Art of Cézanne* of his ideas about romanticism and power. He sent copies of these passages to a variety of people and was elated when Dewey told him he had expressed fundamental and axiomatic things, and that: "In the light of your treatment it is difficult to see how realism could ever be art unless it actualized the romantic in terms of natural objects and events, and it is hard to see how any new movement can in its early stages be without a strong romantic strain . . . An individual departure from convention must be romantic until it has attained expression in terms . . . capable of being perceived and felt by others and thus becoming 'objective.' . . . Bernard Shaw's romanticism was never deep enough to enable him to do more than react against current conventions, and because of his failure to embody a new vision, he will, as time goes by, I fancy, appear as an embodiment of certain conventions more modern than those he attacked."

 LIV

The Art of Cézanne was the last book Barnes wrote, and, to date, the last book that has come from the Barnes Foundation. I once asked why he didn't do a book on Picasso and his answer was: "He lacks the *sine qua non* of the true artist—integrity." When I asked why he didn't do an autobiography he replied: "I'll never show off in *that* way." And when I asked if, some day, he'd let me do a "life and letters," he replied: "OK—but there's no hurry."

At one time he spoke of doing a book on early American furniture and handicraft, in which he was genuinely interested. He and Mrs. Barnes had always collected American antiques, but in the late '30s he began to collect examples of early American handicraft and furniture *systematically*, especially those of the "Pennsylvania Dutch."

One of his prime sources for the latter was Hattie Brunner, who had not yet begun to paint, in the style of Grandma Moses, as she has since. Another of the few antique dealers for whom Barnes had any respect was Arthur J. Sussel, who, I believe, began life as a bell-hop in the Bellevue-Stratford Hotel in Philadelphia. His shop on Spruce Street frequently contained things that belonged in museums, and Barnes learned a great deal from him, invited him to see his paintings, and sometimes had him drop in for a drink. Sussel had a country place at Birchrunville and Barnes and his wife occasionally motored out to see "a new Sussel find."

Sussel often outbid Barnes at local auctions and whenever he did so on something for which Barnes was especially keen, they would bargain excitedly over what Barnes should pay for it, more for the pleasure of sparring with each other than for the money either gained thereby. Their most memorable bouts occurred after the auctions of the collections of George Horace Lorimer, the editor of "The Saturday Evening Post," and Joseph Hergesheimer. At the latter Barnes outbid all the dealers for a sofa he had tried for years to induce the author to sell.

Barnes also bought early American things from the Madison Avenue dealers in New York, almost all of whom misrepresented at one time or another. When Barnes forced them to take things back they retaliated by circulating malicious stories about him.

Barnes always knew exactly what he acquired, for, if there were any doubt, or anything needed repair, Albert Nulty would take it apart and rebuild it as it had been originally. Nulty was an artist in this work and Barnes justifiably boasted that Nulty's restorations were "unrivalled."

The display of the finest pieces of furniture and handicraft in the Foundation's gallery warms the rooms and demonstrates the validity of Barnes' conviction that there is art in everything. Metal hinges hammered out by blacksmiths in Pennsylvania's southeastern counties are not extraneous by the side of even very modern paintings, and chests, tables and chairs fashioned by our ancestors stand *fittingly* below paintings of every period and place.

Barnes also acquired some prime examples of early American cupboards, beds and kitchen artifacts, and these he put into a farmhouse he bought in 1940.

It had been built, in 1774, of Pennsylvania field stone, by two brothers named Vare, and stood amid 180 acres of Chester County's rolling land not far from a tiny settlement called Rapp's Corner. Barnes bought it from a Pittsburgh doctor who had used it as a hunting lodge and subsequently rented it to a squalid Italian family. Barnes had Philadelphia architects redesign it inside and build extensions on both ends, using stone from the barn, which was also rebuilt. A swimming pool, shaped like a flat iron, was created near the house. Nine feet of earth was bulldozed off a hillock to make a particular view possible from a porch attached to one of the new extensions. Barnes called it "Ker Feal," which is Breton for "Fidele's House." Fidele was the little mongrel that made friends with Barnes one year in Port Manech and Barnes adopted on the spot.

Barnes arranged the furnishing at "Ker Feal." Except for kitchen, bathrooms and electricity, everything is early American. Mrs. Barnes was given carte blanche with the grounds, which she transformed into an aesthetic pleasure and a botanically important adjunct to the Foundation's Arboretum in Merion.

 LV

The Foundation's two arboretums, now among the most important in the United States, are Mrs. Barnes' handiwork exclusively, and incontrovertible proof that Barnes was right when he contended that genuine interest in something, pursued intelligently for its own sake, in accordance with scientific principles, results in an aesthetic creation no matter what that "something" is.

When Barnes bought the twelve acres which surround the Foundation's buildings in Merion, Captain Wilson made it a condition of sale that the trees he had planted, after his acquisition of the land in 1880, should be preserved. From his nucleus of a dozen or so species and varieties the Arboretum has grown until it now contains over two thousand species and varieties of woody plants; a collection of perennials which includes wall and rockery plants; a peony garden that has 110 herbaceous peonies surrounded by a hedge of forty-four "tree" peonies, including most of the best forms; and a woodland in which there are 90 species and varieties of hardy ferns.

There is also a collection of 250 species and varieties of lilacs; a representative series of berberis, cotoneaster, viburnum, lonicera, magnolia, cornus, ilex, stewartia and rhododendron; a rose garden containing over 200 hybrid tea roses; 30 hybrid perpetuals, 45 polyanthas and floribundas (75 climbers are distributed elsewhere in various parts of the grounds). The gymnosperms comprise unusual specimens of cedrus libani, libocedrus decurrens, and cunninghamia laneolata; varieties of picea, abies, pinus, and taxus; and more than 200 dwarf conifers.

In 1940 the Arboretum began offering courses in horticulture and botany and in the last two decades has trained hundreds of gardening amateurs and professionals. All courses are free. Eight were offered during the 1962–3 terms: the history of botany; the structure and activities of plants; plant materials; plant growth and activities; plant culture; plant geography; cultivated trees; and landscape architecture. Mrs. Barnes gave the courses on plant materials and cultivated trees, and the other courses were given by experts in their field.

Barnes' attitude toward the Arboretum, in which he never involved himself at all, was ambivalent. He was proud of the beautiful setting Mrs. Barnes created for the Foundation's buildings, proud of the Arboretum's reputation in botanical circles throughout the world, and proud of its ramifying influence on gardens and gardening in the Philadelphia countryside and other parts of the United States.

But he also, I always thought, was a bit jealous. He didn't fear that the Arboretum would eclipse the collection of paintings, or the courses on the appreciation and understanding of art—such a thought would never have entered his mind. His jealousy had to do, I think, with his recognition of the fact that the students at the Arboretum's courses were, on the average, more intelligent and effective human beings than those at the Foundation's art courses.

He once asked why I thought this was, and I replied that horticulturists are realists and aestheticians are romantics. The suggestion lulled him for the moment, but I could see it wouldn't do so permanently.

 LVI

Barnes discovered the property at Rapp's Corners while house-hunting for Bertrand Russell, and he house-hunted for Russell during the euphoria of one of his highest hopes, a hope fated to become one of his bitterest disappointments.

Russell was teaching philosophy at the University of California in Los Angeles when, on February 26, 1940, the Board of Higher Education of New York City appointed him professor of philosophy at the College of the City of New York for eighteen months beginning a year thereafter and terminating on June 30, 1942. In the interval between his UCLA and City College jobs Russell was to be at Harvard University for three or four months as William James Lecturer in Philosophy.

But his appointment to City College aroused widespread opposition. In the words of Bishop William T. Manning, of the Protestant Episcopal Church, who inspired an attempt to have the Board rescind Russell's appointment, he was "a recognized propagandist against religion and morality" who "specifically defends adultery." When the Board refused to rescind Russell's appointment, a Mrs. Jean Kay, of Brooklyn, undertook a taxpayer's suit to vacate the appointment on the grounds that Russell was not a citizen of the United States, had not taken a Civil Service examination, and was an advocate of sexual immorality

The case came before John E. McGeehan, a Tammany judge and a Roman Catholic. On March 30 he ruled that the appointment was revoked on all three grounds, and, in an extended and carefully researched opinion, he quoted passages from Russell's books and articles which advocated or condoned sexual infidelity, adultery, and trial marriage, infantile masturbation and juvenile homosexuality. He then characterized Russell's appointment as "an insult to the people of the City of New York," and declared that in making the appointment the Board of Higher Education was "in effect establishing a chair of indecency."

When the Board announced it would not itself appeal McGeehan's decision to a higher court, a "Committee on Cultural Freedom" was quickly organized to do so. Some of the country's foremost educators, including John Dewey, convinced that academic freedom was being attacked, either joined the Committee or gave it their support. It soon seemed likely that the Committee's efforts to take the case to a higher court would fail, and Dewey suggested to Barnes that he offer Russell a lectureship at the Foundation. No intercession has ever so unequivocally been a matter of principle. Russell had assailed Dewey's philosophy for years.*

Barnes acted on Dewey's suggestion with enthusiasm and wrote to Russell in California, offering him $6000 a year, for five years, for one one-hour lecture a week, October through May. Russell accepted at once, saying: "I cannot tell you what an immense boon your offer is to me. One is almost ashamed, at such a moment, to think of personal things, but when one has young children it is unavoidable."

They endeavored to decide what Russell would lecture on by correspondence, and in one letter Russell said: "I do not

* Often glibly and speciously. For a successful refutation by Dewey of some of Russell's criticisms, see the "Journal of Philosophy" for March 27, 1941.

know whether you want me to lecture on philosophy or on social questions. I should be very reluctant to lecture on sexual ethics, which have quite wrongly been supposed to be my special field. Actually the subject interests me much less than many others and I should be sorry to be diverted from philosophy and history to sociology. I could, if it suited you, lecture on different philosophies of the past, and their influence on culture and social questions. E.g., Platonism and its influence, or the Romantic movement of the nineteenth century."

In August Barnes flew to Lake Tahoe, where Russell was living in a small cabin with his third wife and their four-year-old son (Conrad Sebastian Robert Russell). He took a contract with him and Russell signed it without a change.

On his return to Merion Barnes wrote me with elation: "His subject will be the philosophy and culture of Europe from the Greeks to the present day. His lectures will serve as an ideal background for our studies of the traditions in art." The lectures were to be quite detailed, and not to be completed until the end of the fifth year, at which time they would be published in book form by the Foundation.

I do not remember any prospect Barnes ever found more pleasing. He was confident not only that the Foundation had obtained one of the world's foremost intellects and lucid expositors, but that, in time, he would have another philosopher-friend. He and Russell had been born in the same year, he had read everything Russell had written save some of the mathematical treatises, and he looked forward confidently to many pleasant hours in Russell's company. On Russell's side, the arrangement with Barnes provided an income in exchange for work he would enjoy, and enabled him to remain in the United States for the duration of the war (he was sixty-nine and could contribute nothing to Britain's survival by returning there with his wife and young son).

In one of his early letters in that summer of '40, during which England wondered whether Hitler would invade her,

Russell thanked Barnes for trying to find a house for him and then said:

"It is very good of you to be taking so much trouble on our behalf, and when we come East your preliminary search [for a suitable house] will be a great help to us.

"There are, however, some points that I should like to put to you, as I am afraid that your enthusiasm for lovely places may lead to your not quite realizing my circumstances. In the first place, it is *impossible* for us to buy: I cannot get money from England, and have here only what I have saved during the last twenty months. In the second place, I shall, out of $6000 a year, have to keep my two older children at the university, and perhaps spend money on refugee children; I must therefore have a house which not only has a low rental, but is cheap to run and requires little service. I should not know what to do with 60 or 70 acres of farmland. It is much more important to my happiness to live within my means than to live in a beautiful house; and it is essential both to my wife and to myself to reduce the machinery of life to a minimum.

"Choosing a house is a very personal matter, like choosing a wife. I know that in China the latter is done by proxy, but although people make mistakes, we are apt to prefer our own folly to the wisdom of others. We should neither of us wish to decide on a house until we have seen a considerable selection. I am deeply touched at your even contemplating spending $35,000 on the matter, but I am sure we can be happy at very much lower cost, and we could not possibly pay a rent corresponding to such a price, so that, in effect, you would be paying me a bigger salary than was agreed upon.

"Your offer to pay the fare of one of us to fly East is, again, extraordinarily kind. But we are leaving here very soon, and my wife, at least, will be in Philadelphia about September 13 ...

"Buying furniture is great fun and I hate to disappoint your kindly impulse, but we have enough furniture coming from England ...

"I am very much afraid all this may sound ungracious, but it is not so intended . . . What you have already done in giving me the post is so much that no more is needed to secure my life-long gratitude . . ."

The allusion to furniture referred to Barnes' offer to furnish Russell's house with antiques.

Russell added a postscript, which, in the light of subsequent events, was the first rift in the lute. The postscript said: "When my wife first gets to Philadelphia, she will be staying with some very old friends of ours."

 LVII

Meanwhile Barnes was active in Russell's behalf on another front. In New York the Committee on Cultural Freedom, unable to obtain a higher court review of the McGeehan ruling, decided to publish a symposium in which the implications of his decision would be discussed from a variety of viewpoints. They asked Barnes, through Dewey, to pay the costs, and he asked me to look into it and let him know what the costs would be.

The organizer of the symposium was Horace M. Kallen, who was then teaching philosophy in the New School for Social Research, and he and I arranged to meet in the office of B. W. Huebsch, of the Viking Press. Huebsch's interest in the symposium was strictly ideological, for he was, and had been for many years, treasurer of the American Civil Liberties Union. He and Kallen believed that Russell had been the victim of ecclesiastical authority, and that soon others would be similarly victimized should such an anti-democratic force be allowed to grow unchallenged and unopposed. Huebsch knew as well as I there would be little sale for the sort of book Kallen had in mind. He said the Viking Press was willing to publish but not to absorb the costs. Kallen made an off-the-cuff estimate of the number of contributors and the probable lengths of their articles, and Huebsch calculated the costs would not exceed $2000. When I conveyed this information Barnes agreed, and *The Bertrand Russell Case* was published in the spring of '41, after Russell had begun lecturing at the Foundation.

Dewey wrote an introduction for it, as well as an article, and his and Kallen's names were on the title page as "editors."

Dewey seemed to take what had happened to Russell personally. In his article he called McGeehan's court "an alleged court of justice," and averred that the things McGeehan quoted from *Marriage and Morals* and other Russell books were out of their context. Dewey quoted, from the same books McGeehan had used, passages which indicated that Russell believed marriage to be "the best and most important relation that can exist between two human beings," "custom should be against divorce except in somewhat extreme cases," and "undue preoccupation with sex is an evil."

Kallen's article, entitled "*Behind* the Bertrand Russell Case" (my italics), recounted the facts and then swung into a review of ecclesiastical repression of the freedom of thought through the ages. He disparaged "persons who make their living" by upholding practises which "keep religion going," and presented some dubious statistics to show that "crime and delinquency are directly proportional to the intransigent dogmatism of theological and moral instruction." Needless to say, polemics of that sort alienated not a few of those whom Kallen had hoped to win to the cause of academic freedom.

The best contribution to this symposium was that of Richard McKeon, professor of philosophy at the University of Chicago. It was an ably reasoned statement of "The Problems of Education in a Democracy," and deserves to be read today. Much richer in historical allusions than Kallen's piece, and far more temperate, it was for those reasons incomparably more effective. McKeon's sense of polemical fair play can best be seen in one of his footnotes: "The verdict of posterity for Socrates has been so overwhelming that it is only fair to remark that there has been dissent from it, such as the judgment of Hegel, who argued that the application of dialectic to moral questions involves a serious danger, since it undermines the sense of sacredness of duty by making it depend on individual conviction, and so introduces subjectivity into morals."

McKeon addressed himself to the fundamental issue: how can a society preserve its "moral integrity and spiritual purity" without resorting to the means which "lead to actions more noxious to religion and morality than any of the results of intellectual inquiry and criticism." In his elucidation of this all-important point McKeon employed a variety of diverting asides, like the fact that Augustine thought it "altogether impossible, or at any rate very difficult, to define heresy," and that Augustine had called attention "to the vast diversities in the lists of heresies, and therefore laid emphasis, as has continued to be the case in canon law, on the obstinate temper with which the wrong opinion is defended." McKeon concluded his article with this: "If any lesson is taught unambiguously by the long history of morality by suppression, it is that freedom of thought and of expression are not only privileges consistent with the integrity of a people and a state, but that they are indispensable means for the defense of free institutions and the advancement of a responsible and enlightened morality."

The other contributions were what one would expect from academic liberals of the '30s. Walton H. Hamilton, professor of law at Yale, was heavily witty in a piece entitled "Trial by Ordeal, New Style" ("Fire, water, hot irons have receded; the syllogism, the reference of instance to category, the staccato of an unruly dialectic, have come into their places. In so verbal a ceremonial where a parade of sequiturs separates premises from conclusions, there is many a chance for a 'therefore' to go astray"). Morris R. Cohen, emeritus professor of philosophy at the College of the City of New York, was properly exercised over the fact that appeals from McGeehan's decision had been denied and that Russell himself had not been allowed to testify. But he restrained himself and used only such words as "strange" and "ominous" when he characterized the action of a judge who "on the basis of reading a number of passages in a scholar's works, set up his own judgment as to whether the author is fit for a professorship in a college" and "ventured to overrule the faculty and the educational authorities to whom such determination is expressly delegated by law and who have had more opportunity to study and competently to interpret these works."

Guy Emery Shipler, the editor of "The Churchman," explained why Bishop Manning spoke only for himself (to speak for the Protestant Episcopal Church he would have to have had the authorization of the Church's General Convention, which is composed of bishops and other clergy and laymen); Carleton Washburn, superintendent of public schools in Winnetka, Ill., seized the occasion to argue on behalf of what he called "delegation of power to experts"; the members of the philosophy department at the College of the City of New York jointly saw in the Russell case one more manifestation of the hostility of those who did not want higher education bestowed on "the children of workers and of the lower middle class . . . and immigrant groups"; Sidney Hook, the head of New York University's philosophy department, asserted that since "the economy of the free market in goods and services is gone beyond recall" it behooves us all to see that "a free market in ideas is preserved." The McGeehan decision was printed in full in an appendix, and so was the original statement in Russell's defense of the Committee on Cultural Freedom.

Barnes contributed a short foreword in which he said the

book was neither an attempt to vindicate Russell nor a plea for academic freedom but "simply the record of an inquiry into the *facts* of the case." For, he said, "it is Democracy that needs to be vindicated, not Bertrand Russell . . . In a word, the stake is the lifeblood of Democracy, the right of every individual to be free from the tyrannical acts of dictators which, as in the Russell case, usurp the rights of the people, violate the basic principles of the American Constitution, hamstring education, and bring disgrace upon the whole nation."

 # LVIII

The book came out at a time when Barnes was still professing satisfaction, publicly, with Russell's lectures at the Foundation. I was therefore surprised, after the '41 concert of the Bordentown Chorus, to discover that Russell was not among those asked over to Barnes' house for a drink. When I could do so without being overheard I asked where Russell was. "He had to go home to his wife," Barnes said with a frown. "Is she ill?" I asked innocently. "I wish she were," he replied, and there was so much emotion in his tone that I knew more was seething beneath the surface. But he said nothing further, which was unlike him.

A week or two later he divulged things he had kept bottled up all spring (I don't remember his being so repressed in any other of his conflicts).

The trouble, he said, was Russell's wife.

Patricia Helen Spence had been Russell's secretary and had been named co-respondent in the divorce proceedings Russell's second wife, Dora, brought in '36. Russell had then married the red-haired Patricia and soon thereafter had a son by her. She was half Russell's age.*

As soon as she arrived from California she let it be known that she was *Lady* Russell, although her husband was not then using the title of the earldom he had inherited some years before. She was also gauche in other ways. She spoke imperiously to Nelle Mullen and other members of the staff, and though she had not asked permission to attend her husband's lectures, she did so whenever she felt so inclined, and annoyed the class with the clicking of her knitting needles. I also gathered that she had seen to it that a close friendship had not developed between her husband and Barnes.

"I've told Russell to teach her some manners," Barnes said with some bitterness, "but she's got him round her little finger and he's done nothing about it."

Not long afterward he sent me a copy of a letter that bore her signature, though it had obviously been written by her husband. It was an unusually ingenious letter, and Barnes was not aesthetically unappreciative of the deft touches by which she put the blame on him. It read in part:

"The first sentence of your letter of October 1st has seemed to me incomprehensible. My husband has, however, recalled to me an occasion when Miss Mullen appeared to him to have been annoyed by me; and so, fantastic as the charge appears, I must suppose you are referring to the following incident: On a particular day last winter my husband asked me to be not a moment later than 3:45 in calling for him, as he had an important engagement elsewhere. When, therefore, I called at 3:45, and was told indirectly that my husband was busy talking to a reporter and did not wish to be disturbed, I knew that someone had presumed to interpret my husband's wishes, and that in fact he could not have been told of my arrival. I therefore went into the building and spoke to a white-haired lady who approached me, and whose name I did not know, saying in a normal voice, 'Where is Mr. Russell? Will you

* He later divorced her and in '51 married an Edith Finch.

198

please let him know that I am here?' I then left the building. If this seems to the Trustees of the Barnes Foundation a disturbance of the peace, may they long continue to enjoy the unreal paradise where such trifles may be so accounted, for I cannot suppose that they would have the fortitude to endure a true disturbance of the peace: for example bombs tearing through the roof.

"As for my occasional attendance at my husband's lectures: I have always acted as his assistant in research for and preparation of his lectures, and when, as is usually the case, I am familiar with the subject he is to speak about, he does not desire my attendance. On other occasions, when the subject is not one that I have studied, he has wished me to be present, not for my own sake, but for the sake of his lectures, since I cannot assist him adequately with the preparation of any one lecture without a thorough grasp of the whole course. In every other institution in which my husband has taught since I was his assistant, it has only been necessary for him to mention that he would like to have me present at some of his lectures, and the permission has been most readily and courteously granted. I had understood that my husband had arranged this with the Barnes Foundation, but if he forgot to do so, or understood that permission was granted when in fact it was not so, we can only apologize for my unintentional trespass.

"It is in any case necessary for me to drive my husband to his lectures, as he cannot drive himself, and he had not supposed that the Trustees could wish me to wait outside.

"I cannot imagine anyone regarding the Foundation as 'a place where they may drop in occasionally.'

"As for my knitting: it was with some hesitation that I took it with me—on two or perhaps three occasions—to the Barnes Foundation; but when I consulted my husband he remarked that I had disturbed no one by knitting at far more difficult and technical lectures at the Universities of Oxford, Chicago, California, and Harvard, and that therefore I might assume that I would be giving no offense. I am distressed that in fact

I did disturb someone, and would be glad if you would convey to all the students my sincere apologies.

"It would only have been necessary for you to say to me, 'Mrs. Russell, would you mind not knitting' just as you only need to have told my husband 'If you want your wife to come to your lectures it will be necessary for her to obtain permission of the Trustees.'

"My knitting is in no sense an 'indulgence' and I would not have run the risk of annoying anyone by it, however slightly, but for a purpose that seems to me serious, the wish to diminish the number of those who suffer from the cold.

"If I am sometimes a little cold myself in future, when, having no errands, I wait for my husband outside the Barnes Foundation (outside the *grounds* of course), I will knit with more zest from a nearer realization of what it must mean to be cold and really without shelter; and I will marvel that in such a world anyone should be willing, deliberately, to make one fellow-human cold even for one hour. And I will marvel, too, as I do now, that anyone should wish, in a world so full of mountains of hostility, to magnify so grandiloquently so petty a molehill."

Barnes made one last attempt to save his relations with Russell, but with so little hope of success that he ended a letter to him with this: "When we engaged you to teach we did not obligate ourselves to endure forever the trouble-making propensities of your wife."

To which Russell replied: "I shall continue to do all in my power (including utilization of my wife's valuable help in research) to make my lectures as good as I am able to make them; but, so far as any personal relationship is concerned, you are mistaken in supposing that there is no quarrel with me, since whoever quarrels with my wife quarrels with me."

Russell soon began telling people that Barnes had "an inferiority complex," was only comfortable "with dogs and colored people," and was "crazy." And Barnes began to say Russell was no longer taking pains with his lectures, and was patronizing in his replies to the few students who now ventured to ask questions. Barnes also began to collect criticisms of Russell's lectures from the students, and he invited a variety of people to attend some of Russell's lectures and report their findings. He was pleased when I reported that Russell, at least intellectually, was overtly anti-democratic. "Document it, document it," Barnes said.

Russell finally provided Barnes with a reason for firing him. After accepting from the Foundation $2000 a year more than had originally been agreed upon, in order to be relieved from the necessity of giving "popular" lectures, Russell contracted to deliver a series of such lectures at the Rand School in New York.

Barnes' letter made the dismissal effective on the last day of '42, and Russell at once instituted suit for the $24,000 he would have received for the last three years of his five-year contract.

 LIX

Russell sued in the Federal, not the Pennsylvania, courts, and won a verdict of $20,000. The judge felt he could earn at least $4000 in the three years he did not lecture at the Barnes Foundation.

His victory was due to a bit of law that was hard for Barnes to swallow. He himself—not his lawyer—had drawn up the contract with Russell, and, by particularizing all the points he thought relevant at the time *so specifically*, he had denied himself the right to introduce, at the trial, the fact that Russell had agreed not to do "popular" lecturing. Had Barnes' contract been less specific, he would have had a better chance of getting information of Russell's violation of their understanding into the record. Immediately after the verdict he announced he would appeal, but his lawyer convinced him it would be useless.

Barnes solaced his feelings by writing a pamphlet entitled "The Case of Bertrand Russell vs. Democracy and Education," which he broadcast by mail both here and abroad. Considering the circumstances, the pamphlet's restraint is surprising.

It began with a straight-forward account of how Barnes had become interested in the controversy over Russell's rescinded appointment to the College of the City of New York, and of how he had come to offer Russell a lectureship at the Foundation even though he knew "of Mr. Russell's propensity for getting himself embroiled with established law and order, and was aware that after brief engagements at Harvard, Chicago and the University of California he had been retained nowhere."

About a month after they had signed the original contract stipulating a salary of $6000, Barnes wrote, Russell "called at my office and told me that he would be compelled to abandon popular lecturing if he were to do his work for us properly, but that the sacrifice of income would present him with a serious financial problem. When I asked him exactly what the amount of the sacrifice would be, he told me that it would be $2000 a year, and added that he was sick and tired of popular lecturing and wished to devote all his energies to serious work. Upon my further inquiry whether he meant that if I could arrange for an increase of his salary . . . he would agree to discontinue all popular lectures and give the time thus saved to work for the Foundation, he eagerly assented, reserving only the right to deliver 'a very occasional lecture to some university audience.' "

Barnes' account of Mrs. Russell's role was factual and included the quotation from his letter to Russell in which he said that by engaging him to teach the Foundation "did not obli-

gate ourselves to endure forever the trouble-making propensities of your wife." He also mentioned the fact that Mrs.
Russell had been sent a formal notice to stay away from the
Foundation, and asserted that after the trouble with Mrs.
Russell her husband's lectures so declined in interest that of
the sixty students who had attended them at the beginning,
only eleven were left by the end of '42.

The concluding lash of the pamphlet was that if the Foundation's students had "learned anything whatever of democracy in education from Russell, it was because he presented
them with the perfect example of its antithesis."

It should be borne in mind that the Bertrand Russell who
lectured at the Barnes Foundation was in full possession of his
mental powers and was not at all like the Lord Russell of recent years who has oscillated between recommendation of a
preventive atomic war against the Soviet Union and uni-
lateral atomic disarmament by the West.

 LX

As a philosopher-foe of the then Mrs. Russell maliciously remarked, it may have been the strain of surviving the war in
the safety of the United States that caused her to set off the
Russell-Barnes imbroglio. The war affected everyone, in one
way or another.

But it dealt gently with Russell, and with Barnes. The latter
had no children or grandchildren to worry about, and he had
early resolved that the gallery in Merion was as safe a place as
any for his pictures. Had not the National Gallery elected to
store its rarest things in the empty Stotesbury mansion in

nearby Whitemarsh? Besides, Barnes said, how could the Foundation's classes function without its pictures?

Beneath these surface reasons, however, was his conviction that the United States would be neither bombed nor invaded, and that Germany's second bid for world hegemony would be no more successful than her first. Barnes thought Churchill's famous phrase, upon which so many changes have been wrung—"never have so many owed so much to so few"—was literally true, in the sense that the "battle for Britain" in the summer of '40 was the turning point of the war, since Britain's survival made a temporary truce unnecessary, and forced Germany to invade Russia.

I saw him soon after that Sunday morning of June 22, 1941, on which German tanks and troops crossed the Russian border, and he asked me how long it had taken the American Communist Party, which had been opposing our entry into the war, to urge our immediate entry into it. "They did it that very day," I replied. "Do you *now* believe it's controlled by Moscow?" he demanded. "How could anyone not," I replied, and added sheepishly, "Thanks for not saying 'I told you so.' " "I was just about to," he replied.

Barnes followed the progress of the war with active interest, and was sure we would get into it. He was in favor of our doing so, I think, chiefly because he believed Woodrow Wilson's slogan for World War I—"to keep the world safe for democracy"—was an actual issue of World War II. As I have pointed out, he was under no illusions about the Soviet dictatorship, but he thought it could, in time, be brought more toward democracy than could the Nazi, Fascist and Japanese tyrannies, since the Soviets were obliged to pay lip service to the sovereignty of the people, and the fascist dictatorships openly espoused the rule of the many by an elite.

I had a very interesting conversation with him shortly after the Japanese attack on Pearl Harbor.

When I remarked that it was obvious Roosevelt had let it happen in order to get us into the war, he said reprovingly:

"Can you prove it?" I replied that of course I couldn't and asked: "Do you have any doubt about it?"

He evaded the question and inquired whether I thought it was in the national interest of the United States for Germany to be defeated (in both of our minds the defeat of Italy and Japan was implicit in the defeat of Germany). When I answered in the affirmative he asked why I thought so. I replied that Germans comprised a young and vital nation which believed its destiny was to rule the world and that despite their discipline, and the primacy of science in their culture, there was a barbarous element in their rationalization of militarism, and, anyway, I said, I didn't want to be told by lackeys of a Goebbels or Himmler or Hitler what I could say and do.

"Since you agree we should have gotten into the war," Barnes said quietly, "does it make any difference how we did?"

"It does to Admiral Kimmell and General Short," I replied. "They're being blamed for not forestalling an attack that we practically arranged."

"I advise you not to say that in public," Barnes said gravely. "We're at war. It gives aid and comfort to the enemy."

"You're right," I murmured. "Forget it."

"Before I do," he said less gravely, "there's a lesson here for you. It's tough on Kimmell and Short, but history will exonerate them. It wouldn't have been possible for Roosevelt to have done what you say he did if the American people didn't feel about the war the way you do. Here's the sermon for today: war is confusion, and so is life, and that's why you and I like art—it sorts things out and puts them straight."

Although it never entered Barnes' head that we could lose the war, he was avidly interested in the details of individual engagements as well as whole campaigns.

For example, in November '42, while taking Army basic training, I received a letter from him in which he said: "It wouldn't surprise me if, by the time you are ready to be shipped overseas, Eisenhower, with the aid of the British, might leave nothing for you but the mopping up. It certainly was most gratifying news to have the Solomons naval battle and the North African expedition take place at about the same time, and apparently with results all to our good. Like everybody else, I don't like the Darlan end of the situation, and I certainly hope that the rats who have deserted the sinking ship at Vichy, and have gone to Africa, won't have even a slight look-in. I know some of those fellows and they are indescribable moral derelicts."

I cannot remember his immediate reaction to Hiroshima, but some time later he said that with such a weapon up our sleeve Roosevelt's agreements with the Soviet Union at Yalta were certainly unnecessary. And four years later, after Truman's announcement that the Soviets had set off an atomic explosion, he said: "We were masters of the world—for four years."

Except for the drafting of several of the Foundation's instructors, and the inconveniences of rationing, the war touched Barnes only by preventing him from going to Europe. There are those who think it was this inability to go abroad, from '39 to '45, that accounts for his interest in early American furniture and handicraft. I am not one of them. I think this interest had been latent for many years, and was as deep as his fondness for the Methodist hymns he so often sang when he was happy. It is significant, I believe, that the last paintings he acquired were two Chardins, and that instead of paying money for them he traded two Cézannes.

 LXI

It was during the war, and some months before he fired Bertrand Russell, that Barnes had a disappointing, but in some ways an amusing, brush with "The Saturday Evening Post."

On Russell's first day at the Foundation Barnes arranged for him to be interviewed by Carl McCardle, a feature writer for the Philadelphia "Evening Bulletin" who had helped one of the Wideners get out a book. Barnes liked what McCardle wrote about Russell—at that time he was still zealous on Russell's behalf—and in the course of the acquaintanceship which developed McCardle asked if he could do a series of articles on the Foundation for a magazine of national circulation.

Although Barnes had turned down a similar request from Archibald MacLeish some years before, at a time when MacLeish was writing for "Fortune," Barnes told McCardle he would cooperate with him, and would lend him color photographs which he had allowed his protegés, the Pinto brothers, to make of some of the Foundation's paintings, provided McCardle would promise two things: first, to concentrate on the educational aspects of the Foundation, and second, to let Barnes approve his copy before it was submitted to a magazine. McCardle agreed, and soon thereafter contracted to supply four articles to "The Saturday Evening Post."

The "Post" editors, apparently, did not think their readers would be too interested in the educational work of the Foundation, and McCardle soon found himself concentrating on anecdotage, including myths then current about Barnes and myths Barnes had disseminated about himself. He showed some of his manuscript to Barnes, while he was still in the stage of extracting information from him, and when Barnes protested that it was not the sort of material he had agreed to cooperate on, McCardle implied that he had merely been trying to intrigue the "Post" editors and that everything would be all right in the final draft. However, as soon as he finished collecting data from Barnes he showed him no more manuscript, and it was only by threatening to sue, a few days before the first article was to go to press, that McCardle showed him *the galley proofs.*

When Barnes protested and threatened to have the courts enjoin the distribution of the issues containing McCardle's articles, the editors correctly replied that no court would issue such an injunction since Barnes had no contract with the "Post" covering his verbal agreement with McCardle. If Barnes felt he had been libelled, he could sue only after the libel had been published. The "Post" editors did agree, however, to correct some minor factual mis-statements.

When Barnes' lawyer—then Robert T. McCracken—confirmed what the "Post" editors had said, Barnes resorted to a newsworthy way of informing the public that McCardle's articles did not have his approval. He appeared at several newsstands which stocked the March 21, 1942, issue of the "Post" and publicly protested against its sale—in the presence of reporters from the Philadelphia newspapers.

He also wrote and published a pamphlet entitled "How It Happened," in which he said the title of the "Post's" series— "The Terrible Tempered Dr. Barnes"—was a plagiarism of the title of one of the "Bulletin's" comic page features ("The Terrible Tempered Mr. Bangs" by Fontaine Fox). And after recounting how his protests to McCardle about "distortion and falsification of facts" and "over-emphasis of sensational elements of events at the expense of their true meanings" resulted in his being allowed to remove "only the most glaring falsifications," he declared that the "whoppers" and "phantasies" in the articles were more a "portrait of McCardle" than of himself.

He had considerably better luck at the end of '42 with "House and Garden," which put a picture of him and Mrs. Barnes on the cover of its Christmas issue and inside published a profusely illustrated article on the Foundation and "Ker Feal."

It came out while I was in the Army and Barnes urged me to get a copy and read it. "House and Garden" was not one of the magazines sold at the "PX" and it took some time for my wife to get a copy to me. I wrote Barnes that I thought it described the Foundation's work in the right way. He replied:

"I am glad you liked the 'House and Garden' account of the Foundation. My experience with 'The Saturday Evening Post' provided me with a method of preventing them from getting away with the same kind of dirty trick the 'Post' pulled. This is what happened:

"The editor asked to see 'Ker Feal' and when he did he asked for the privilege of writing an account of it for his magazine. He then followed that up with a desire to have an article written showing the relationship between the Foundation and 'Ker Feal' as regards the various values intrinsic to art, craftsmanship, composition, etc. I thought this would be a good way to counteract some of the bad effects of the 'Post' articles so I provided him with books, pamphlets and stacks of information from other sources that would give him the necessary data to do an honest and competent job. But I was careful to get in writing the magazine's agreement that I was to OK everything before it was published.

"I had a hell of a time getting the article out of them and when it came it was a feeble imitation of some of the bad features of the 'Post' articles, especially in its glorification of me as a hero and more or less of a nut. I returned the article and told them 'it stinks' and was ready to apply to the courts for an injunction that would sew them up completely. When they saw that I had them in the corner, they asked me to write the article about the Foundation and we had only a couple of days to do it. I turned the job over to Miss de Mazia and, as you will recognize, much of the matter had already been published. However, it does tell the story adequately. The incident has convinced me that there is an intrinsic, ineradicable, putrid core to journalistic methods as practised."

 LXII

The phrase in the foregoing letter, "more or less of a nut," should be noted more than casually.

Barnes was well aware that McCardle's title, "The Terrible Tempered Dr. Barnes," aptly suggested the "image" which much of the public attached to his name. That the public didn't put a halo over his head didn't bother him, for he knew that anyone who told "art lovers" they are poseurs and emotional ignoramuses, and that genuine appreciation of art requires study, and told museum directors and trustees their pretentious indolence prevented the public from learning what art is really about, is sure to be regarded, at best, as an annoying gadfly.

Barnes did not regard himself as a gadfly, however. He was a messianic man, confident until the moment he died that he had evolved a method by which art could be *made* to have meaning for even the uncultivated. But though he knew, theoretically, how hard it is to "re-educate," he was only intermittently mindful of the personal factors entailed in bridging the gap between a man like himself, who had spent all of his maturity seriously collecting, studying, analyzing and discussing paintings, and a man, say, like Sturgis Ingersoll, much of whose time was necessarily given to business and social affairs, or an earnest young stenographer devoting her Saturday afternoons to "culture."

Barnes might have elected to fabricate a benign public "image" for himself had he not been convinced that kindness is no way to circumvent the infinite resources of the human mind for evading intellectual and moral effort. In his own life he had worked out a regimen from which he never deviated, and he felt it his *duty* to appear to the public as the implacable foe of all that contributes to intellectual stultification and inanition.

This is not to say he didn't have light moments. Some of them occurred at the meeting of the Rhode Island Philosophical Society at Brown University he addressed in January of '43, at the invitation of Dr. C. J. Ducasse, then head of Brown's philosophy department and a friend of Dewey's.

Barnes insisted on titling his address "Having a Hell of a Good Time Playing with Art, Education, Science and Philosophy" in order to alert the Society's members to the fact that though art and philosophy are serious matters one should never be solemn about them. And further to "bridge the gap" the introductory phases of his address emphasized the poverty of his boyhood, and utilized such apocrypha as having had to learn how to box in order to protect himself from the toughs of South Philadelphia. Only then did he attempt to discuss abstruse philosophical and aesthetical things—in a homely but vigorous way.

He said the commonest instance of an aesthetic experience is "when you are having a good time," and that watching a prizefight or a baseball game can yield an aesthetic experience, though its quality will not be as high as that which can occur in front of a truly great picture. Whenever we handle a problem of everyday life, he continued, like parking a car or a mother-in-law, simplifying household routines or secretarial duties, covering a roof or teaching algebra, or whatever, and do it not only effectively but *with grace*, we have had an aesthetic, and possibly a creative, experience. The reason, he explained, is that we have succeeded in adapting our "instinctual drives" to an environmental situation not designed for the satisfaction of those instincts. It's facing and solving a problem presented by the environment, not avoiding or evading it, which provides the opportunity for us to *enjoy* utilizing our capabilities and skills, and thereby to experience what a writer feels when he succeeds in making words express thought, or a painter when his brush makes his vision visible to others. The art in life, Barnes said, is learning how to be *interested* in what we do, no matter what it is. "Inspiration," he said, "is being so excited about something you have an urge to do something about it."

The audience liked his humanization of aesthetics and the questions after his address were to the point. One questioner inquired how he felt when his opinion decided whether a painting is good or bad. He replied equivocally by saying some people thought he was one of God's anointed and others thought he didn't know a damned thing. Another questioner asked how people are to learn how to appreciate modern art if he wouldn't let his pictures be seen. By coming to the Foundation's classes, he said, and he offered a scholarship to anyone with a genuine interest who couldn't afford to study at Merion on his own.

Barnes also told the Rhode Island Philosophical Society that great painting must have a purpose, and that everything in a painting, subject matter as well as plastic means, must contribute to that purpose.

His position on this point has often been misunderstood, even by some who have studied with him. He did *not* believe that subject matter is of no importance, though he did believe that *exclusive* interest in subject matter is wrong. The whole body of his thought, and *many* of his specific utterances, testify to his conviction that the artist's vision is the beginning, the middle, and the end, of a work of art. He also believed that the artist's vision, no matter how introspective, must relate to the real world.

Nor was this a development in the last decade of his life. I have already cited his early attack on Leo Stein for declaring that subjective judgments of painting are irrelevant, and he always resented it when anyone tried to box him into that arid corner. He especially resented Craven's attempt to do it in his review of *The Art of Henri-Matisse*. "Another of Craven's grave misrepresentations," Barnes wrote me at that time, "is the accusation that we make of 'pattern' or 'plastic form' the object of a work of art. We devote a whole chapter to an exposition of the fact that plastic form is valuable only as the medium for the expression of the human values which Craven says we ignore or mention only negligibly. Another bit of colossal ignorance is his emphasis upon our 'dissecting' of a work of art and considering the components separately before we consider them as an 'organization.' That idea, by the way, he stole from what T. S. Eliot said about I. A. Richards' methods of literary criticism."

In view of the many emphases of the importance of a painting's subject matter that abound in *The Art in Painting*, one suspects that those who misrepresent Barnes on this point may have an ulterior purpose. One such ulterior purpose is using Barnes and the Foundation to justify so-called abstract art. The nearest Barnes was willing to approach "abstract" art was to acknowledge that "forms may be charged with aesthetic feeling even when they represent nothing definite in the real world or when what they represent is clearly without appeal in itself." But even that he qualified a page or two later by stating that more often than not such forms are merely "technical exercises, sterile, and of a new kind of pedantry."

On the other hand, he was dedicated to the proposition that the artist's mind, like the scientist's, explores the frontiers of human knowledge and is sensitive to intimations of a reality about which the human race is still ignorant. In *The Art in Painting* he summarized a theory of Buermeyer's that non-representational painting *may* represent *generalized qualities*, "as a paradigm of the visible essence of all things may hold in solution the emotions which individual things provoke in a more highly specialized form."

But that opened the door to Platonic archetypes, in which Barnes did not believe.

 LXIII

Barnes never missed a chance to correct the error that his method of studying pictures de-emphasized subject matter and its representation. In '44 he complained to the Philadelphia Board of Education when its director of fine and industrial arts, Earl B. Milliette, gave that impression in a monograph entitled *Art Annals of the Central High School of Philadelphia.*

Rembrandt Peale had taught at the Central High School and its graduates included not only Glackens and John Sloane but also Thomas Eakins, and such collectors as P. A. B. Widener, John G. Johnson and Barnes. In discussing Barnes' pictures and theories Milliette quoted a criticism that had appeared in "Art News" of *The Art in Painting:* "It remains a cold recital of causality, behaviorism, mechanism and descriptive medical journal writing."

Whatever Milliette's reason may have been, Barnes felt he had contributed to the perpetuation of the delusion that his method dealt with everything about a picture except what it *said.* His letter to the Board complained of such misrepresentation. Milliette was told to apologize, and he did.

Barnes had another purpose in raising this issue, which Milliette's apology frustrated. He wanted to get before the public the fact that the art courses in Philadelphia's public schools treated art as something apart from life, instead of as something that should permeate everything we do, as, in fact, a way of thinking, seeing, doing, and being. He even contemplated suing Milliette for misrepresentation in order to gain an arena in which to expose the thoughtless and lackadaisical approach to art instruction in the Philadelphia schools.

Furthermore, Barnes believed the Philadelphia Museum of Art should give light and leading to the public school system, and that it should not be necessary for him, or any other private citizen, to have to try to force the Board of Education to introduce techniques that foster the all-important truth that art, and the art spirit, enrich and ennoble individual lives and increase mankind's cultural patrimony.

Barnes could never reconcile himself to "the lethargy of the Museum's trustees." He acknowledged that most of them were busy men who had a genuine sense of social responsibility. But he thought it wrong of them to let the museum staff doze in the mornings and cocktail-party in the afternoons. It was all very well for Fiske Kimball to give elaborate "soupers" in the Museum for people who might donate money or works of art, but *in addition*, Barnes thought, Kimball and his staff should concern themselves with such things as improving art instruction in the public schools, and everywhere else that the minds of the next generation could be won to art.

So much could be done, he always said, if only the will to do it were in the Museum trustees! How could it be put there?

Barnes tested several possibilities over the years. One of them was the occasional public prodding of Sturgis Ingersoll, especially after Ingersoll became the Museum's president.

It was Philadelphia's loss that Ingersoll had come to regard Barnes merely as a nuisance. Had he adhered to his earlier belief that Barnes' "contribution to life here has been immense," and not allowed the things Barnes said and did to get under his skin, the two men could have revolutionized art museum procedures and art education not only in Philadelphia but throughout the country. It is true Barnes was not the easiest man in the world to understand, or work with, but it is equally true he was a man who was passionately dedicated to the belief that art is man's most valuable tool. There wasn't anything he wouldn't have done to help the Museum bring that message to the humblest citizen of Philadelphia.

Ingersoll didn't understand Barnes, and was put out by Barnes' impatience with "the Establishment," and Ingersoll's own personal uncertainties caused him to do things which abetted their alienation.

In the spring of '44 he published a tribute to Henry Mc-Carter, a well-loved Philadelphia artist who had taught for many years at the Pennsylvania Academy of Fine Arts. The volume consisted largely of quotations from McCarter's letters, which are worth reading, and deserve a larger audience than they have had.

In a none too relevant context Ingersoll, seemingly determined to pay Barnes back in his own coin, inserted this: "A patent medicine manufacturer, Albert Barnes, had been accumulating some contemporary paintings under the advice of Mac's friend Glackens."

The result was a mimeographed "Message to Students at the Pennsylvania Academy of Fine Arts from Albert C. Barnes of Merion, Pa.," which Barnes caused to be distributed, by hand and mail, to many who were not Academy students, including Ingersoll and the Museum trustees:

"I was dismayed to learn that the story of the career of an honorable man, revered for his artistry, probity and personal charm—and a deceased man at that—has been garbled and flagrantly exploited by R. Sturgis Ingersoll in his book entitled *Henry McCarter*. The author runs true to form in his false statements about me.

"Ingersoll's book gives the names of rich snobs and bad painters who hang on the coat-tails of art. His snappy stories of gay drinking parties fail to mention the sexual orgies which, according to current legends, often followed these sprees. McCarter was never present at the orgies. Some years ago Ingersoll tried, by flattery, to entice me into joining this local band of artistic and mental cripples, and into allowing them to contaminate our gallery by their presence."

He quoted Ingersoll's praise for *The Art in Painting* and Ingersoll's tribute to his contribution to the cultural life of Philadelphia. He recounted his controversies with the Museum in the '30s, and he quoted Ingersoll's crack about a "patent medicine manufacturer" who needed advice on what to buy. He explained that Argyrol had never been patented and is a definite synthetic chemical "listed as such in the scientific annals of all nations" and he denied he had ever bought a painting "under the advice" of anyone.

He concluded the broadside with this taunt:

"I also challenge Ingersoll to refute the statement that a painting for which he paid a high price, and which he exhibits as the work of a famous foreign artist now dead, was painted by a man living in America."

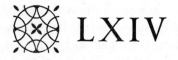 LXIV

I was on "Fortune" at that particular juncture and was traveling about the country a great deal, but I occasionally managed, between assignments, to weekend with Barnes at "Ker Feal." On one such weekend we had quite a to-do when I suggested that he and Ingersoll had so many purposes in common they should cooperate, not feud. He said that even if Ingersoll were willing to work with him on a new program of art education for the Museum, the other trustees wouldn't let him. I said that couldn't be known until it had been tried. Barnes said he had tried it with Stogdell Stokes. I remarked that Ingersoll knew more about art than Stokes, but Barnes dismissed that by saying Ingersoll's greater knowledge only made it easier for him to rationalize away the Museum's indolence.

A week or so later I received one of the letters he sometimes wrote by hand, with the stub of an indelible pencil, on the porch of "Ker Feal." They always expressed the gentler, and winning, side of his nature. This one read:

"It's wonderfully cool, sunshiny and serene here, but no harvesting of wheat, and no you, as we had last Sunday. And that's too bad, for it was nice to have you here. As I looked at you, I kept thinking of your various stages between 1927 and 1944—grub, caterpillar, butterfly, the early ones positive and short-sighted, but still pervaded with the basic quality that makes the butterfly more solidly worthwhile than a grub or caterpillar of other composition, would have been. In short, the real survived the ravages of the frothy ephemeral. And that's good.

"It's a pretty swell world if one likes to observe, dream, and fight for the real. I got a new fight on. This time with the top members of the time-serving politicians in the Philadelphia Public School System. They trod on our toes by trying to exploit the Foundation's name in a publication that's just another of their counterfeits. I let out—not to the public, just to them—a blast that puts them on a spot so hot they sizzle. If they reply they'll get another that will burn them up. If it gets to that stage, I'll send you copies of the cause and effect."

I soon received a sheaf of data from which I learned that Jack Bookbinder, one of the teachers at the Foundation whom Barnes had twice sent abroad, sold antiques to at cost, and permitted to teach in the Philadelphia public school system, at night and during the summer, had written a pamphlet entitled "Invitation to the Arts" which the Board of Education was distributing to its teaching personnel. Bookbinder's connection with the Barnes Foundation was mentioned in it, Barnes explained, without the Foundation's permission, and was deployed not only to enhance Bookbinder's personal prestige but also to give the impression the Foundation endorsed his pamphlet.

I perused "Invitation to the Arts" and thought it an elementary and sentimental, but well-meaning, attempt to quicken an interest in art in adult-education circles.

Subsequent letters from Barnes kept me informed of developments as I traveled about the country. Bookbinder, I gathered, had been told to ask the Board of Education to recall the pamphlet and remove the Foundation's name, and had refused and been fired. Barnes, I learned, was writing letters to the Superintendent of Schools, Alexander J. Stoddard, who had written an introduction for Bookbinder's pamphlet, and to others connected with the public school system, in the hope that they'd sue for libel and thus open the door for "drastic legal action" by Barnes which would enable him to "get out a pamphlet on the status of education in the public schools in Philadelphia and show the working alliance between the Board of Education and the Philadelphia Museum of Art. A suit for libel will furnish the opportunity and I think we can do a good job."

No one rose to his bait, but he decided to issue a pamphlet anyway. He sent me a rough draft of it and I told him he was wasting his intelligence, time and money. Which elicited this:

"I cracked a smile when I read your post card—cracked two of 'em, one for each idea expressed. I smiled also when I read your former card impugning my honesty. The smile in each case had the same cause and it's an old story with you: lack of integration of heart and head. I never asked you what you thought of my article, and I never doubted your affection for me, and certainly not mine for you. I am sore at you only on one score: you didn't come over, as you promised you would do, at the end of your vacation. Sore because I wanted to use your 'But you don't tell me why Roberts resigned' as a text to drive home to you 'how you get that way.' At the farm I gave you the significant elements of the

219

situation—all you had to do was to establish the *relationship* between them.*

"This particular instance, I think, is symbolic of the way your heart bumps your head—and has ever since I have known you. The explanation is that in forming opinions you, like everybody else, let emotional elements function. Emotion, you know, is synonymous with heart, and with you it often gets in the saddle and rides roughshod over the intellectual factors. That's disorderly thinking.

"Now don't tell me I'm wrong in this—it would be no use because I have seen it happen time and time again. It annoys me at times, but firm organic integration always reestablishes my equilibrium.

"Coming down to my article, which goes out in pamphlet form next week: the facts are as stated and have been verified by a number of competent people. It is certainly a rotten situation that affects the public. The importance for us is that for twenty-three years I have devoted many millions of dollars to the establishment of an educational institution, and we've made our mark in the world. Now, wouldn't I be a sucker, a poltroon, if I let those ignorant, limelighting ————use my name and that of my enterprise to promote charlatanry? . . . Bookbinder wrote the brochure while he was on our payroll and never said anything to me about it. The first knowledge I had of it came from school teachers who had received it and said it was tripe. You may say, and I agree with you, that there is plenty of emotion entering into my decision to publish the article. But you cannot say the emotion is not integrated with the facts and that the fusion is not a real judgment. You don't know all the facts —can't get the 'feel' of the situation as a whole.

* I had expressed skepticism when he said Owen J. Roberts had resigned from the United States Supreme Court because he was out of sympathy with the decisions a majority of the Justices were then rendering. My point was that similar feelings had not prompted Holmes or Brandeis to resign.

"Now, you damn fool, shut up, and come to see me whenever you can, for you are always welcome."

The pamphlet, entitled "Sabotage of Public Education in Philadelphia," was an able review of his controversies with the Philadelphia Board of Education and the Philadelphia Museum of Art, going as far back as the survey of art instruction in the schools he had published in the Foundation's "Journal" in 1925. It aroused no significant public response. The Board of Education remained silent and continued to distribute Bookbinder's brochure. However, a series of articles extolling the Board's new "progressive" policies suddenly appeared in the Philadelphia "Inquirer." Barnes quickly got out a printed broadside which characterized the series as a "whitewash." Some years later Bookbinder was promoted to Milliette's job as director of fine and industrial arts in the Philadelphia public school system.

 LXV

I think it was Marx who said that everything happens twice —first as melodrama and then as farce. Whoever said it, the *mot* has relevance to Barnes' last sally against the Philadelphia Museum of Art. It occurred after he had given up all hope that he would ever affect either the Museum's trustees or their policies.

He decided to have some fun. It did not altogether come off.

In February of '48 Henry Clifford, the Museum's curator of paintings, wrote him and said that although he knew "the Barnes Foundation rarely lends," he did remember, with pleasure, having seen some of the Foundation's examples of

Maurice Prendergast's work at the memorial exhibition for that painter put on by the Whitney Gallery. Clifford then said the Museum was planning a big Matisse exhibition for April and asked whether the Foundation would consider lending "Joie de Vivre," "Still Life—1907" and "Music Lesson—1916." Clifford added that he had recently seen Matisse in Paris and that Matisse had expressed a hope that "the Barnes Foundation would be disposed to lend to his show."

With two exceptions, Barnes had not lent any pictures since he was so roundly denounced for doing so to the Pennsylvania Academy of Fine Arts. This was less because of pique than because his pictures were in constant use by teachers and students in the Foundation courses, which had begun about a year after the Pennsylvania Academy's 1923 show. The two exceptions were memorial exhibitions of the work of Maurice Prendergast and Glackens, both of whom were Barnes' friends. By the stretch of no one's imagination could Matisse be regarded as a close personal friend of Barnes. He had visited with the Barnes when in this country, and they had visited him at his home when they were in Paris. But Barnes and Matisse did not click personally. At the time of the installation of the Matisse mural in the Foundation's gallery Barnes thought Matisse coddled his ego "too damned much."

Barnes did not turn Clifford down, at least not flat. He did not offer to lend the three pictures Clifford had specified, but he offered to lend three others—with a condition. And he made the offer in so tentative and complicated a manner Clifford may not have known an offer was being made. But I think he did know, and declined because of the condition Barnes attached to it.

Barnes told Clifford that of all the artists he had ever known "Matisse is the best informed, the most worldly-wise, he knows what goes on in the art world and has an unerring sense in spotting phonies, a wit and humor that is both subtle and penetrating . . . It is difficult for me to believe he was not spoofing you . . . He surely knew you would inform me of what he said, and was probably more interested in imagining my reaction to it. I even venture the hypothesis that in a tête-à-tête with me he would suggest that I offer to loan to your exhibition the triptych, "The Three Sisters," on condition that on one side of the central painting you would hang the documents dated November 26, 1934 [see page 122] and on the other side of the same painting you hang a copy of the analysis of the triptych that appeared in our book, *The Art of Henri-Matisse.*"

Matisse, of course, was *not* spoofing Clifford, and Barnes knew that very well. In fact, Matisse was very grateful, as he should have been, to Clifford and others at the Philadelphia Museum of Art for putting on so major an exhibition (it included 300 or so examples of Matisse's work), and he wrote Clifford a long letter designed to be a foreword to the exhibition catalog. Clifford so used it, and prefaced it with this sentence: "We are fortunate in having the blessing of Matisse himself."

When the show had been on a few days Barnes took some of his students to it and analyzed in plastic terms its more important paintings and drawings. After which one of the students, who had been primed to do so, asked why Matisse had given "his blessing" to the Philadelphia Museum of Art. Didn't he know the Museum "is a place where both art and education are prostituted?" The query gave Barnes a chance to reiterate all the Museum's shortcomings, including one that was new, to wit, reproduction in its current bulletin of a photograph of one of Barnes' Matisses without his permission. Barnes subsequently wrote, and had mimeographed, a resumé of all this, which he sent to the newspapers and to his ever-growing mailing list.

About a week before the exhibition closed Fiske Kimball lectured on it. His lecture had been well publicized in advance and Barnes attended with a retinue of Foundation students and alumni—to have fun at Kimball's expense. But what ensued was too cruel to be comic.

Kimball knew about architecture but little about painting, and he should never have undertaken to lecture on the Matisse show. In fact, Clifford, who had gotten it up, and was the Museum's curator of painting, should have given it.

In a two-page mimeographed report of what happened, which he later distributed widely, Barnes said that "practically the entire staff of the Museum, including the official bouncer, and some armed Park Guards—all paid by taxpayers' money" had lined the walls of the Museum gallery in which the lecture took place.

Kimball's lecture began, Barnes said, "with a lengthy recital of his qualifications to talk about art," and quotations from books on art, philosophy and aesthetics which "had no rational relation to what he subsequently said about Matisse's paintings. Whenever he characterized a particular canvas as a 'great masterpiece,' which he did frequently, he did not disclose what in the painting made it a masterpiece." In short, Barnes declared, "the stenographic record of his lecture embodies an incredible farrago of *ipse dixits* that reveal mental confusion, incompetence and transparent sham."

After about thirty minutes of such "futile rambling," Barnes continued, Kimball was questioned from the floor about certain of his statements. What did he mean by saying Matisse imparted life to a still-life? What did he mean "the only specific thing about Matisse is his being Matisse?" (In answering this one Kimball said Shelley was different from Keats and Keats was different from Shelley, whereupon Barnes, trying to keep things light, called out: "You mean Kelly and Sheets, don't you?".) This led, a moment or two later, to Kimball saying to Barnes: "I wish you'd interpret your Matisses to me," and Barnes saying he would if Kimball entered "our first-year class."

When a questioner asked Kimball whether what he had said about Matisse might not apply equally to any modern artist and Kimball answered: "Yes, it could," there were gasps of surprise and audible exclamations of "My God!" Kimball hastily added that he made "no pretense, as I said, of being a master of interpretation," and asked a member of the audience, who had addressed several questions to him, to "talk to the audience, why don't *you* enlighten these people." This questioner was Abraham L. Chanin, a former student at the Barnes Foundation who had become a lecturer who "interpreted" paintings for visitors to New York City's Museum of Modern Art.

Chanin at once began an analysis of Matisse's "The Blue Window," and after what Kimball regarded as a fitting length of time, he interrupted Chanin with: "My dear boy, I am sure we have all enjoyed—"

"You can't interrupt him!" Barnes cried out. "He has the floor! It's not polite—and you know, Mr. Kimball, *I* am *never* impolite."

"I am director of the Museum," the hard-pressed Kimball was foolish enough to say.

"That doesn't mean you own the Museum," Barnes quickly countered. "It's tax-supported and you are expected to serve the tax-paying public. Besides, you asked the man to speak and he has the right to finish what he wants to say."

"Unfortunately," Kimball said hastily, "I have to go."

And did.

It was not a funny scene. Kimball's rout was too complete.

About a month or so later, when the Museum issued a monograph called "The College and the Museum," in which professors of art in six colleges in the Philadelphia metropolitan area told how they and their students made use of the Museum's resources, Barnes called them "mama's little helpers in the Museum's deception of the public." And though he referred to Kimball as a "mental delinquent," this broadside lacked his usual fire. He told me he almost felt sorry for Kimball, and almost sorry he had gone to his lecture.

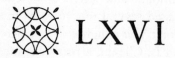 LXVI

Barnes was not a vindictive man, and although he believed pugnacity contributes to mental health, by discharging pent-up emotion in the direction of its cause, I never knew him to start a fight. Nor, as he said, to back away from one. I do not agree with those who think he picked up challenges for the hell of it, or to relieve boredom.

As I have indicated earlier, Barnes had a messianic streak which caused him to do things that sometimes *seemed* to others to result from boredom, an innate bellicosity, or an inferiority complex. He believed every human creature is constantly making psychical decisions which lead to effective behavior or to lethargy, stultification and worse. Since he was convinced everyone *could* acquire the habit of using intelligence in making adjustments to their environment, if they *would*, he was unable to tolerate indolence and self-deception and the rationalizations thereof. He believed the Philadelphia Museum of Art and the University of Pennsylvania, for example, *could* be more effective institutions if enough people expended enough energy with enough intelligence.

I once suggested to him that it was his wealth, rather than his wisdom, that enabled him to be so implacably intolerant of human weakness.

Suppose it is, he replied, that only proves my case. Wealth *can*, but not always *does*, enable an individual to live more widely and develop his potentialities more fully. So, in my salad days I analyzed my abilities and capabilities and used my intelligence in choosing an activity that would lead to wealth. This led to Argyrol, a commodity that answered a need, a *recurrent* need, not an errant desire. Then, with my economics taken care of, I used my intelligence to choose the sort of life that would be right for me. I did not choose booze, chorus girls, yachts, gambling or dope. I chose philosophy and art and I've had a wonderful time. Do you want me to say I'm a special kind of genius? I don't say it or think it. I think *everyone* can live effectively, and happily, if they'd utilize the principles of James and Dewey as I have."

Stated thus, his case was not easily contested, especially since he at once launched an attack on my reasons for suggesting that it was his wealth, instead of psychological principles, that allowed him to be intolerant of what he called the "half-way mores" of most of humanity. I had put forward such a hypothesis, he declared, in order to evade the very thing he was preaching, to undermine the whole idea of self-improvement, to apologize for laziness, in fact, to *propagandize* for it. My own life, he said, was a good example of mental dawdling and day-dreaming. If I would sit down and not get up until I had come to a clear conception of what I wanted, and of how to get it, I would do myself, and him, more good than I did by babbling about his wealth and not accepting and applying his ideas. It was because of his ideas, not his money, he said with conviction, that he could tell me off and the Museum and the University "and everybody else who uses a half of one per cent of the intelligence God gave them."

His use of the word "God" was metaphorical. He was never bothered by the mystery of life or the possibility that human creatures may be so constituted they will *never* understand life ("pessimism results from maladjustment to the environment"). And though he admitted the world's major religions are poetry which provide personal comfort for individuals and a very necessary support for society (by abetting the morality which makes social life possible), Barnes' theological and philosophical bent was almost exclusively pragmatic. But he was very understanding of the *emotion* which is best described by the adjective "religious." Any devotion to a cause larger than ourselves, and which includes ourselves, he called a religion. Art, he said, was his.

Nor did "loneliness" bother him too much, as some have thought and said. He sometimes complained that the Philadelphia milieu did not provide the sort of companionship he needed, but I doubt if any other milieu would have been any better. He was, and I suspect had been since before adolescence, a lone wolf. In his way, however, he enjoyed people and always found time to fraternize with very disparate personalities—*vide* Charles Laughton, William C. Bullitt and Owen J. Roberts. He could also find time to attend the annual dinner in the firehouse of the Narberth Volunteer Fire Company, the costs of which he sometimes paid.

His enemies have said his interest in the fire company was the ulterior one of predisposing it to save his paintings in case of fire. I doubt it. The gallery is as fireproof as it is possible for a building to be, and smoking was forbidden to everyone but himself. As a matter of fact, he was quite fatalistic about the danger to the paintings from fire. He did not insure them because, he said with truth, if fire destroyed them no amount of money could replace them. His affection for the Narberth Volunteer Fire Co. was not complicated at all. Albert Nulty had belonged to it and through him Barnes discovered it to be an association of simple, valiant men united by a sense of social responsibility for a socially essential and praiseworthy purpose.

Barnes did not insure his pictures against burglary, either. His reason was that those who steal paintings as well known as his do not do so in order to sell them, which they know would result in arrest, but to shake-down insurance companies, which sometimes settle with thieves for less than they would have to pay the owners of the stolen paintings. But Barnes spent, and the Foundation continues to spend, a large sum to maintain a staff of watchmen who police the gallery and grounds twenty-four hours a day.

Barnes did not, as some rich men do, live in fear of theft and violence. There was a revolver in the glove compartment of his Packard roadster, but that is the only precaution of the sort he took. He did, however, especially in France, let it be known that he never carried cash on his person. And he affected old clothes, for protective coloration as well as comfort. On shipboard he dressed the first, or the second, night out, to let people know he had evening clothes, but he didn't dress for dinner thereafter, and at home he never did.

He liked good food, but watched his weight, and good wines and Scotch, but in small amounts. Only once, in all the years I knew him, did I ever see him "high." No matter how late he went to bed, and usually it was not late, he was up by six if not before, and he took his morning walk in all weathers, except gales and heavy rain and snow.

His health was excellent and I don't think his body ever inconvenienced him, except for a very occasional cold, until the fall of '50.

 # LXVII

Why, if Barnes was so self-disciplined, public-spirited and well-meaning, are there so many denigrating stories about him?

The answer is that half the stories are false and are circulated by dealers he denounced, incompetent museum officials he exposed, or individuals whose personal pretensions he punctured. A fourth of the stories are partly false, and the strand of truth they contain is twisted to put the teller in the better role and Barnes in the worse one. The remainder quote blunt truths, but usually out of context.

Most of the stories have to do with things Barnes said, or wrote, to people who asked to see his pictures and were refused. Stories about the many who got to see his pictures are almost never told. And they were many—from Einstein and Thomas Mann and Greta Garbo down to very humble people of all races and creeds. Bertrand Russell was recriminatory, not veracious, when he said the Barnes Foundation had been set up for the purpose of preventing people from seeing the pictures. Had that been Barnes' purpose he needn't have created the Foundation at all, nor, when he lived at "Lauraston," have allowed people to go through his home practically every day.

Occasionally, but only occasionally, mistakes were made, and someone who was genuinely interested was refused. If the mistakes could be corrected, they were.

Barnes would not admit art dealers, overt or covert enemies, curiosity seekers, day-dreamers, social-climbers or other self-seekers. The great bulk of applicants in these categories received a printed slip which stated that the Barnes Foundation "is not a public gallery. It is an educational institution with a program for systematic work, organized into classes which are held every day, and conducted by a staff of experienced teachers. Admission to the gallery is restricted to students enrolled in the classes."

But to some applicants in those categories he replied personally. If a society matron wrote and said she was having the so-and-soes for the weekend and could she bring them to see the pictures, and Barnes, or Miss Mullen, or a stenographer, or Barnes' little dog Fidele, replied that on the date specified the gallery would be given over to a striptease contest for the season's shapeliest debutantes, didn't the punishment fit the crime? If the somewhat weak-wristed son of a genuinely creative industrialist wrote with patently insincere, self-abasing flattery, was it altogether inappropriate for him to be told the date was awkward because Dr. Barnes would be practising goldfish-swallowing?

Some of Barnes' letters were shrewdly calculated to elicit the very sort of publicity they have received, and were concocted in accordance with the rules and principles laid down in Whistler's *The Gentle Art of Making Enemies*, a work which does not deserve its present neglect. And some of Barnes' letters were written just to have fun. In fact, it annoyed him that so few recipients of his fun-letters had the wit, inclination, or time, to reply in kind and keep the correspondence going.

Alexander Woollcott was one who had all three, plus a well-developed publicity sense. He was a native of Philadelphia, and, like Barnes, a graduate of its Central High School.

When he was touring in *The Man Who Came to Dinner*—in which he played the title role—Woollcott sent Barnes a *collect* telegram asking for permission to see a dozen of the Foundation's pictures, which he specified.

The reply he received was a letter signed "Fidele de Port Manech, secretaire de Dr. Barnes," and in it the little dog told Mr. Woollcott he had been alone in the house when Western Union phoned to say they had a collect telegram for Dr. Barnes and would he accept the charges. "My reply," Fidele wrote, "was that Dr. Barnes was out on the lawn singing to the birds and that it would cost me my job if I should disturb him at his regular Sunday-morning nature worship." However, Fidele added, Western Union had read him the telegram anyway because the local manager did not want "to thwart a man of your eminence."

Which evaded, but did not refuse, Woollcott's request.

The publicity man for *The Man Who Came to Dinner*, I believe, sent Woollcott's telegram and Fidele's reply to the press, which occasioned more letters to-and-fro, until the play's run was over. In Woollcott's last letter he informed Barnes peremptorily he no longer had time for pointless correspondence and would present himself at the Foundation, to see the pictures, the next time he visited Philadelphia.

Barnes replied with a warning that "thousands of birds inhabit our park and swoop down on every visible lump of suet and pick it to pieces."

James Michener was another who knew how to play the game according to Whistler's rules.

In an article on the Philadelphia suburbs called "The Main Line," in "Holiday," Michener said a student in nearby Swarthmore College in the late '20s, who had applied to see the Barnes Foundation's pictures three times without success, then wrote as though he were a steelworker and had the letter mailed in Pittsburgh. The Foundation replied at once, Michener said, and granted permission.

Barnes consulted the Foundation's records and discovered Michener had been admitted to the gallery in the late '20s as one of a group of Swarthmore students. He therefore wrote Michener a letter in which the following was one of the milder charges:

"In short, you write fiction and sell it as factual reporting, glamorize ordinary people and lick their boots *ad nauseam*, and comfort the smug complacency of snobs."

In his reply Michener thanked Barnes for his "warm and friendly note" and the good wishes it contained. He said he himself had been "the four-flushing swine who pulled that Pittsburgh iron-worker routine on you some 25 years ago, and I remember the trip to Merion as about the best intellectual part of my years at Swarthmore with A. M. Brooks, who first told me of the indecent number of good paintings you have."

He then said he was sure *he* would not again be admitted to the Foundation's gallery but "since the vitriol of your pen seems to be diminishing with age, and since you have appeared to mellow with the passing years, do you think there's any chance that my wife—who is a damned good artist and not at all like me—might get a chance to see what you're sitting on over there behind the wall? If you can name a date she'd be delighted to trek your way, because, as I said to her last night, 'It just don't matter how much of a bastard a guy is, if he had the good sense in the first place to collect such art, why it don't behoove you and me to let him know what a stinker we think he is.' How about it?"

Barnes' reply was not mailable and was delivered by hand to Michener's home in Bucks County. In it he alluded to the fact that one of the photographs illustrating Michener's "Holiday" article "was of a group of parasites who infest the fringes of art, among whom was a notorious fairy"; referred to "the woman you *say* is your wife"; and ended with a characterization of Michener which is unprintable.

To make sure Michener received this Barnes personally took a copy of it the following night to a lecture on the novel Michener was delivering at the University of Pennsylvania. Barnes had also hoped to bait Michener during the question period, but the chairman adjourned the meeting before questions could be asked. Barnes thereupon went to the base of the platform and handed Michener the copy of the letter. As soon as Michener saw Barnes' name on the letterhead, he grabbed his hand, pulled him up on to the platform, and, smiling, gave him an embrace. Barnes, also smiling, reciprocated.

 LXVIII

In the fall of '46 I had a serious conversation with Barnes about his plans for the future of the Foundation.

I had long wanted his opinion of a friend whose opinion of Barnes I had also long wanted, and was finally able to arrange a time that suited all of us. After lunch Barnes and I sat on for almost two hours, talking of my friend, the state of the world, ourselves, and his problems at the Foundation.

He had become disenchanted with a new teacher for whom he had had hopes. This was Roderick Milton Chisholm, who was then just turning thirty and is now the head of Brown University's philosophy department. He had studied philosophy at Harvard, and, while in the Army, during World War II, had written to Barnes to inquire how he could get a copy of *The Bertrand Russell Case*. He had also become acquainted with Dewey, who thought him well grounded in philosophy, liked several articles he had written on philosophical subjects, and considered him capable of the right sort of growth. So had Barnes, and, after Chisholm got out of the Army, he had Chisholm take Miss de Mazia's course and offered him a lectureship at the Foundation. Barnes also spent much of that summer working out a new relationship with the University of Pennsylvania whereby Penn students could take Chisholm's course at the Foundation. The course, Barnes announced, would provide "the essentials of philosophy, psychology and scientific method," and do so by means of objective studies of the paintings in the collection.

"Harold [his nickname for Buermeyer] and I have been attending his lectures and they're not at all what I had in mind," Barnes told me in New York. He said he felt let down, inasmuch as he had thought he had at last found a way to improve the instruction provided by Penn's Fine Arts Department. I asked what the matter was, specifically, with Chisholm's lectures. He replied that they were "superficial" and a "rehash." "Don't take my word for it," he added bitterly, "ask Dewey. He has all the data." I did ask Dewey and he said he thought Chisholm and Miss de Mazia did not get on. Sometime later Barnes sent me a seven-page, single-spaced stenographic report of one of Chisholm's lectures. It was elementary, but earnest and lucid. I could not tell whether it was a rehash—that depended on what had gone before and came after. I did note that the students had been allowed to do considerable needling.

Barnes' disappointment with Chisholm was dual: he would have to find a new teacher, and he would not be able to say to the University's president, then George W. McClelland: "See this is what I mean by art education, this is what you should have been doing all along. This is what I want Penn to do at the Foundation after I'm gone."

Despite all his ups and downs with Penn, Barnes had left unchanged in the Foundation's by-laws the provision that after his and Mrs. Barnes' deaths Penn's trustees would nominate the Foundation's.

But he was profoundly disappointed in '48 when the Republicans then backing the Presidential aspirations of Harold E. Stassen got him elected president of the University of Pennsylvania in order to provide him with status in an Eastern state that has considerably more votes in the Electoral College than Minnesota, of which Stassen had been Governor. Barnes thought his alma mater had "degraded" itself by allowing Stassen, "a political stuffed-shirt," to parade around as its president.

I don't know how much time and attention Stassen was able to devote to the University's affairs in the midst of his maneuvers for the Republican Presidential nomination of '52, but he certainly did not spend enough on Dr. Albert C. Barnes. And the attention he did pay him could not have been clumsier.

Various prominent Pennsylvania alumni, and some of the more intelligent members of the faculty, had spent considerable time cultivating Barnes in those years, and several of Mrs. Barnes' lecturers at the Arboretum were Penn professors, including Dr. John M. Fogg, Jr., who was not only professor of botany but also, in the late '40s, Penn's vice provost. Fogg had hoped Stassen *might* turn out to be a new broom and urged Barnes to help Stassen "raise the educational status of Penn and regain some of its lost prestige." Barnes said he would be eager to help if only he could believe real improvement would result.

So Fogg had Stassen write to Barnes. The letter, alas, was patently mechanical and revealed that Stassen had no idea of how to deal with intellectuals in general, or Barnes in particular. It began with patently factitious statements about being "pleased to note the general observation [sic] of Professor John Dewey's ninetieth birthday," and wondering whether Dewey had ever written or spoken on "Prime Minister Nehru's approach to the international situation." Only then did he invite Barnes to lunch and explain: "I now have the reported recommendations as to the School of Fine Arts and would like to discuss them with you." With which he should have begun, and to which he should have confined, his letter.

Barnes replied that he had shown Dewey all the correspondence he had had with Dr. Fogg and that the way Dewey "sized up the situation expresses my attitude so well that I quote what he wrote me: 'It would be wonderful if Stassen had the insight and foresight to break away and do something sound in educational policy on his own.' " Barnes then said: "It is not only your Fine Arts Department that is at fault, but several sections of other departments, and all of these defects are directly traceable to the men who are responsible for the present state of affairs. To expect you, a man not trained in educational science and not having around him anybody who has evidenced such knowledge, to bring about the desired results, is practically a confession of a belief in miracles. And your suggestion to discuss with me 'the reported recommendations as to the School of Fine Arts' would be like a Frenchman and a Chinese trying to convey to each other, each in his own language, the essentials of a problem in which both are interested. Your problem, I think, is the very old one of how to eat your cake and have it too, and is, it seems to me, not unlike that of Hercules when he had to clean out the Augean stables."

Four *months* later Stassen replied that he had appreciated

the "bluntness" of Barnes' letter and had "given much thought to the situation." He did not allude to Barnes' Augean reference but he did say that "though I lay no claim to being a twentieth century Hercules, I am determined to make progress on the task." He said his invitation to lunch still stood and he concluded with this absurdity: "I think the State Department made a mistake in Picasso's case." Stassen had said nothing in public about the State Department's refusal to allow Picasso to come here under Communist sponsorship, and he evidently did not know that Barnes thought Picasso played the Communist game for the publicity he could get by so doing.

Barnes sent Stassen a ribald joke, the point of which was that Stassen's offer to discuss Penn's 'Fine Arts Department' was merely a suggestion that they discuss the transfer of the Barnes Foundation from Barnes' control to Penn's.

Barnes did not completely close the door, however, and from time to time thereafter sent Stassen copies of any of his correspondence which related in any way to Penn. So Stassen made one more clumsy attempt.

"I am sorry," he wrote, "that you are afraid to go ahead and help me improve the Fine Arts situation at the University of Pennsylvania. You have stated that it is difficult to build up and referred to it as a Herculean task. I am working at it and am determined that it will be strengthened. I wish I could have your help in bringing it about, but if you are afraid to tackle it, because of its many difficulties, that of course is your privilege. I did have the impression, however, that you were a man of courage and determination.

The taunt was so childish, Barnes told Stassen, it proved he still wore "the dunce cap that Tom Dewey placed on you in the 1948 Presidential campaign." And by means of various circumlocutions Barnes gave Stassen to understand he regarded him as the worst president the University of Pennsylvania had ever had, and that Penn should send him "back to the sticks."

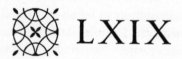 LXIX

That fall the Barnes Foundation gave a course on the relationship between art and philosophy for a selected group of students from Lincoln University, a Negro institution twenty or so miles south of Philadelphia which has an enrollment of around 350. Barnes had given money to it in the past, as he had to Fisk University, the National Urban League, the magazine "Opportunity," and other Negro causes.

His interest in the Negro began in 1902 when he happened to start his factory in a Negro neighborhood, and thereby happened to employ Negro help. He came to like the Negro's spontaneity, imaginative qualities and sense of rhythm, and the fact that he is uninhibited in ways the white man is not. Barnes began to help individual Negroes, and, as I have said, during the Depression he gave sizable sums, through the Tindley Temple, to alleviate the distress of Philadelphia Negroes.

In '40 he went out of his way to promote the career of a Negro artist named Horace Pippin. He bought several of his canvases, induced others to buy them, and wrote a foreword to catalogs of Pippin shows in Philadelphia and New York, the latter of which he arranged. Pippin was a veteran of World War I with a crippled right arm who lived in Chester, Pennsylvania. He had been astonished when Christian Brinton, the art critic, saw one of his canvases in a shoemaker's window and brought him to the attention of a Philadelphia dealer, who brought him to the attention of Barnes.

"One feels in Pippin's painting," Barnes wrote, "a purpose, possibly not a conscious purpose, to attain a particular end, set by himself and pursued without leaning, or even drawing upon, the resources of previous painters. This explains why his work has the simplicity, directness, sincerity, naïveté, and vivid drama of a story told by an unspoiled Negro in his own words. It is probably not too much to say that he is the first important Negro painter to appear on the American scene, and that his work shares with that of John Kane the distinction of being the most individual and unadulterated painting authentically expressive of the American spirit that has been produced during our generation. To hold against Pippin his present inability to make pigment express his ideas and feelings with refinement and finesse, is equivalent to finding fault with Andrew Jackson because he never went to college."

Although there are several sentimental ideas in that paragraph, especially the seeming equation of folk art with the kind of art which requires no qualifying adjective, Barnes was not usually sentimental about Negroes, and had few illusions about them. He once said that not one of those to whom he had lent money had repaid it, and he was fully cognizant of the cultural differences which separate the black and white races.

But he believed American democracy is capable of withstanding the stress of the Negro's greed as he rises in white civilization, and the strain on the white race as he does so. He also believed democracy as a governmental form would be vindicated or convicted according to whether or not the Negro minority attained social equality. He regretted that the tender plant of democracy should be exposed so early to so great a tempest, but he was completely confident it would be standing, more firmly rooted than ever, after the storms of Negro ascension had passed.

His experiment with the Lincoln University students was far from an unqualified success. As he wrote to J. Newton Hill, the man at Lincoln most responsible for the cooperative effort with the Barnes Foundation:

"The only possible way to make our resources really serv-

239

iceable to Lincoln is by the method of 'trial and error' and to fulfill conditions which experience shows are indispensable. These are: 1) a rational philosophic foundation; 2) a trained teacher; 3) selected students; 4) a first-year class in fundamental principles of orderly thinking, scientific method, authentic experience. This year the experiment with Lincoln failed in practically all of these requisites, in spite of your zeal and intelligent cooperation, and my efforts to start it right. When I saw that the teacher was inadequate, I suggested that you enter the Tuesday class in order to see what can be done, and *how*."

Nevertheless, it was this experiment with Lincoln students which started him thinking that perhaps a small *Negro* university, rather than a large white one, was the sort of educational institution with which to link the Foundation if the kind of art education he so passionately believed necessary was to be made standard operating procedure in American colleges. Lincoln University had fewer deeply vested interests resisting change, greater reason to prove itself worthy of so important a trust, and, in the political maelstrom of the future, an association of Lincoln and the Foundation might even affect the turn democracy would take.

Accordingly, in October of '50, a month before he entered the hospital for the removal of his prostate, Barnes changed the by-law which establishes how candidates for the office of trustee of the Barnes Foundation were to be nominated after his and his wife's death. Lincoln University's trustees, not Penn's, he decided, would nominate them.

 LXX

Late in April of '50 Barnes pinned to the bottom of a letter in which he praised "Films in Review," the magazine which the National Board of Review of Motion Pictures had just started and which I now edit, a slip of onion-skin paper on which was typed: "CONSULTATION WITH DR. DYER. A.C.B.: "What do you advise?" Dr. Dyer: "If you were my *father* I would advise you to have an X-ray taken." A.C.B.: "What if I were your son?" Dr. Dyer: "I would put you in a reform school."

This jocularity was his only reference to the annoyance which led, in November, to the removal of his prostate. That operation is usually a debilitating one but Barnes was in the Presbyterian Hospital on Powelton Avenue in Philadelphia only two or three weeks, and, after several more recuperating weeks at home, he seemed like his old self.

I last heard from him in June of '51 when he wrote that Lincoln University had given him an honorary degree—Doctor of Science—but that he had not gone to receive it since he regarded honorary degrees as a racket, harmless to be sure, but a racket. And he enclosed carbon copies of some of his recent correspondence, as he had throughout all the years I had known him.

One of the copies was of a letter to Ralph J. Bunche, who had apparently expressed an interest in Barnes' experiment with Lincoln University students. Bunche had recently received the Nobel Peace Prize, at the same time Bertrand Russell had received a Nobel Prize for Literature. So Barnes sent Bunche his pamphlet on the Russell affair, to correct, I gathered, any erroneous impressions Russell might have given him. "Russell is unquestionably brilliant," Barnes told Bunche, "but in the sense Goethe meant when he said it's easy to be brilliant if one respects nothing."

The reference to Russell seemed to be redolent of the Barnes of old—Bunche had been in contact with Russell, this fact had revived unpleasant memories in Barnes, who had thereupon discharged his psychological tension by informing Bunche about his side of the controversy. It was Barnes' tried-and-true method for the maintenance of psychological comfort and mental health. Nothing in any of the other letters indicated any diminution of Barnes' intellectual prowess, or made one lift an eyebrow and think: "After all, he's seventy-nine and has had a serious operation."

I was therefore astonished when I learned from a New York newspaper that he had been killed instantly when his Packard roadster, in which he had been driving alone, except for Fidele, had been hit by a ten-ton loaded trailer-truck only a mile or two from "Ker Feal."

On the morning of July 24, 1951, he had driven out to "Ker Feal," he told Mrs. Barnes, who had preceded him there, to "settle my mind," and, after a light lunch, had sat on the porch engrossed in thought until about half past two, when he took off in order to keep an appointment to talk to two new instructors at the Foundation in Merion. Mrs. Barnes, who was supervising the packaging of chickens for the freezer at Merion and was not ready to leave, said she would drive down later in her own car, with the three Merion gardeners she had brought to "Ker Feal" that morning, as she had planned.

She left a half hour after Barnes did and as she drove out of the driveway of "Ker Feal" onto the Old Conestoga Pike (now Route 401) she had nothing on her mind more pressing than the peace of a sunny mid-summer afternoon after household chores were done. But as she approached the main route between Phoenixville and West Chester (Route 29) and became aware there had been an accident, a premonition assailed her and a moment later she learned it was her husband who had been killed. His body had already been taken to an undertaking establishment in Malvern, and little Fidele had been put out of his misery by a State Trooper's bullet.

That evening Albert Nulty assumed the duty of making sure the body in the undertaking establishment in Malvern was that of Albert Coombs Barnes.

It was cremated, and, in accordance with Barnes' wish, there was no funeral service. His ashes were buried in a woodland he had helped to preserve and develop.

His will left a personal estate of about $1,000,000 to his widow, who succeeded him as president of the Barnes Foundation.

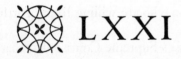 # LXXI

Barnes' lifelong faith in democracy would indeed have been put to the test had he seen how quickly the wreckers began to try to destroy what he had created and given to the public.

He had been dead only a few months when the Philadelphia "Inquirer," which is published by Walter Annenberg, announced that one of its employes would institute legal proceedings "so the public can see the pictures in a tax-free institution." Such demagogy did not at first succeed. The Courts ruled that only the Attorney General of the Commonwealth of Pennsylvania could raise the question of improper administration by trustees.

It is widely believed that the publisher of the "Inquirer," because he resents Barnes *personally*, then prevailed upon the

Attorney General to bring such a suit, and that the case quickly became political football.

All of which was unnecessary, for the Foundation's by-laws provided that *after Barnes' death, and that of his wife,* the gallery and arboretum should be open to the public on Saturdays, except during July and August, and open five other days "for educational purposes to students and instructors of institutions which conduct courses in art and art appreciation which are approved by the Foundation's trustees." And as has already been shown, seriously interested members of the public had *always* been admitted to the gallery while Barnes was alive, and continued to be after his death.

It should also be remembered that Mrs. Barnes still lived on the Foundation property, in a building which had been her home for almost thirty years, and that at the time of the "Inquirer's" first harassment she was seventy-seven years old. Also, that Barnes had given his pictures to the Foundation *because* it was an educational institution and *because* he wanted them used primarily by those who are willing to put forth the effort to study them.

Nevertheless, Pennsylvania's Supreme Court ruled that the Foundation administered *two* trusts—an educational institution and an art gallery—and that the donor's wishes as to how the latter should be administered, while he and his wife lived, were to be set aside. This was tantamount to saying that a man cannot make a gift to the public in his own way, which is but a small legal step from saying a man cannot bequeath his property as he sees fit. And *that* strikes at the foundations of the private property edifice.

This decision has not yet been appealed to the United States Supreme Court, and the Barnes Foundation's gallery has been open to the public on Fridays and Saturdays, September through May. When the Foundation announced it would have to charge admission to pay for the extra guards required, and for its other new expenses, the "Inquirer" and the Attorney

General's office sought a court injunction. In doing so one of the Attorney General's assistants made mock of the Foundation's Arboretum as an unnecessary expense, saying, "Who looks at trees?" She also suggested that the Foundation shift its investments from bonds to common stocks despite the fact that at that very moment (May '62) the value of common stocks was falling drastically.

Such ignorance in a public official is a menace to public peace and security and I could not help wondering, as I learned of each new maneuver of the "Inquirer" and the Attorney General, what Barnes would have said and done. Here indeed was an instance of how Toynbee's "internal barbarians" disintegrate the culture of any society which allows them to go unchallenged and unchecked.

"The insolence of office" is one of the things it is necessary to combat, Barnes believed, if men are to remain free. It is also one of the things that once made him say every city should have a man like himself, who, being financially independent, can devote time and attention to the preservation and increase of a community's cultural welfare.

Every city does not have an Albert Coombs Barnes, and Philadelphia has not seen his like again, for he was a unique phenomenon. Dewey said that in a lifetime of association with scholars he had not encountered a finer intelligence.

INDEX

A. C. Barnes Co., 43, 44, 76, 115.
Alexander, F. M., 65–6.
Altman, Benjamin, 57.
American Civil Liberties Union, 6, 193.
American Legion, 6.
Anderson, Sherwood, 69.
Annenberg, Walter, 243.
Apollinaire, Guillaume, 126.
Arboretum of the Barnes Foundation, 77,
  83, 96, 118, 187–9, 235, 244–5.
Argyrol, 5, 35–7, 38 et seq., 47, 94, 116,
  226.
Armory Show, 52–5.
Art in Painting, The, 20, 84–94, 111,
  122, 128, 133–6, 141, 165–6, 172, 213,
  214, 217.
Art of Cezanne, The, 176–185.
Art of Henri-Matisse, The, 127–133, 213.
Art of Renoir, The, 140–153, 155, 183.
"Art News," 162, 214.
"Arts à Paris, Les," 19.
"Arts and Decoration," 55–9.
"Arts, The," 82–3, 84.

Ballard, Spahr, Andrews and Ingersoll,
  122.
Barbizon Gallery, 137.
Barnes, Albert Coombs: Merion "slum,"
  5–6; suffering fools, 7–8; 9, 13, 14;
  motives, 16; on Titian, 16; the time
  of happiness, 17–8; and the Steins, 18;
  non-admittance to gallery, 22; influence of James, Santayana and Dewey,
  24; his character, 24; as a teacher, 27–
  8; and Laurence Buermeyer, 28; relation with Dewey, 29; birth, 31;
  Methodism, 32; Central High School,
  33; University of Pa. Medical School,
  33; intern, 34; medical practice, 34;
  first trips to Europe, 35; early jobs, 35;

Argyrol, 35 et seq.; courtship and
  marriage, 36–8; Nelle Mullen, 43;
  Negro employes, 45; move to Merion,
  47; never painted, 47–8; first acquisitions, 48; horseback riding, 48–9;
  friendship with Glackens, 49–51; early
  opinions on collecting, 55; on Renoir,
  57; World War I, 59–60; and *Democracy and Education,* 60–3; at
  Dewey's seminar, 64; field study of
  Polish assimilation, 65–7; Provincetown Players, 68; on communism, 69–
  70; on New Deal, 70; mature goals,
  71; exhibition at Pa. Academy of Fine
  Arts, 73–76; indenture of Barnes
  Foundation, 76–80; and architect Paul
  Cret, 80–2; *The Art in Painting,* 84–
  94; the necessity of controversy, 99–
  101; his proposed courses for the
  Univ. of Pa., 102–3; and *The French
  Primitives and Their Forms,* 106–7;
  tax-exempt bonds, 115; sale of A. C.
  Barnes Co., 115–6; Matisse mural,
  119–21; Matisse's "Trois Soeurs," 122–
  3; and the Depression, 123–4; *The
  Art of Henri-Matisse,* 128–133; and
  Leo Stein, 133–7; Dewey's dedication
  of *Art as Experience,* 139; *The Art of
  Renoir,* 140–53; on Renoir and Cézanne, 150; and Spanish civil war,
  156–8; self-created myths, 158–9;
  Phila. Museum of Art, 163–73, 215 et
  seq.; Federal Arts Project, 167–70;
  The Art of Cézanne, 176–85; "Ker
  Feal," 186–7; and the Foundation's
  arboretum, 188–9; and Bertrand Russell, 189–202; World War II, 203–6;
  and atomic bomb, 206; and "Saturday
  Evening Post," 207–8; and "House
  and Garden," 209–10; at Rhode Is-

248